DICTIONARY OF COLLECTIVE NOUNS AND GROUP TERMS

DICTIONARY OF COLLECTIVE NOUNS AND GROUP TERMS

Being a Compendium of More Than 1800 Collective Nouns, Group Terms, and Phrases That from Medieval to Modern Times Have Described Companies of Persons, Birds, Insects, Animals, Professions, and Objects

SECOND EDITION

IVAN G. SPARKES, Editor

GALE RESEARCH COMPANY
BOOK TOWER ● DETROIT, MICHIGAN 48226

Ivan G. Sparkes, *Editor*

Carol Blanchard, *Production Director*
Arthur Chartow, *Art Director*

Frederick G. Ruffner, *Publisher*
James M. Ethridge, *Executive Vice-President/Editorial*
Dedria Bryfonski, *Editorial Director*
Ellen T. Crowley, *Director, Indexes and Dictionaries Division*

Library of Congress Cataloging-in-Publication Data

Sparkes, Ivan George, 1930-
Dictionary of collective nouns and group terms.

Subtitle: Being a compendium of more than 1800 collective nouns, group terms, and phrases, that from medieval to modern times have described companies of persons, birds, insects, animals, professions, and objects.
Bibliography, p.
Includes index.
1. English language—Terms and phrases—Dictionaries.
2. English language—Collective nouns—Dictionaries.
I. Title.
PE1689.S69   1985   423.'1   85-16195
ISBN 0-8103-2188-2

Printed in the United States of America

Contents

Foreword

Dictionary of Collective Nouns and Group Terms, second edition, lists more than 1800 entries, a 50% increase over the first edition. It includes several kinds of collectives, which are described in the editor's preface following this note; most of the terms have been selected because they are unusual, or interesting, or fun.

Collecting Collectives

At some earlier stage of English, collectives like *herd, flock, gam,* and others evolved quite naturally; it is difficult to cite the earliest instances when poets and other writers first concocted conceits like Shelley's "exaltation of larks" (which he borrowed from Lydgate, 1430), for it is often impossible to separate the citation of a denotative use from that of a connotative or facetious use. Thus, *flock* has long referred not only to sheep and birds but to the members of a religious congregation. The Bible is rife with such metaphor: "The Lord is my Shepherd...." And a *minister* (itself metaphoric) is referred to as *pastor* (Latin for 'shepherd'). There are many such metaphoric uses in English, and we can assume that Shelley was availing himself of a naturally productive poetic opportunity in singing thus of larks.

More recently, the coining of collectives has become a pastime for some. Several years ago, *An Exaltation of Larks* by James Lipton appeared (Viking, 1968; Brit. Ed., 1970; 2nd Ed., 1977); it contained some established collectives, but also a number of "originals," facetious collectives like *an anthology of pros,* referring to a collection of prostitutes, and, in less than flattering reference to elected officials, *an odium of politicians.* Whether these qualify for citation along with the established, literate, and literary language may be debatable, were this an attempt to offer a scholarly disquisition on the subject of collectives. As it is, this book is a collection of collective nouns, without pretense to be anything it is not.

Gathered here, then, are the fruits of collecting collectives, as garnered from as many sources as he could harvest by Ivan G. Sparkes, Collectives Collector.

Features in This Edition

This second edition differs from the first mainly in that it: 1) contains hundreds of new entries and, 2) has been amplified in regard to the citations and other evidence (such as dates) adduced to identify, as best could be done, the use of the entries. In addition, an Index provides a complete alphabetic listing, by every significant word, of "things collected," allowing one to find, say, *flowerage of architectural fancy* both under **flowerage** in the text and under *architectural fancy* and *fancy, architectural* in the Index.

Preface

Group terms have been in constant use since medieval times, and much of their richness is derived from the language of the chase in use among the knights and esquires of that day. When Sir Arthur Conan Doyle wrote his historical novel entitled *Sir Nigel,* he put into the mouth of an old knight these words of advice: "But above all, I pray you Nigel to have a care in the use of terms of the craft, lest you should make some blunders at table."

The terms we use today come mainly from those days, and carry a lingering quaintness in their turn of phrase. Many are culled from a rich medieval treasury of hunting terms called *The Boke of St. Albans,* which was compiled by Dame Juliana Berners and printed in 1486. There, in their gothic script, are listed the words in common use and their proper value propounded. Dame Juliana is most anxious that the correct term be found, adding that this is a point which distinguishes the "gentylman from the ungentylman." Some of these terms were straightforward words in use for many years; others, I suspect, were somewhat critical comments which reflect the view of medieval man. We may accept the poetic truth in a *descent of woodpeckers* or a *watch of nightingales,* so I imagine there is equal truth in the rather bitter *an abomination of monks,* referring to that large body of clergy who roamed the countryside from monastery to monastery claiming the benefit of clergy whenever trouble raised its ugly head.

Since those days we find that the use of collectives has diminished until at present they appear lost in the mists of time, practised only in the prose of authors and journalists. Yet they are often colourful and add considerably to the descriptive power of the English language.

During the past century a handful of slim volumes has fortunately recorded new phrases and faithfully reprinted the old, but until now, no systematic dictionary of these terms has been compiled. The words themselves fall into several groups:

(a) Ancient phrases such as *an exaltation of larks* or *an abomination of monks,* reflecting some of the views of the original users.

(b) General terms such as *flock, pile, heap, herd,* or *shoal,* which can apply to a wide variety of persons, animals, or objects.

(c) Words or names that are made collective by the addition of an

9

ending such as -*y* or -*age;* for example: *froggery, fruitery, assemblage,* or *brigandage.*

(d) Terms that, through misuse or some quirk of change in terminology, relate to one particular group; for instance, *a charm of goldfinches* arises from the archaic *chirm* (i.e., 'din or chatter').

(e) Modern punning terms such as *a dilation of pupils* and apocryphal comments made in Oxford on seeing a group of prostitutes: *a flourish of strumpets, a jam of tarts,* or the more subtle *an anthology of pros.*

(f) Finally are included several terms of quantity, number, or capacity that seemed of interest to the compiler.

There is a tendency nowadays for the punning phrase, especially an alliterative one, to be composed and used in articles or in smart collections of group terms that appear from time to time in the glossy magazines. These are usually passing fancies, and have not the determination to survive found in the older terms. Occasionally a poetic phrase will find favour and by constant repeating implant itself more firmly in the memory; this is what has happened with *a host of golden daffodils* or *the monstrous regiment of women.*

In compiling this dictionary, I found my personal knowledge of words was stretched to the limit, and that as others read the proofs they were able to contribute other uses of terms that I had completely overlooked. I feel that you, the reader, will suddenly spot an omission or see an extra use of a group term not listed to date, so do not hesitate to send suggestions for inclusion in any future edition.

For those fascinated by the original medieval terminology, I would recommend Dame Juliana's *Boke of St. Albans,* reprinted in 1881. Those wishing to pursue the etymology of the collective noun will find items of interest in James Lipton's *An Exaltation of Larks* (Viking, 1968; Brit. Ed., 1970; 2nd Ed., 1977). But to those who seek to find the right term to use at the right time, or who are caught in the middle of an intricate crossword puzzle, I dedicate this volume, hoping that one day I might qualify to join *a labour of lexicographers* or maybe even achieve my ambition by claiming inclusion in a happy *consort of authors.*

Sources

Adams, J. D. *The Magic and Mystery of Words.* 1963.

Berners, Dame Juliana. *The Boke of St. Albans.* 1486. Facsim. ed. 1881.

Brewer, E. Cobham. *Brewer's Dictionary of Phrase and Fable.* 1952 ed.

Century Dictionary. 1890.

Gepp, Edward. *An Essex Dialect Dictionary.* 1923. Facsim. ed. 1969.

Goss, Helen and Philip. *Gathered Together.* 1928.

Hare, C. E. *The Language of Field Sports.* 1939. Rev. ed. 1949.

Johnson, Dr. Samuel. *Johnson's Dictionary, a Modern Selection.* By E. L. McAdam and George Milne. 1963. New ed. 1982.

Lipton, James. *An Exaltation of Larks.* 1970.

Lydgate, John. *A Lytell Treatye of the Horse, the Sheep and the Ghoos.* 1499. Reprint 1906.

Lynch, S. *Group Terms of the Chase.* Chambers Journal.

Mensa Society. *Bulletin.* (Article quoted by James Lipton, p. 93.)

Oxford English Dictionary on Historical Principles.

Slang Dictionary. 1874.

Strutt, J. *The Sports and Pastimes of the People of England.* 1835.

Webster's New International Dictionary. 1926 ed.

Wright, Joseph. *The English Dialect Dictionary.* 1899. Reprint 1970.

Grateful thanks are also given to the following for new terms included in this second edition: Christine Jeffery, M. A. Madden, Frederick G. Ruffner, W. Safire, and Ian Wilkes.

A

abominable sight   of monks: a large company of monks
—*Bk. of St. Albans,* 1486.

abundance   a profusion, a great plenty, an overflowing quantity. See also **exuberance.**
Examples: of superfluous breath, 1593; of valuable information, 1824; of mercy; of worthless and fabulous scoundrels, 1687; an abundance of good things.

academy   a society of learned men; a school of learning. See also **college, institute.**
Examples: an academy of fanaticism, 1761; the living academy of love-lore, 1754; academy of learned men.

accrescence   a quantity formed by continuous growth; something that grows from outside itself. See also **accretion.**
Examples: an accrescence of belief; of objectivity, 1819; of gentile superstition, 1649.

accretion   the coherence of particles to create a solid mass.
Examples: accretions of age, 1853; of bad humours, 1653; of earth; of ice, 1853; of particles, 1794; of snow, 1853; of water, 1853; of casual writings [the Bible], 1866.

accumulation   an accumulated mass; a heap; a pile or quantity formed by successive additions. See also **collection, hoard.**
Examples: an accumulation of capital, 1843; of energy; of evils; of fortunes; of honours; of ire, 1490; of knowledge, 1760; of power; of snow; of waters; of wealth; of wrath.

ace   a small quantity —*Johnson,* 1755.

acervation   a heaping up; an accumulation, especially in the form of a tight cluster —*Wilkes.*

acne   of adolescents —*Lipton,* 1970.

acrobacy   acrobats *collectively.*

aeon   an indefinitely long period of time.
Example: aeons of time, 1647.

aerie, eyrie   a brood of birds of prey. See also **brood, nest.**
Examples: aerie of children, 1602; of eagles; of hawks, 1598; of pheasants, 1604; of ravens.

agglomerate   a group or mass of things loosely thrown or huddled together or gathered into a ball or cluster; a mass of volcanic fragments linked through the action of heat.
Examples: an agglomerate of all duchies, 1865; of all facts, 1831; of volcanic fragments.

agglomeration   a mass or clump of things gathered together; an unmethodical assemblage; a cluster. See also **cluster, conglomerate.**
Examples: an agglomeration of self-loving beings, 1866; of granite houses, 1859; of turrets, 1774.

agglutination   a combination of simple words to express compound ideas —*Wilkes.*

aggregate   an assemblage collected into one body, e.g., a house is an aggregate of bricks, timber, etc. See also **collection, combination, compound, sum.**
Examples: aggregate of activities, 1855; of small bubbles, 1677; of confusions and incongruities, 1878; of all past experience.

aggregation   a collection of parts of a whole; a natural group or body of human beings. See also **assemblage, collection, gathering.**
Examples: an aggregation of believers, 1638; of isolated settlements, 1863; of species.

agora   an assembly place, e.g., a marketplace, *hence,* the people assembled, 1820.

agreat   in gross, 1502; by the lot, 1622; en masse, agreat or altogether, 1580.

aircraft   flying machines *collectively,* 1850.

airfleet   a group of aircraft, *collectively.*

aisle   *Dialectal.* double rows of wheat sheaves set up to dry. *Example*: aisle of wheat, 1817.

alag   *Sporting.* a flight of geese, 1898.

alliance   a union between families, states, or parties; the persons allied; a combination of common objects; a group of natural orders of plants, e.g., *glumal alliance* includes grasses and other allied orders.

allies   a group of nations allied against another nation or group of nations.

althing   a whole assembly, *specifically,* the General Assembly of Iceland.

amalgam   an alloy of a metal or metals — *Wilkes.*

amassment   accumulation; the result of amassing, e.g., money. See also **heap, mass, pile, stack.**

ambigu   a banquet at which a medley of dishes is set together, 1753; from the word *ambiguous,* 1688.

ambush   a group of troops of persons concealed or lying in wait for their prey.
Examples: ambush of amber coloured darts [referring to a lady's hair], 1592; of envy, 1751; of error, 1852; of tigers; of widows — *Lipton,* 1970.

ammullock   piled untidily in a confused heap, 1890.

ana   a collection of the sayings of a person, 1727; literary gossip.
Examples: *ana*—an assembly brew'd of clerks and elders, 1651;

of loose thoughts dropped by eminent men collected by their friends —*Johnson, 1755.*

anadem   a wreath, chaplet, or garland.
Examples: anadems of flowers, 1604; sweet anadems to gird thy brow, 1613.

anagraph   an inventory; a description of the contents of something; a record or breviate, 1656.

analects   literary gleanings.
Examples: analects . . . is taken for collections of scraps out of authors, 1658; analects in verse and prose, 1770.

ancientry   elders *collectively*; antiquities *collectively*; elders of a parish.
Examples: nobility and ancientry of their houses, 1580; the ancientry of the parish, 1589; cram full of ancientry ['antiques'], 1866; wronging the ancientry, 1611.

ancienty   the ancients; people of olden times.
Example: The anciety did sin in the Ark of the Lord's covenant, 1556.

angerie   *Dialectal.* a crowd; a multitude.

anthology   a collection of flowers; items culled from literature. See also **garland, treasury.**
Examples: anthology of causes and effects, 1878; of epigrams; of flowers, 1755; of hymns, 1775; of poems; of pros' ['prostitutes'] —*Lipton, 1970;* of prose.

anthood   ants *collectively*, 1897.
Example: a mass of struggling anthood, 1881.

apery   a collection or colony of apes.
Example: more apish than all the ages of all aperies —*Kingsley, 1862.*

aquarium   a place for keeping fish; a collection of tanks for fish, *hence,* the fish themselves *collectively* —*Wilkes.*

appendix, appendices   something attached as if by being hung on; appendage.
Example: the ark . . . the heavenly fire, and the rest were ceremonial appendices, 1665.

archery   a company or corps of archers.
Examples: he rode through a hundred archery, 1465; signal for England's archery to halt and bend their bows, 1814.

archipelago   the Greek islands in the Aegean Sea, *hence,* any sea or broad sheet of water containing many islands.
Examples: archipelago of isolated communities, 1862; of the Polar Ocean, 1830.

archive, archives   a collection of documents, esp. a historical collection of written or printed material, nowadays including audio recordings and visual material.
Examples: archives of their ancient records, 1645; a living archive in that business, 1865; the universities, archives of all the errors of the age, 1878.

areopagy   a secret tribunal; a conclave.
Examples: an areopagy of hell, 1646; conscience sits in the areopagy and dark tribunals of our hearts, 1682.

aristocracy   the nobles or chief officials in a state; the privileged class.
Example: aristocracy is the ruling body of the best citizens, 1531.

ark   clouds in lines converging to two points on opposite parts of the sky.
Example: an ark of cloud, 1839.

armada   an armed force; a fleet of ships of war, *specifically,* the fleet sent against England by Philip of Spain in 1588.
Examples: an armada of ships, 1533; of aircraft.

armental   of or belonging to a drove or herd; *hence,* a herd of cattle, 1731.

armentose   full of great cattle; abounding with herds of beasts, 1731.

armoury   armour *collectively*; an armed force.
Example: the king had ordained his armour, knights . . . all ready for to go, c. 1400.

army, armies   a collection of men armed for battle; a naval armament, armada, or fleet; a great number of something. See also **array, force, host, multitude, troop.**
Examples: army of ants; of arguments; of caterpillars, 1611; of idlers, 1855; of locusts, 1857; of lovely looks, 1596; of martyrs, 1543; of misfortunes, 1675; of people, 1500; of pestilence, 1593; naval army [manned with sailors and marines], 1751; sea army [sailors and marines], 1751; army of sins, 1751; of speeches wise, 1596; of waiters, c. 1890; of words, 1628; of good words.

aroma   bakers *collectively* —*Lipton,* 1970.

array   an orderly collection; an imposing series of things or group of persons; a disposition of troops. See also **display, host, militia, series.**
Examples: array of attorneys [in court]; of Doric cities, 1846; of cliffs, 1856; of facts; of figures [numerals]; of hedgehogs; of sapphire and gold, 1814; of soldiers; of teeth, 1843.

ash-holt   a small grove of ash trees — *Wright.*

assemblage   a collection of individuals or things; a number of persons gathered together, a gathering. See also **assembly, cluster, collection, concourse, group.**
Examples: assemblage of all ages and nations, 1741; of grace; of ideas, 1704; of mighty heroes, 1877; of ladies, 1809; of rocks, 1748; of skaters.

assembly   a company of persons together at one place, esp. for one purpose; a legislative body; any set of things. See also **assemblage, bevy, company, diet, gathering, group, throng.**

Examples: assembly of huge crags and hills, 1642; of stock jobbers, 1711.

association   a group of persons to promote some idea, sport, or object. See also **alliance, fellowship, league.**

assortment   a group of things; a selection; a group of things of the same sort; an assorted set. See also **medley, miscellany.**
Examples: assortment of gift-horses, 1823; of shades ['colours'], 1611.

attic   a collection of Greeks —*N. Y. Times,* 1983.

attroopment   a disorderly or tumultuous crowd.
Examples: attroopments of houseless lazaroni ['lepers'], 1795; attroopment of people, 1822.

auctary   an addition or augmentation; something superadded.
Example: a large auctary ['donation of books'], to the library, 1580.

audience   a group or assembly of listeners, viewers, or spectators; a formal interview with a person of importance, *hence,* those present at such an interview.
Examples: an audience with the pope; an audience of readers; of secular men, 1407.

auditory   an assemblage of listeners and spectators. See also **audience.**
Examples: he chose to speak to small auditories, 1715; here is a learned auditory, 1548.

aumlach   a small quantity —*Wright.*

avenue, avenues   a double row of trees or pillars acting as a passageway, also used figuratively.
Examples: avenues of research; of thought; of wealth.

aviary   an enclosure for live birds, *hence,* the birds themselves, *collectively.*
Examples: aviary of birds; aviary of errors, 1647.

Axis   the association of the countries that formed the German/Italian/Japanese alliance in World War II.

B

babble   barbers *collectively* —*Lipton,* 1970

babel   a confused mixture of sounds, voices, or languages; a confused assembly. See also **charivari, hubbub, pandemonium.**
Examples: babel of follies, 1529; of past idle objurgations, 1884; of sectaries, 1731; babel towers of chimney, 1848.

bachelory, bachelordom   a group of bachelors; young knights as a class.
Example: a fair host of boys bachelerie, 1297.

badelyng, badling   a brood of ducks.
Example: a badelyng of ducks, 1486.

bag   a measure varying in size and quantity; the amount of game killed at one time.
Examples: bag of almonds [three hundredweight], 1751; of hops, 1679; of potatoes [three bushels to the bag]; of sugar [75 kilos]; of tricks; bag and baggage ['all the property of an army'].

bal   *Cornwall.* a collection of mines.

bale   a large bundle or package; a measure of varying quantity, 1502.
Examples: bale of cloth; of coffee [two to two and a half hundredweight]; of cotton; of crown paper [14 reams]; of dice [a pair or set], 1822; of turtles —*Lipton,* 1970.

balk   a ridge or heap on the ground. See also **bank, bar.**

Examples: balk of earth; of good ground, 1605; of money, 1652; of sand, 1538.

ball   a round or roundish body or mass. See also **clew, globe, orb.**
Examples: balls ['rings'] of cowslips, daisies, 1648; of fire; of nutmegs, 1583; of rosemary [750 lbs], 1796; of twine, 1841; of wool, 1884; of yarn, 1572; of live crabs, 1875.

balustrade   a row or assemblage of balusters or turned pillars —*Johnson,* 1755.

band   a company of persons or, sometimes, animals; a company of musicians. See also **company, party, troop.**
Examples: band of camels, 1611; of fold, 1490; of followers; of fugitives, 1876; of gorillas [a male with one or more females and young]; of men; of music, 1660; of musicians; of outlaws; of pilgrims [hymn]; of plovers; of robbers, 1826; of strangers, 1601; of violins.

banditti   a company of bandits.

bank   a mound, pile, or ridge; a group or series of objects; an amount or stock of money; a batch of paper money. See also **balk, bar, heap, mass.**
Examples: bank of ants; of books, 1577; of clouds, 1626; of electric lights; of fog, 1848; of hill ants, 1747; of judges [a full court in which the judges are "in bank"]; of mist, 1840; of money, 1878; of mussels, 1861; of oars, 1884; of organ keys, 1884; of oysters, 1861; of rememberances, 1576; of sand; of snow; of swans [on the ground].

banner   a body of men or troops who follow a banner; a group of knights.
Example: banner of horse, 1818.

bar   a bank of sand or gravel, esp. at the mouth of a river; barristers or lawyers *collectively.*
Examples: bar [barristers *collectively*], 1559; bar of gravel, 1586; of sand, 1586.

baren   a pack or herd of mules [from *barren,* i.e., 'not capable of producing young'].
Example: baren of mules, 1486.

baronage, baroney, barondy   the whole body of barons *collectively.*
Example: baronage of heaven ['angels'], 1340.

barring   bars *collectively,* i.e., decorative bars or stripes.

basinful   a burden, load, or overwhelming amount.
Examples: basinful of troubles; of worries.

bask   of crocodiles —*Hare.*

basket   A collection of various representative types, as for deriving an average.
Example: The value of the pound sterling may be averaged against a basket of currencies —*The Times,* 1984.

batch   a group or collection of persons or things of the same kind, taken or made at the same time. See also **lot, sort.**
Examples: batch of beers [a brewing], 1713; of bread [quantity baked at one time], 1461; of letters [usually a bundle] 1782; of notes; of politics, 1840; of prize money, 1838; of soup, 1878; of visitors, 1793.

battalion   the main body of an army; an infantry command of two or more companies forming part of a regiment; a large number.
Examples: battalion of men, 1705; of soldiers; of sorrows, 1603; of tunnyfish, 1603.

battery   a number of similar machines or devices arranged in a group; a succession of blows or drum beats; a number of hens housed together to encourage the laying of eggs. See also **bank, bench.**
Examples: battery of boilers; condensers; of drum beats; of dynamos; of electric lights; of guns [gun emplacement]; of hens, 1879; of kitchen untensils, 1819; of prisms or lens; of Leyden jars; of lights; of looks, 1823; of three mortars, 1688; searchlight battery.

bavin   a bundle of brushwood, 1580.

bayonet   a group of soldiers armed with bayonets, 1780.

beach   pebbles *collectively,* 1538; sand at the seaside, 1597; a ridge or bank, 1598.

beaconage   a system of beacons, 1862.

bead-roll, bede-roll   a list of persons to be prayed for, c. 1500; a list or string of names; a catalogue; a long line; a pedigree.
Examples: bead-roll of cousins, 1826; of offences, 1644; of living oracles, 1884; of prayers.

beam   a ray or collection of parallel rays.
Examples: beam of comfort, 1742; of glory; of heat, 1860; of light rays; of sunlight; of truth, 1674.

beat   a quantity to be beaten or processed at once; a bundle of flax or hemp made up ready for steeping, 1616.

bed   a layer or bed-like mass; small animals, especially reptiles, grouped together. See also **layer.**
Examples: bed of adders; of ashes; of clams; of coal; of cockles; of eels, 1608; of mussels; of oysters, 1682; of sand; of scorpions, 1692; of snakes, 1731; of worms, 1666.

beggary   beggars *collectively,* 1615. Also **beggardom,** 1884; **beggarhood,** 1843.

bellowing   bullfinches *collectively.*

bellyful   excessive amount.
Examples: bellyfull of bores —*Lipton,* 1970; of trouble.

belt   a continuous series of objects, usually encircling something; also a broad strip of any kind usually bordering something.
Examples: belt of lechery, 1483; of mirrors, 1857; of paternosters or "Our Fathers," 1844; of trees.

belting   belts *collectively.*

bench   officials *collectively*; judges *collectively*. See also **bank.**
Examples: bench of aldermen; of bishops, 1742; of judges, 1592; of magistrates; of organ keys; of dogs [at a dog-show].

bestiary   a medieval written book which collects together verse, prose, and illustrations of real and fabled animals —*Wilkes.*

bestial   collective term for domestic animals, 1393; replaced by *cattle* in the 17th century.

bevy   a drinking company; an assembly or collection. See also **covey, flight, flock, herd, swarm.**
Examples: bevy of beauties, of bright damsels, 1725; of conies, 1486; of fair women, 1667; of fairies, 1603; of girls; of ladies, 1470; of larks, 1470; of maids of honour, 1808; of otter; of powdered coxcombs, 1765; of quails, 1630; of renegades, 1848; of roes [six head of roe deer], 1470; of slaves, 1611; of swans.

bew   a flock of partridge.

bibliography   a collection of book titles arranged in a special order or relating to a special subject.

bijouterie   bijoux *collectively*; collective term for jewellery, trinkets, and articles of vertu, 1831.

bike   a swarm or crowd of people; a nest of wild bees; a bee-hive shaped stack of corn chaff; a teeming crowd; a "crew."
Examples: bike of ants; of beggars, 1785; of bumble bees, 1759; of wild bees.

bind   a unit of measurement for salmon or eels.
Examples: bind of eels [ten strike or sticks, i.e., 250 eels], 1667; bind of salmon [fourteen gallons].

bing   a heap or pile, particularly of metallic substances.
Examples: bing of alum, 1679; of lead ore [eight hundredweight], 1679; of metallic ore [eight hundredweight], 1679; of stones, 1513.

bishopdom   bishops *collectively*.

bite   a piece bitten off; a mouthful, 1535; *Thieves' cant.* cash or money.
Example: a bite of mites (modern pun).

blackening   shoemakers *collectively*. See also **bleche.**

blarney   bartenders *collectively* —*Lipton,* 1970

blast   a company of hunters, 1486 [a pun on the blast of the hunter's horn].

bleche   of Sowters, 1486 [translated as a 'blackening of shoe-makers' —*Lipton,* 1970].

blend   a mixture which is mingled inseparably —*Wilkes.*
Examples: blend of coffee; of tea.

bloat   of hippopotami —*Lipton,* 1970.

block   a quantity, number, or a section of something; a large quantity of anything dealt with at once, in a mass, wholesale; a group of houses or a building consisting of flats.
Examples: blocks of bonds; of flats; of shares.

blow   a quantity of steel dealt with at one time in a Bessemer converter, 1881.

blush   a group of young boys, 1486 [15th-century pun on the shyness of adolescent youth].

board   a council convened for business; a number of persons appointed or elected to sit on a committee.
Examples: board of commissioners; of directors, 1712; of governors; of guardians.

boarding   boards *collectively,* 1552; planks joined together.

boast   a number of soldiers, 1486 [15th-century pun on exploits recounted by returning soldiers].

boatage, boatery   boats and similar craft *collectively,* 1662.

bob   a knot or bunch of hair, *hence,* a bunch or cluster of leaves, flowers, fruit, etc. See also **bouquet, bunch, nosegay.**
Examples: bob of cherries, 1460; of flowers, 1570; of fruit; of

grapes, 1400; of hair, 1680; of hawthorn, 1807; of leaves, 1570; of primroses, 1807; of crimson ribbons, 1837; of worms, 1882.

bodge   a measure of oats [about half a peck].
Examples: bodge of beans, 1520; of oats.

body   a number of individuals spoken of *collectively*; a general collection of things or ideas; a mass of matter; the main portion of a collection or company.
Examples: body of inferior clergy, 1732; of cold air; of dialects, 1875; of disciples of Christ, 1886; of discourse, 1599; of divinity, 1659; of facts; of horse, 1769; of laws, 1699; of light; of natural history, 1711; of opinion; of philosophers, 1647; of precepts, 1860; of principles, 1860; of scriptures, 1593; of troops.

boll   measure of capacity for grain [six bushels in Scotland]; a measure of weight [140 lb.].
Examples: boll of corn, 1651; of grain; of malt, 1725; of oats, 1590; of salt, 1691; of wheat, 1875.

bolt   a bundle; a compact packet; a roll of woven fabric.
Examples: bolt of canvas [40 yards], 1638; of cloth [40 yards]; of fabric; of glass [molten cylindrical jet]; of osiers [willow twigs], 1725; of satin, 1592; of silk [40 yards]; of straw; of worsted, 1407.

bolus   a small rounded mass of a substance.

boodle   all of one's possessions; a disorderly mass; a crowd; a lot; stock in trade; capital.
Example: whole kit and boodle, 1625.

book   collection of tablets, sheets of paper, or similar material strung or bound together.
Examples: book of beauty, 1595; of bitter passion, 1532; of gold leaf [separated by vellum leaves]; of knowledge, 1667; of love, 1592; of nature, 1830; of precepts, 1380; of scorn, 1847; of silk [bundle of skeins of raw silk].

bookery   a collection of books, 1812; a library.

booly   a company of herdsmen wandering to find pasturage for their cattle, 1596.

boom   a fixed line of floating timber, 1702.

boredom   bores *collectively,* 1883.
Example: boredom of briefs [modern pun on legal briefs].

bosk, bosquet, bosket, boscage   a grove or plantation of shrubs or trees, 1737.
Examples: bosk of flowers, 1878; of holly, 1833; of laurel, 1833; of shrubs, 1737; of trees, 1737; of wildernesses, 1847.

bottle   bundle of hay or straw, 1386.
Examples: bottle of furs, 1578; of hay, 1486; of lupins, 1601; of straw, 1798.

bouquet   a nosegay or bunch, cluster, etc. See also **bow.**
Examples: bouquet of beaters [game beaters], 1875; of feathers; of fireworks [a large flight of rockets], 1879; of flowers; of herbs, 1846; of jewels, 1716; of pheasants [the flight of the flock from the beaters —*Lipton,* 1970]; of rockets, 1879.

bourgeoisie   bourgeois *collectively* or as a class, the French middle class, 1707; also extended to other nationalities.

bourock   a stone heap; a mound; a confused heap, 1807.

bow   a herd of cattle; the cattle on a farm [the livestock], c. 1300; bowmen or archers *collectively,* 1511.
Example: bow of ky [*Scots* 'cattle'], 1568.

bow, bowpot, boughpot   a bouquet of flowers or boughs; a bunch of flowers, 1848; a pot for holding boughs or flowers for ornament, 1583.

boyhood   boys *collectively,* 1802.

brace   a pair; a couple, originally of dogs, rarely used for people; a coat of armour. See also **cast, yoke.**
Examples: brace of bishops; of brethren, 1655; of bucks; of bullets, 1725; of chambers [rooms], 1642; of deer, 1570; of ducks;

of dukes, 1768; of fish, 1867; of foxes; of game, 1751; of geldings, 1651; of orthopaedists —*Mensa*; of partridge, 1741; of
pheasants; of pike; of pistols, 1832; of trout, 1715; of wives,
1606.

bracketing   brackets *collectively*, 1876.

brake   a clump of brushes, brushwood, or briars. See also
thicket.
Example: brakes of fern, shrub, and fallen trees, 1772.

branchage   a collection of branches, 1868. Also called
branchery, 1847; branching, 1882; also used figuratively.
Examples: branchery of mystic belief and superstitious practices, 1847; branching of rivers, 1684 ['the tributaries'
collectively].

brash   a mass of fragments or debris; a sudden outburst of
rain.
Examples: brash of bitter waters, 1856; of hedge clippings; of
ice, 1837; of rain, 1849; of twigs; of stone; of wooing, 1724.

brass   army officers *collectively*, 1899 [used in phrases *top brass*
or *brass hats*]; memorial brasses *collectively*, 1613; musical instrument of a brass band type *collectively*, 1382; copper coins
collectively, 1599; money in general, 1601.

break   a large quantity; a lot or consignment; a great number; a burst of sound.
Examples: break of folk, 1808; of honeysuckle, 1880; *Billards.* of
points, 1865; of stars, 1884; of tea, 1864; of trumpets, 1750.

breed   a race or variety of animals; a class, sort, or kind of
men, things, or qualities; a number produced at one time. See
also **brood.**
Examples: breed of bees [a brood], 1580; of duckling, 1802; of
thinkers; of wits, 1588.

bretheren   bretheren, brothers *collectively*; fraternity —*Wilkes.*

brewage   a mixture of various things —*Johnson*, 1755.

Examples: brewage of best Spanish wine, 1848; of tempests, 1821.

brewery   the brewing trade or a body of brewers, 1714.

brewing   a collection of black clouds which signal a storm.

briar, brier   briar bushes *collectively*, 1340.

brigade   a company or band of people; a body of troops; any body of persons acting together for a purpose, e.g., fire brigade.
Examples: brigade of firemen; of papists, 1649; of people, 1650; of foot (soldiers) 1642; of sappers, 1806; of trappers, 1837.

briggandage   brigands or robbers *collectively,* 1875.

brood   the young of animals or of birds, hatched or reared at the same time or from the same dam. See also **aerie, breed, fry.**
Examples: brood of birds, 1530; of blackgame, 1805; of smallboats; of chess players [modern pun on *to brood —Lipton,* 1970]; of chicken, 1611; of daughters, 1896; of ducks, 1711; of eels, 1558; of eagles; of eggs; of folly, 1632; of game; of grouse; of guilty wishes, 1863; of hawks; of heath fowl, 1805; of hens, 1486; of kittens; of lies, 1798; of oysters [in second year], 1862; of petty despots, 1867; of poisons, 1719; of presbyterians, 1706; of salmon, 1389; of serpents, 1697; of silkworms, 1760; of time, 1597.

brotherhood   an association or guild; a profession, person, or things of like kind or interest; a fellowship. See also **fraternity.**
Examples: brotherhood of blood, 1860; of lofty elms, 1814; of monks and friars, 1528; of mountains, 1843; of the sons of God, 1526.

brow   a collection of scholars —*Lipton,* 1970.

brush   a bundle of light rays; the loppings of trees and hedges, 1330; a faggot or bavin of brushwood, 1690; a thicket of small growing trees or shrubs, 1553.

Examples: brush of rosemary, hyssop, fennel or other herbs, 1609; of light rays, 1817.

budget   a bag or sack with its contents; a stock or accumulation; an estimate of expenses; a leather or skin bottle.
Examples: budget of freshwater ['leather bottleful'], 1580; of general knowledge, 1822; of inventions, 1692; of nails ['a bag'], 1677; of news; of olives, 1653; of paper, 1729; of paradoxes, 1867; of tools ['a bag'], 1879.

building   a flock of rooks, 1470 [from their nesting habits].

bulk   a main mass or amount; a heap; a cargo; a considerable amount. See also **mass.**
Examples: bulk of people, 1711; of pilchards [a pile awaiting salting], 1822; of popery, 1641; of seals, 1881; of ships, 1658; of tobacco [a pile arranged for curing].

bullary, bullarium   a collection of papal bulls or documents, 1674.

bulwark   a collection of persons acting as a defense or safeguard to protect an ideal or way of life.
Examples: bulwark of Christendom, 1577; of our laws, 1614; of our liberties, 1789; to theology, 1837.

bumf, bumph   *British.* documents *collectively*; waste or unnecessary documents *collectively*, 1899; [short for *bumfolder* 'toilet paper'].

bunch   a cluster or tuft, properly of things of one type growing or fastened together; a group of things or animals of the same type gathered close together. See also **bundle, nosegay.**
Examples: bunch of bananas; of cards, 1563; of cattle, 1884; of charity, 1633; of cherubs, 1832; of ducks [up to 130 in a group], 1835; of fives ['a clenched fist']; of flowers, 1570; of grapes, 1842; of hair, 1590; of imbecility, 1874; of judges, 1622; of keys, 1587; of kings, 1622; of linen yarn [60 hanks]; of copper or tin ore, 1815; of machinery, 1984; of patriarchs, 1622; of prophets, 1622; of raisins, 1719; of reeds, 1863; of slate, 1865; of straw, 1450; of teal [small group on the water];

of teazles, 1863; of tunes; of vapours, 1873; of violets, 1821; of waterfowl; of widgeon.

bundle   a number of things bound together as a loose package or roll; a given quantity of some articles. See also **bolt, bunch, collection, package.**
Examples: bundle of archdeacons; of calumnies, 1646; of glass plate, 1831; of herbs, 1796; of ideas, 1690; of iron rods, 1831; of keys, 1474; of linen yarn [20 hanks], 1875; of notes [money]; of myrrh [sorrow], 1388; of principal nobility of the Christian world, 1564; of paper [two reams]; of papers, 1636; of qualities, 1863; of rags; of rays; of sensations, 1785; of sins, 1633; of sticks; of straw; of superstitions, 1768.

burden   a fixed quantity of a commodity; a heavy load; the chorus of a song. See also **charge, load, trust.**
Examples: burden of armour, 1595; of brass [debts], 1601; of corn, 1523; of despair, 1812; of gold, 1440; of rushes, 1560; of sin, 1303; of sorrows, 1374; of steel [120 lb.]; of thorns, 1449; of verse, 1598; of weeds, 1527.

bureaucracy   government officials *collectively*, 1848.

burgonet   a headpiece; a protection for the head, *hence,* a bodyguard.
Example: burgonet of men, 1606.

burrow   a heap or mound; esp., an animal's hiding- or dwelling-place, *hence,* the animals themselves *collectively*.
Examples: burrow of conies, 1669; of foxes, 1538; of puffins, 1832; of rubbish, 1875; of rabbits, 1540; of soil, 1784; of barking squirrels or prairie dogs, 1814.

burst   a vehement outburst.
Examples: burst of applause; of gratitude, 1775; of ill humour, 1838; of laughter, 1838; of merriment, 1751; of passion; of sunlight, 1854; of thunder, 1671.

bury   a burrow of conies; rabbits *collectively*.

bush   bushes *collectively*; a cluster of shrubs; a brush-like mass

such as foliage or feathers, woodland, or rural countryside *collectively,* as contrasted with the town. See also **brush.**
Examples: bush of broom, 1670; of ivy (used as inn sign); of ostrich feathers, 1530; of spears, 1513; of thorns; of wood, 1639.

bushel   *loosely,* a large quantity or number.
Examples: bushel of curled hair on his head, 1718; of girls, 1873; of honours, 1680; of money, 1683; of venom, 1374.

business   of flies; flies *collectively.*

busyness   of ferrets; ferrets *collectively* —*Bk. of St. Albans,* 1486.

butchery   butchers *collectively,* 1475.

butt   a small piece of land; a bundle or pack.
Examples: butt of land, 1475; of linen [1500 yds.], 1705; of olives, 1653; of Malmsey wine, 1477.

buzz   of barflies; barflies *collectively* —*Lipton,* 1970.

C

cabal   a small group engaged in a secret intrigue; a political clique. See also **camarilla, conspiracy, faction, party.**
Examples: cabal of artists, 1859; of cardinals, 1715; of intriguers; of politicians. [Its origin was popularly related as an acronym referring to 1670, when the English Government ministers included *C*lifford, *A*shley, *B*uckingham, *A*rlington, and *L*auderdale.]

cabinet   a body of persons, usually a limited number, of the ministers of state of a country, 1630; a secret store-house, *hence,* its contents.
Examples: cabinet of animal functions, 1667; of my secret thoughts, 1549; of his secret will, 1634.

cabiri   a group of deities of Samothrace.

caboodle   *U. S. Slang.* the whole amount; the lot, usually in *(the whole) kit and caboodle.*

cache   a hiding place, *hence,* the items hidden; the stores of provisions hidden by travellers or explorers on their journeys.
Examples: cache of green boughs, 1866; of jewels; of meat, 1865; of a barrel of pork, 1842; of provisions; of silver, 1860; of treasure.

cade   a cask or barrel containing a quantity of 720 herrings, later 500 herrings; a quantity of 1000 sprats.
Examples: cade of herrings, 1440; of sprats, 1704.

cadre   a group or skeleton crew of trained men who would absorb untrained men to form an efficient unit in an emergency; 19th century.

cafila, kafila   convoy of travellers in Arabia, Persia, or India, 1594. See also **caravan.**

cagmag   scraps, odds and ends, 1874; decaying refuse, 1859.

cairn   a pile of stones, usually erected to mark a spot as a memorial or to mark a cache of provisions, etc., 1535.

cajolery   of taverners —*Bk. of St. Albans,* 1486.

cake   a mass of matter moulded into a solid shape; used figuratively.
Examples: cake of customs, 1872; of dynamite, 1884; of ice; of laws and customs, 1879; of paint; of soap; of tobacco; of wax, 1528.

calendar   an orderly list of persons, things, or events; a list of offenders in the Newgate Calendar or in similar prisons or at Quarter Session Courts; a list or record.
Examples: calendar of academics; of crimes, 1856; of documents; of my past endeavours, 1601; of martyrs, 1781; of saints, 1631; of sins, 1633.

calling   a group of persons following a profession, *specifically,* the church, medicine, or nursing.
Example: calling house of wits, 1860.

camarilla   a company of secret or irresponsible councillors, e.g., the king's circle of advisors. See also **cabal, clique, coterie.**
Examples: camarilla of advisors; of councillors; of politicians, 1867; of priests, 1839.

camelry   troops mounted on camels, 1854 —*Wilkes.*

camorra   a secret society of lawless malcontents in Naples and other Neopolitan cities, 1865 —*Wilkes.*

camp   a body of troops on campaign; a collection of tents; the company who are encamped; a great number; a body of people who join together to promote some theory or doctrine; a body of people engaged in some occupation or sport who are encamped together; a conical or ridge-shaped pile or heap; used figuratively.

Examples: camp of allegations, 1871; of arguments; of facts, 1566; of ideas, 1885; of lumbermen; of nomads; of potatoes ['a heap'], 1700; of surveyors; of troops; of turnips ['a heap'].

canaille   the rabble; a mob; the lowest class of people, 1676.
Example: canaille of miscreants, 1680.

candy   to form into congelations —*Johnson,* 1755; to be in a congealed state.
Example: candied with ice —*Shakespeare.*

cannonry   cannons *collectively*; cannoneers, *collectively,* as a force, 1886.

canon   a collection of rules or laws; a set of mathematical tables; a collection or list of books of the Bible accepted as genuine and inspired; any set of sacred books; a piece of music with different parts taking up the same subject successively in strict imitation. See also **code.**
Examples: canon of laws; of mathematical tables; of monastic rules; of rules; of saints.

canopy   an overhanging shelter or shade; used figuratively.
Examples: canopy of clouds, 1855; of heaven, 1869; of plumage, 1843; of trees; of virtue, 1603.

canteen   a chest or case for carrying culinary utensils, *hence,* a collection of the utensils themselves; a small tin or wooden vessel with the capacity of three to four pints carried by soldiers on the march; by workmen, or by travellers.
Examples: canteen of coffee, 1851; cutlery; with a tea service, 1839; of water, 1744; of wine flasks, 1737.

canvas   paintings *collectively*; sails *collectively*; tents *collectively*; also used figuratively to mean 'a wide range, a large expanse.'
Example: canvas of fancy, 1822.

capelocracy   *from Greek.* the shopkeeping class, 1841.

caper   of kids —*Lipton,* 1970.

capful   as much as a cap will contain.
Examples: capful of quartz, 1873; of wind, 1719.

capillament   the hair, *collectively,* 1681.

capitulary   a collection of ordinances, esp. of the Frankish kings; e.g., the capitulary of Worms, 829.

car   the seven stars in the constellation of the Great Bear, 1633.

caravan   a number of people travelling together; a moving company; a fleet of merchant ships. See also **cafila, convoy.**
Examples: caravan of camels, 1601; of merchants, 1602; of pilgrims; of merchant ships; of travellers, 1599; an aerie caravan [birds], 1667.

cardinalate   the state of being a cardinal, *hence,* cardinals *collectively.*

cargason, cargazon   a cargo; freight of a ship, 1645; used figuratively.
Examples: cargason of cloth, 1645; of compliments, 1642; of corrupt humours, 1645.

cargo   a shipload, 1657; a load. See also **burden.**
Examples: cargo of brown sugar, 1705; of ginger, 1705; of lampoons, 1762; of novels, 1806.

cark   a load or weight of three to four hundredweight; a burden.
Examples: cark of alum, 1473; of anxiety; of ginger, 1502; of pepper; of wool, 1637.

carnage   a heap of dead bodies; men slain in a battle, 1667; carcasses *collectively.*

carol   a band or company; a circle or ring of things; a ring dance with songs; *hence,* the songs themselves; a ring of standing stones; a company of singers; an assembly. See also **choir.**

Examples: carol of maidens; of singers; of songs, 1300; of standing stones; of virgins, 1483.

carpet   a covering or expanse, as of grass or flowers; used figuratively.
Examples: carpet of flowers, 1854; grassy carpet, 1593.

carrot   a group of objects in the shape of a carrot.
Example: carrot of tobacco, 1808.

cartel   political or economic combination between parties or business organizations; *hence,* the parties themselves. See also **combine, syndicate.**

cartload   a large and mixed quantity; a load or heap, 1577.
Examples: cartload of complaints, 1577; of grievances, 1577; of lies, 1645; of monkeys ['artful as a cartload of monkeys'].

cascade   something suggestive of a fall of water. See also **cataract, spray.**
Examples: cascade of fireworks; of hair; of ice, 1860; of jewels; of lace, 1882; of molecules, 1878; of rockets; of stones, 1687; of volcanic ash, 1869.

case   set or pair; a box and its contents. See also **brace.**
Examples: case of books, 1639; of coxcombs; of instruments; of lies, 1599; of pistols, 1579; of rapiers, 1590; of teeth, 1824; of wine.

casket, casquet   a small chest, as of jewels; a selection of literary or musical gems.
Examples: casket of jewels; of literary selections; of musical selections; of songs, 1850.

cast   the things or quantity created or produced at one time; a group of actors in play; a set or suit of armour; a couple of birds. See also **brace, brood, set.**
Examples: cast of actors; of armour [a suit]; of bees [an afterswarm], 1662; of bread [baked at one time], 1470; of corn [a yield], 1787; of counters, 1591; of dust, 1697; of eagles, 1615; of falcons, 1826; of goshawks; of grain [amount harvested]; of hawks, 1470; of hay, 1450; of herrings [number

thrown in vessel at one time], 1887; of merlins, 1881; of oysters, 1808; of seed [amount scattered at one time]; of stones, 1481; of vultures, 1611; of wood.

castle   any structure or pile of objects more or less in the shape of a castle.
Examples: castle of cards (modern); of fine manchet [the finest kind of wheaten bread], 1791; of march-pane ['marzipan'], 1627.

catalects   a collection of short poems, e.g., ascribed to Virgil; fragments or detached pieces.

catalogue   a list of names, titles, or articles arranged systematically. See also **calendar.**
Examples: catalogue of books, 1669; of calamities, 1792; of disasters, 1824; of endowments, 1611; of librarians [modern]; of martyrs, 1483; of popes, 1460; of sins; of virtues; of woes, 1719.

cataract   a violent downpour or rush; anything likened to a waterfall. See also **cascade.**
Examples: cataract of nastiness; of evil news, 1864; of panegyrics; of water.

catch   the quantity caught or taken at one time; a fragment or scrap of anything; used figuratively.
Examples: catch of fish; of songs, 1830; of favourite stories; of pretty stories, 1665.

catena   a chain or a connected series; a string or series of extracts from the writings of the Christian Fathers. See also **chain.**
Examples: catena of conscious observance, 1868; of difficulties, 1884; of opinion; 1862; of tory platitudes, 1886; of writers, 1862.

cateran   common people of the Highlands in a band; brigands, freebooters, or marauders *collectively.*

cattle   bovine animals *collectively;* other live animals, as fowl, bees, etc.; slaves; people considered to be rubbish or trash; the mob; lazy servants —*Slang Dictionary,* 1874.

caucus   an inner committee, usually political, that works behind the main party.

cavalcade   a procession of persons on horseback; a procession or parade of carriages.
Examples: cavalcade of carriages; of devils, 1709; of horsemen; of songs; of sewarry [Indian mounted troops], 1616.

cavalry   horses or horsemen *collectively*; horse soldiers *collectively* as contrasted with infantry, 1591.

cave   a small group of politicians who break away from the main party; a splinter party.
Example: cave of Adullam, 1866.

cell   a small religious group or community connected to a monastery or convent; a unit of persons forming part of a network in a political party; a communist cell; a cell of workers.

cellar   a place for storing wine, *hence,* the wine bottles *collectively.*
Example: cellar of bottles, 1627.

cellarage   cellars *collectively,* 1602.

cenoby   a religious community, 1475.

centgener, centeener   a large number [properly one hundred plants or animals] of common parentage —*Webster.*

cento, centones, centoism   A literary or musical composition made up of selections; a string or rigmarole; a composition formed by joining scraps from other authors, 1605; a patchwork of coloured cloths, 1610.
Examples: cento of blunders, 1780; of borrowed thoughts, 1859; of commonplaces, 1822; of literary works, 1605; of musical composition; of uncircumcised nations, 1647; of patchwork, 1610; of revolters of popery, 1626; of scriptural phrases; of verses, 1882.

century   a group of a hundred things; a period of one hundred years; a body of one hundred men or troops.
Examples: century of copies, 1867; of sultrying passions, 1598; of prayers, 1611; of sonnets, 1855; of troops; of words, 1737; of years.

cete   a meeting or assemblage of badgers.
Examples: cete of badgers —_Bk. of St. Albans,_ 1486; of greys.

chain   a series of things linked together into a chain, actually or figuratively. See also **catena, cordon, series.**
Examples: chain of buckets; of causes, 1829; of charity, 1377; of deductions, 1664; of discourse, 1651; of events; of human beings; of ideas; of islands; of lakes; of mountains; of proof; of reasoning, 1809; of shops or supermarkets; of spangles, 1841; of storms; of succession, 1655; of thought, 1711.

change   the order in which a peal of bells can be rung, _hence,_ the collective sound of the bells; _Mathematics._ a permutation for a different order in which a set or series of things can be changed.
Examples: change or peal of bells; a change of clothing [modern].

chantry   a body of priests who say masses for the dead in a chantry chapel.
Example: chantry of priests, 1775.

chaos   any confused or disorderly collection or state of things; a conglomeration of parts or elements without order or connexion. See also **clutter, confusion.**
Examples: chaos of accidental knowledge; of foul disorders, 1579; of green and grey mists, 1878; of laws and regulations, 1781.

chapel   a choir or body of singers; an association of printers, 1688; a chapter of a printers' union at a certain press [modern].

chapelry   a congregation of nonconformist chapel-goers, 1707.

chaplet   a string of beads or a garland, or something that resembles it; a rosary, *hence,* the prayers recited over it.
Examples: chaplet of beads, 1653; of domestic affections, 1827; of flowers, 1590; of olive leaves, 1839; of prayers; of precious stones, 1450; of roses, 1711; of sharp nettles, 1480; of toad's eggs, 1835; of laurel, 1691; of rue, 1864.

chapter   the body or community of an organized branch of a society or church, monastic or religious order, or of any order of knights; a unit that is a sequential part of a series; used figuratively.
Examples: chapter of accidents, 1773; of canons, 1305; of friars, 1679; of knights, 1842; of the Noble Order of the Garter, 1681; of noble virgins; of possibilities, 1769.

charge   a load, burden, or weight; a quantity of ammunition powder for the firing of a gun; metallic ore to fill a furnace; a mental or moral load. See also **burden, trust.**
Examples: charge of curates —*Bk. of St. Albans,* 1486; of electricity, 1782; of gunpowder, 1653; of intelligence, 1713; of lead ore, 1858; of money, 1653; of snuff, 1712; of shot, 1863; of taxis —*Lipton,* 1970.

chariotry   warriors who fought from chariots *collectively,* 1828.

charivari   a medley of discordant sounds; "rough music." See also **babel.**

charm   a medley of goldfinches, 1430; the blended voices of a choir; a noise or confusion of voices as of children or birds.
Examples: charm of angels, 1530; of birds [a group of singing birds]; of choristers; of goldfinches, 1430.

chartulary   a collection or set of charters, 1571. See also **archives.**

chattering   a company of choughs; starlings *collectively.*

chautauqua   an educational assembly modelled on that at Lake Chautauqua, 1874.

cherubim   cherubs collectively or plural, 1613.

chest   a box; the quantity or the things contained. See also
case.
Examples: chest of clothes, 1865; of tools, 1854; of viols, 1611.

chice   a small quantity; a taste. See also **smidgeon**
—*Gepp.*
Examples: chice of salt; of sugar.

chiliad   a group of 1,000 things or years.
Examples: chiliad of cross fortunes, 1598; of years before
Christ, 1876.

chiliarchy   a body of 1,000 troops.

chime   a peal of bells; a set of bells in a church tower.

chirm   a din or chatter, *hence,* finches *collectively,* 1430. See
also **charm.**

choice   a choice or picked company of people.
Example: a brave choice of dauntless spirits, 1595.

choir   an organized company of persons or things; a company
of singers; a band or company of dancers; an order or division
of angels. See also **carol, chorus.**
Examples: choir of angels, 1667; of cherubim, 1667; of choristers; of cosmical science, 1855; of dancers; of echoes, 1592; of
muses, of planets, 1692; of teeth, 1704; of tents, 1382.

chorus   a company of singers; a simultaneous outburst of
speech. See also **carol, choir.**
Examples: chorus of bad language; of complaints; of conversation, 1845; of Greek actors; of laughter; of planets, 1660; of
porpoises, 1698; of singers, 1656.

chrestomathy   a selection of choice literary passages from one
or more authors, 1832.

christendom   Christians *collectively,* 1131; A particular body
or community of Christians, 1205.

circle   a set or series of parts connected to form a whole; a

company assembled about a central point or topic of interest; a circular ring of persons or things. See also **company, ring.**
Examples: circle of action, 1752; of admirers, 1793; of acquaintances, 1752; of doctrine, 1531; of fallacy, 1646; of foliages, 1713; of glory, 1595; literary circle; circle of onlookers, 1875; of pleasures, 1759; of passion, 1768; of possibilities, 1644; of probability, 1851; of sciences, 1854; of stars, 1611.

circuit the action of moving round about; those persons making a circuit; used figuratively.
Examples: circuit of judges and barristers, 1494; of deductions, 1594; of reasoning, 1836; of speech, 1605; of words, 1672.

citadel a fortress; mole burrows at different levels; used figuratively.
Examples: citadel of mole burrows; of smuggling, 1774; of superstition, 1826.

citizenhood citizens collectively, 1871; citizenry, 1819.

clam a stack or pile of bricks; a heap of oysters.
Examples: clam of bricks, 1663; of earth, 1554; of oysters.

clamjamphine a rabble of worthless people, a mob; things of no value, 1825; rubbish — *Wilkes*.
Examples: clamjamphine of actors, 1821; of the mob, 1816.

clamour a company of rooks; a flock of birds; a loud collective noise of musical instruments, 1592; a loud noise of birds and animals; loud shouting; a mingling of voices.
Examples: clamour of disapprobation, 1830; common clamour of the Englishman, 1480; of rooks; of storms, 1876.

clamp a compact heap or pile of bricks for baking; a heap of earth to cover potatoes; a pile of ore for roasting.
Examples: clamp of bricks, 1679; of coal; of dung, 1771; of limestone, 1795; of mangolds, 1881; of metal ore; of potatoes; of turf, 1753.

clan a social group of common descent; a collection of animals, plants, or lifeless things; a body of persons with a common interest. See also **set, society.**

Examples: clan o' bairns ['children'], 1855; of the enlightened, 1790; of false traitors, 1552; of hounds, 1735.

claque   a group of admirers; always ready to applaud the person they follow; *esp. in France,* a group of paid applauders.

class   a rank or position of society; a division into units in a school or college; *in the United States,* those students who enter college the same year; a number of persons with similar qualities or skills grouped together; a range of items or things graded according to quality.

clatter   a scattered mass of loose stones; a confusion of voices. See also **clutter.**
Examples: clatter of grey rock, 1873; of stones; of tongues in empty heads, 1851.

clattering   a flock of choughs, 1430.

claut   a handful or rakeful, from the verb meaning 'claw' or 'scratch.'
Examples: claut o' siler [silver], 1793; claut o' cauld porridge [cold porridge], 1818.

cleft   a group of stars [modern].

clerisy, clericity   learned men as a body; scholars, 1818.
Example: the clerisy of a nation, that is its learned men, whether poets, or philosophers, or scholars, 1834.

clerkage, clerkery   clerks *collectively,* 1829.

cletch   a brood or hatching; a clutch; *Contemptous.* a family.
Examples: cletch of chickens, 1691; of ducks, 1868.

clew   a globe, ball, or spherical bunch; a tangled cluster of things; a ball of thread, etc.
Examples: clew of bees, 1616; of cord; of thread; of yarn; of worms, 1669.

clientage   a body of adherents; supporters, 1611.

clientelage   a body of retainers or followers, 1879.

clientele, clientry   a body of clients, 1594.

clip   something that clips or clasps things together, *hence,* the group of items so clipped; a springholder for letters or papers — *Wilkes.*
Example: clip of papers [modern].

clique   a narrow circle of friends; an exclusive set, 1711. See also **coterie, faction.**
Example: clique of admirers.

clobber   belongings; personal clothes and goods.

clod   a mass or lump of any solid matter.
Example: clod of earth, clay, iron, brass, turf.

closing   of taverners; a group of innkeepers, 1486.

clothing   clothes, suits, etc., *collectively,* 1275.

cloud   a mass or volume of smoke, flying dust, etc.; a body of insects or birds; a mass of rock; a great crowd; a vast collection. See also **drift, plague, swarm.**
Examples: cloud of arrows, 1776; of disdain, 1591; of dust; of flies, 1855; of foxes, 1883; of gnats, 1590; of grasshoppers; of incense; of information, 1705; of insects; of locust, 1667; of rain; of rock; of sails, 1748; of seafowl, 1885; of smoke; of starlings, 1882; of witches; of witnesses, 1382.

cloud drift   a body of drifting clouds across the sky.

cloudfield   an expanse of cloud, 1840.

cloudrack   a collection of broken clouds, 1847.

clowder, cludder, clutter   kendle or kindle of cats, 1801; a group of cats.
Example: clowder of cats.

club   a meeting or assembly for social discourse; an association of persons of like sympathies usually interested in the promotion of some object, sport, etc.; a combination; a clique.

cludder   See **clowder.**

clump   an unshaped mass; a heap; a cluster of trees; a tuft of shrubs; a compact mass or patch of any growing plants; used figuratively. See also **group, thicket.**
Examples: clump of bananas, 1845; of bread, 1868; of flowers; of frog-spawn, 1721; of grass; of houses, 1870; of plants, 1822; of reeds, 1766; of salt, 1767; of stitches [needlework], 1870; of trees, 1586.

clunch   a lump; a heavy, unshapely mass.
Example: clunch of snow, 1888.

cluster   a number of like things growing together; a number of similar things collected together; a rounded mass; a clot or clutter; a body of people collected together; a crowd; group. See also **bunch, crowd.**
Examples: cluster of apples, 1400; of bees, 1609; of blood, 1548; of churches; of churls, 1486; of curls, 1798; of crystals; of eggs, 1555; of rich parasitic fancies, 1856; of feelings, 1855; of grapes, 1486; of houses; of icebergs, 1860; of ideas, 1768; of islands, 1697; of jewels, 1712; of knots, 1486; of civil law, 1607; of memories, 1884; of nuts, 1483; of pines, 1797; of spiders; of stars, 1854; of towers, 1400; of woes, 1742.

clustering   a group gathered together in a cluster.
Examples: clustering of calamities, 1576; of humble dwellings, 1858; of verdure, 1842; clustering together in companies, 1541.

clutch   a nest of eggs or brood of young. See also **brood, cletch, family.**
Examples: clutch of chicken; constables [modern]; eggs, 1721; geese, 1885; partridges; squalls, 1825; tempests, 1825.

clutter   a confused collection; a clotted mass; a crowded and confused group; a collection. See also **clowder.**
Examples: clutter of bodies, 1674; of business, 1649; of cats; of citations, 1666; of consonants, 1791; of narrow crooked, dark, and dirty lanes, 1792; of drops against the glass, 1841; of spiders; of thick and deep grass, 1670.

coacervation   the result of piling or heaping things together; an accumulation; a mass — *Wilkes*.
Examples: coacervation of proofs, 1852; of texts, 1641; of tough humours, 1650.

coalesque   to grow into one body; to unite; to grow into lumps; to cake.

coagmentation   a mass formed by things being cemented or joined together — *Wilkes*.
Examples: coagmentations of matter, 1678; of words, 1636.

coalition   the union of a mass of separate bodies; an alliance of political parties, states, or persons. See also **combination, fusion, league.**
Examples: coalition of interests, 1779; of parties, 1715.

cob   a bunch of hair; a stack of grain or hay; a rounded heap or mass; a small heap of anything.
Examples: cob of grain; of hair [a bunch or chignon]; of hay, 1616; of jelly, 1876.

cock   a conical heap of produce or vegetation, e.g., of hay in the field in stacks.
Examples: cock of barley, 1718; of corn, 1483; of grass, 1750; of hay, 1483; of oak (trees), 1473; of turf, 1881.

code   a collection of laws, rules, or signals; a body of writings. See also **canon.**
Examples: code of cyphers; of ethics, 1841; of laws, 1577; of good manners of perfection, 1875; of rules; of scriptures, 1794; of signals; of Christian writings, 1795.

codex   a collection of recipes for the preparation of drugs; a collection of the scriptures written down on parchment or papyrus in their earliest texts.
Examples: codex of the law, 1622; of Christian precepts, 1659.

coffle   a train of slaves or of beasts driven along together.
Examples: coffle of asses, 1799; of beasts; of horses, 1873; of slaves, 1799.

cohort   a division in the Roman army; a band of warriors. See also **band, company.**
Examples: cohort of acquaintances, 1719; of bright cherubim, 1667; of Christian fathers, 1858; of infantry, 1489; of priests, 1874; of social regenerators, 1871; of warriors, 1500.

coil   a series of rings; a selection; a spiral; connected pipes in rows or layers.
Examples: coil of hair, 1888; of hay, 1800; of lace, 1858; of lava, 1869; of men, women, and children, 1856; of proper men, 1574; of bubbling springs, 1816; of teal [in flight].

collation   things brought together, as different varieties or denominations of money, of food, etc., the possessions of a person. See also **contribution, hotch-potch.**
Examples: collation of chicken; of food (e.g., *cold collation*); of money, 1382; of salad.

collect   a meeting for worship; an assembly; a collection; a gathering.
Examples: collect of money; of Tuscan hieroglyphics, 1651.

collectanea   a miscellany of passages collected from various authors, 1791. See also **anthology.**

collection   a gathering of objects or of persons, as works of art, literary materials, etc.; a quantity of anything collected together into a mass; an assemblage. See also **accumulation.**
Examples: collection of literary material, 1460; of floating vapours, 1747; of waters, 1697; of works of art, 1651.

collective   a collective body; a gathering; a collection of extracts; a number of individuals working or acting together; *specifically in the USSR,* a farm created by pooling together a number of small holdings. See also **aggregate, body.**

college   a body of colleagues or students; a collective body of a profession or religious order; a society of students or scholars. See also **academy, institute.**
Examples: college of bees, 1790; of canons; of cardinals; of clergy; of courtesans, 1621; of executioners, 1655; of hand-

maidens, 1430; of heralds; of paradise, 1502; of scholars; of undergraduates.

colligation   conjunction; alliance; union; the binding together or the linking of a number of isolated facts — *Wilkes*.
Examples: colligation of facts, 1837; of kingdoms, 1651; of [blood] vessels, 1646.

collocation   a group or sequence formed by placing things side by side or in a place or position. e.g., words in a sentence or sound in music — *Wilkes*.
Examples: collocation of intervals and pores, 1684; of magazines, 1813; of poetry, 1873; of various metals, or inlaying them by way of ornament, 1881; of vowels and consonants, 1751; of words, 1750.

colloquium   a conference; an assembly for discussion [from *colloque*, 'a place for conversation in a monastery,' 1844].

colluvies   a medley; a rabble, 1647; a collection of foul matter; a conflux of filthy water. See also **hotchpotch, medley, rabble.**
Examples: colluvies and sink of human greatness, 1730; of remaining humours, 1651; of all nations, 1678; of filthy lecherous people, 1671; of rain water, 1655; of recrements ['dross, waste substances'], 1710.

collonade   series of columns, 1718; row of trees or pillars, or other objects, as elms, 1830; chestnut trees, 1784.

colony   a group of people transported to another place or part of the world; a collection of people associated with a craft, occupation, decorative art, etc.; a number of animals or plants in a group. See also **community.**
Examples: colony of ants —*Lipton*, 1970; of artists; of auks [on land]; of avocets; of badgers; of bats; of bees, 1713; of beggars, 1737; of chinchilla; of cormorants; of frogs; of gulls; of ibises; of lepers; of mice; of monks, 1844; of musicians,1711; of penguins; of sparrows, 1840; of voles; of vampires.

column   anything resembling a vertical or horizontal column; an upright mass of water or air. See also **pillar.**
Examples: column of accountants —*Lipton,* 1970; of air, 1833; of atmosphere, 1700; of infantry [on the march]; of majesty, 1619; of mercury, 1878; of numbers of ships, 1805; of smoke, 1715; of society, 1862; of state, 1725; of troops, 1677.

combination   a union of people to achieve an aim; a collection of connected ideas, letters, or incidents. See also **alliance, coalition.**

combine   a group of persons, originally coming together for a conspiracy or for fraudulent purposes, now usually a very large commercial company or group of companies. See also **cartel, syndicate.**

comfort   of cats.

comitadji   a band of irregulars.

comitatus   a body of companions; a retinue of warriors attached to a king or chieftain. See also **posse comitatus.**

comitia   an assembly of people to act on matters before them, 1734; an assembly, 1625; the principal assembly at Oxford where public disputations took place and degrees were conferred, 1714.

command   a military or naval force; a body of troops under a commander, 1592.

commission   *in the United Kingdom,* a committee or advisory body created by Royal Warrant to conduct a special enquiry; *in the United States,* a committee, advisory board, or governmental department.

committee   a group of people appointed or elected to administer, discuss, or make reports concerning a subject on which its members are authorities.

commixture   a mixture or compound.
Examples: commixture of good and evil acts, 1607; of intellectual delights, 1643; of virtues and vices, 1601.

commonalty, commonty   the community; the common people; the corporate body of a town or city.

commonwealth   the body of the public constituting a state or community; a body united for some special interest and common benefit.
Examples: commonwealth of all Christendom, 1551; of angels, 1608; of learning; The British Commonwealth of Nations; The Commonwealth [English history 1649—1660].

commune   a body of the commons; a group forming an interim government. e.g., in Paris in 1794 and 1781; a group living together in a common community.

communion   a body of Christians with a common faith and ritual. See also **fellowship, sect.**
Examples: the Anglican Communion; Communion of holy men, 1573; of Saints, 1394.

community   a body of people living in the same locality or having a common language or interest. See also **cluster, combination.**
Examples: community of feeling, 1823; of flies; of good, 1645; of interests, 1875; of power, 1561; of studies, 1841; of ulcers, 1541; of wives, 1564.

compages   a system or linking of many parts.
Examples: compages of the Christian faith, 1724; of forces, 1860; of pipes and vessels; of body and spirit, 1740.

compagination   a union of parts; a structure; the whole that is made up of parts, e.g., the human body.
Examples: compagination of icy islands, 1691; of many parts and members, 1655; of sin.

companionship   a body of companions; a company of compositors, a guild or union.
Examples: companionship of compositors; of twenty to thirty boats, 1865.

company   a band, retinue, or fellowship; a retinue or train; a

collection, assemblage, or multitude of people, beasts, birds, etc. See also **assembly, band, bevy, party.**
Examples: company of actors [often used collectively as "the company"]; of apostles, 1548; of fair maidens, 1325; of fowls, 1393; of fine glasses, 1621; of islands, 1677; of moles; of musicians; of parrots; of players; of prophets; of small roots, 1577; of ships [merchant fleet]; of soldiers; of turbot, 1864; of widgeon, 1856.

compilation   a heaping or piling together; an accumulation; a literary work compiled from various sources.
Examples: compilation of foreign memoirs, 1794; of the mass, 1728; of theological systems, 1837.

complement   the full amount; a set; the total number of personnel of a ship or military establishment; a cargo; the amount needed to fill a conveyance.
Example: complement of cloves, 1697.

complex   an object or framework made up from parts; a group of buildings forming part of related whole.
Examples: complex of doctrine, 1862; of fluid atoms, 1652; of planets, 1672; of psychoanalysts —*Lipton,* 1970.

compliment   of sycophants —*Madden.*

composition   an aggregate; a mixture; objects or persons of different natures associated together.

compound   a union; a chemical bonding of elements —*Wilkes.*
Example: compound of two liquids, 1710.

concatenation   a chain; a sequence of things or sounds dependent on each other. See also **catena, chain.**
Examples: concatenation of bungles and contradictions, 1880; of causes and effects, 1753; of explosions; of felicity, 1622; of ideas, 1867; of orgiasts; of straight lines, 1845.

concent   a concord or harmony of sounds. See also **concert, consort.**
Examples: concent or consort of authors, 1654; of birds [their

music], 1601; of flutes, 1697; of minds, 1865; of scripture, 1588; of voices, 1694.

concentration   a concentrated collection or mass; a distillate.
Examples: concentration of broken beams, 1634; of lunar beams, 1691; of related species, 1881; of hostile tribes, 1841; of forces, 1804.

concert   a harmony of sounds, things, or persons; a set of instruments; an agreement.
Examples: concert of angels, 1727; of terrific vociferation; of trumpets, 1674; of voices and instruments, 1732; of Europe [agreement of power on the Eastern Question]; cat's concert [caterwauling, *hence* any hideous combination of sounds]; Dutch concert [in which each performer plays a different tune].

conciliable   small or private party or assembly, usually of illegal religious groups. See also **conventicle.**
Example: convecticles and conciliables of heretics and sectaries, 1589.

concilium   a convocation of three or more experts to confer and give advice, as of medical specialists.

conclave   an assembly of cardinals for the election of a pope; a close or secret meeting.
Examples: conclave of bishops, 1568; of cardinals, 1625; of prelates; of rabbins [rabbis], 1635; of teachers.

concourse   an assembly of things or persons brought together; a moving group of people or things. See also **assemblage.**
Examples: concourse of atoms, 1692; of books, 1855; of humours, 1604; of spiritual joy, 1628; of particles of matter, 1677; of all nations, 1642; of people, 1440; of dependent plebeians, 1781; of the world, 1558.

concretion   a lump, nodule, or clot; a cohesion of particles.
Examples: concretion of ceremonial matters, 1634; of marine shells, 1796; of salt, 1697; of slime, 1626.

condensation   the grouping together or making thicker or

denser, *esp.* by evaporation; the action of crowding together —*Wilkes.*
Examples: condensation of manufacturing populace, 1828; of thought and expression, 1794; of water drops.

condescension   a company of actors —*Hare.*

cone   a cone-like shape; used figuratively. See also **cock.**
Examples: cone of flame, 1813; of prelacy, 1641; of rays, 1831; of shade, 1667.

cone-in-cone   a series of parallel cones.

confection, confectionery   sweetmeats, pastry, etc.; a composition of a light nature, either musical of literary.

confederacy   a combination of persons, of states or nations. See also **alliance, league.**
Example: confederacy of Dunces.

confession   a religious group; a body or church united by a particular confession of faith. See also **communion, congregation.**

configuration   a pattern of stars, of muscles, etc.; a particular form of organization of a number of separate elements.

confluence   a flowing together or the result of such an action; a merging; a large number of persons, animals, or things gathered together from various quarters; a concourse; a crowd; a multitude.
Examples: confluence of association [historical], 1856; of blood, 1635; of brooks, 1794; of dissenting clergymen, 1847; of all comforts, 1654; of ethereal fire, 1742; of young gentlemen, 1673; of grace, 1711; of joys; of shady lanes, 1863; of men, 1596; of particles, 1865; of people, 1818; of prosperous successes, 1606; of rivers, 1828; of rivulets, 1692; of visitants, 1751; of visitors, 1697; of waters, 1615.

conflux   a flowing together, or into each other, as rivers or their tributaries; a confluence.
Examples: conflux of company, 1647; of eternities, 1831; of ill

humours, 1658; of misery, 1779; of the mob, 1710; of riches, 1694; of second causes, 1654; of several populations, 1875; of several springs, 1612; of sick persons, 1836; of splendid actions, 1877; of strangers to the city, 1699; of waters, 1698.

confraternity   an association of men united together for some profession or object. See also **brotherhood, clan, fraternity.**
Examples: confraternity of aldermen, 1654; of chimney sweeps, 1688; of men-milliners ['dandies'], 1885; of monks and friars, 1688; of potters, 1601; of traitors, 1872.

confriary   brotherly union or guild, 1525; a religious group, 1882.

confusion   a confused collection or assemblage. See also **chaos, clutter.**
Examples: confusion of blocks of stone; of piled blocks, 1835; of persons, 1791.

congelation   a coagulated mass resulting from the congealing of a substance.

conger   a group of booksellers.
Example: a conger, set or knot of booksellers —*Bookseller,* 1977.

congeries   a collection of particles, parts, or things; a heap; a group of things heaped together.
Examples: congeries of ballads; of furniture shops; of repugnant affections, 1619; of rocks, 1793; of dead and stupid matter, 1679; of towers, halls, churches, and chambers, 1875; of stars, 1849; of watery particles, 1725.

congest   an accumulation; a number of separate people or things crowded very closely together; a heap.
Examples: congest of floods, 1651; of methodical arguments, 1657.

congestion   a gathering or accumulation; a heap or pile.
Examples: congestion of population, 1887; of traffic, 1883; of unmethodized matter, 1843.

congiary   a present or largess given in Roman times to soldiers or people. [from *congius,* 'a measure of three quarts']
Examples: congiary of corn, 1697; of oil, of salt, 1601; of wine.

conglobation   gathered together into a spherical shape. See also **conglomerate.**
Example: conglobation of gravel and sand, 1697.

conglomerate   a mass of separate items collected into a ball; things closely crowded or gathered together into a coherent mass or whole.
Examples: conglomerate of anecdotes; of flowers; of fragments; of fruit and leaves, 1572; of geologists —*Lipton,* 1970; of gravel and ice, 1856; of useful or useless knowledge, 1864.

conglomeration   a cluster; things joined into a compact body, coil, or ball.
Examples: conglomeration of buildings, 1858; of chances; of Christian names, 1842; of men, 1866; of sounds, 1626; of threads of silk worms, 1659; of vessels, 1697; of words.

congregation   an assembly of persons or things; a group of religious persons under a common rule; the Christian Church *collectively;* those attending a religious service. See also **community, confession.**
Examples: congregation of holy apostles, 1526; of gaseous atoms, 1883; of birds; of cardinals; of elves, 1809; of fish, 1865; of goods; of hypocrites, 1611; of holy maidens; of monasteries [e.g., Congregation of Cluny]; of oyster and scallop shells, 1717; of people, 1486; of plovers, 1430; of princes, 1539; of fine qualities, 1878; of saints, 1535; of soldiers, 1598; of vapour, 1602; of water, 1526; of winds; of worshippers.

congress   a formal assembly of a union, trade body, or similar organization; the assembly of a society; the national legislative body of the United States of America, 1798.

conjugation   a united series; a combination; a sequence.
Examples: conjugation of atoms, 1692; of labours, 1824; of letters, 1626; of men in society, 1605; of miracles, 1660; of probabilities, 1718.

conjunction   a combination of events or circumstances.
Examples: conjunction of alleys, courts, and passages, 1722; of circumstances, 1866; of events, 1862; of grammarians —*Lipton,* 1970; of planets, 1375; of all good things. 1644.

conjuncture   the meeting of events or circumstances.
Examples: conjuncture of accidents, 1736; of affairs, 1768; of atmosphere or other circumstances, 1853; grand conjuncture (when several planets or stars are found together); of principles.

connexion, connection   a religious society; a body of persons connected by either political (1767) or religious ties (1753); a circle of clients; a group of fellow worshippers. See also **denomination, faction, set.**

conrey   a company equipped to fight; a detachment of battalion, 1300.

consection   a series of things that follow in sequence; a train of reasoning.
Examples: consection of action, 1863; of experiments, 1651; of glory, 1601; of mental phenomena, 1836; of tenses [grammar], 1871.

consent   a party united by a common agrement; adherents to an opinion *collectively.*

conservatory, conservatoire   a school of advanced studies, usually in one of the fine arts, *hence,* the students and professors *collectively;* a repository of knowledge.
Examples: conservatory of gauds and baubles, 1656; of law, 1642; of music [*Conservatoire de Paris,* 1795]; of rights and privileges, 1790; of senses, 1656; of snow and ice, 1626.

consistory   a solemn council; a court; an ecclesiastical senate. See also **conclave.**
Examples: consistory of bishops, of martyrs, 1641; of saints, 1641; of senators, 1660.

consociation   a confederation of churches or religious bodies; an alliance or confederation.

Examples: consociation of acts of providence, 1645; of churches, 1646; of many of the worst acts, 1649; of good spirits, 1656; of tribes for plunder or defence, 1804.

consolidation   combination of two or more Acts, Bills, or Statutes to be placed before Parliament; a combining of two or more sources of income, the union of two benefices or offices of State — *Wilkes*.

consort   a number of people consorting together or in a company; a company or set of musicians; an assembly; a divan or consultation —*Johnson*, 1755.
Examples: consort of authors, 1654; of bird calls, 1711; of birds, 1712; of fiddlers, 1656; of knavery, 1598; of musical instruments; of musicians, 1616; of parasites, 1702; of plaudits, 1667; of praise, 1705; of ships [sailing together], 1591; of viols, 1883; of virgins, 1604.

consortia, consortium   a partnership; a union; a fellowship.
Examples: consortium of local authorities [to undertake some project jointly between them]; a housing consortium; a consortium of university libraries.

conspiracy   a body or band of conspirators, 1386.
Examples: conspiracy of graces, 1580; of honesty and virtues, 1538; of things, 1691.

constabulary   constables or the police force *collectively*, 1824.

constellation   a fixed group of stars; an assembly of great splendour; a group of famous people; a fixed pattern of individual elements functioning in a related way.
Examples: constellation of fair ladies, 1665; of genius; of computer programs; of prophets, 1860; of stars; of wax lights, 1739.

consternation   of mothers —*Lipton*, 1970.

constituency   the body of voters represented by a legislator or elected official; the constituents, 1831.

consult   council meeting for consultation, 1634; a meeting for conspiracy or intrigue. See also **conspiracy.**
Examples: consult of catholics, 1762; of coquettes; of doctors, 1700; of Jesuits, 1823.

consultation   conference of lawyers, barristers, or medical practitioners; a deliberation; a conference or consultation.
Examples: consultation of doctors, 1800; of lawyers,1882.

contesseration   a contract of friendship signified by a tessera, or symbol of the relationship — *Wilkes.*
Example: contesseration of elegances, 1671.

contribution   something given to a common stock or fund; a sum of money or item voluntarily contributed, 1582.

convent   an association of religious persons secluded from the world; an assembly or meeting; a body of monks, friars, or nuns; a company of twelve (or with a Superior, thirteen); an assemblage or gathering of people.
Examples: convent of apostles, 1526; of courtiers, 1484; of friars, 1554; of merchants, 1534; of monks; of nuns; of veins and arteries, 1578; of warriors, 1383; of witches, 1652.

conventicle   a small or private assembly, 1382; a meeting for religious worship, 1649; a clandestine or irregular meeting. See also **conciliable.**

convention   an assembly, especially a meeting of representatives of some profession, society, or religious political organization, 1552. See also **congress.**
Examples: convention of estates, 1651; of islands, 1651; of exquisite lineaments, 1592; for prayer, 1649.

converting   a company of preachers, 15th century — *Lipton,* 1970.

conversazione   a private assembly; an assembly for conversation or social recreation; a soirée given by a learned society — *Wilkes.*

convocation   an assembly of persons convoked or called

together, as the Convocation of Canterbury; a group of high-ranking clergy; *in Cornwall,* a group of tinners.
Examples: convocation of clergy; of eagles; of political worms, 1603.

convoy   a party of ships escorting unarmed vessels; a wedding party or funeral train or cortège; a supply of provisions.
Examples: convoy of friends, 1596; of honour, 1866; of meat and drink, 1691; of rude men, 1681; of mourners, 1523; of mules, 1827; of provisions, 1839; of ships, 1626; of wedding guests.

coopery   collection of cooper's wares, 1695.

copse   a thicket of underwood and small trees; the underwood of a wood or forest.
Example: copse of trees, 1578.

cord   a string composed of strands which are woven or twisted together, a central idea or link that strings things together; a measure of cut wood, stone, or rock.
Examples: cords of discipline, 1883; of friendship, 1535; of poorness, 1382; of rock, 1882; of stone, 1703; of wood, 1616.

cordon   a continuous line or circle of persons or objects forming a barrier around a person, place, or building; a string or row of stones. See also **chain.**
Examples: cordon of admirers, 1854; of strike pickets; of police, 1883; *cordon sanitaire;* of troops.

core   a number of people or objects that form the centre or main part of a group, organization, or society; players in a curling match; miners in one shift, *hence,* core of people, 1622.

corps   a body of men assigned to a special service, usually military; a number of students; members of an organization who wear uniforms, as St. John Ambulance Corps.
Examples: corps of actors [Dramatic Corps], 1831; of anatomists —*Mensa;* Corps de Ballet, 1845; of counsellors [legal], 1803; of giraffes; of instructors, 1859; ragged corps of labourers, 1832; of writers, 1882.

corpus   collection of writings on a subject; writings by an author or group of authors.
Examples: corpus of Christian tradition, 1865; of civil law, 1727; of Oriental numismatics, 1886; of the Greek poets, 1727; of scripture, 1876.

corroboree   a hilarious assembly, based on the Australian dance, 1793.
Examples: large chattering corrobories . . . of kingfishers, 1885; of lyrebirds, 1892.

cortège   a procession; a train of attendants; *later,* a funeral procession.
Examples: cortège of labourers and harvest waggons, 1828; of mourners; the Imperial cortège, 1864.

cosmocracy   the people of the world — *Webster.*

cotchel   a small quantity; a niggardly gift — *Gepp.*
Example: cotchel of saltpetre, 1870.

coterie   a circle of persons associated together and separated from outsiders; an association for political or social purposes; a number of people meeting familiarly, usually for social or literary reasons, 1738. See also **clique, company, set.**
Examples: coterie of orchids, 1849; of revolutionaries, 1764.

couchee   an evening reception; an assembly of company in the evening, usually connected with royalty or nobility.

council   an assembly elected or appointed to administer a county, district, or city; the governing body of various professions, institutions, societies, etc.

counsel   a body of legal advisors, 1393.

court   the retinue of a sovereign; an organization for the administration of justice; directors, managers, delegates, or courtiers *collectively.*

coven   a company or assembly, 1500; *esp.,* a group or convent of witches, 1662; see also **covin.**

covert   a flock of birds; a flock or company of coots, 1430.

covey   a flock of birds; a brood or hatch of birds; a family, party, or set of persons or things. See also **bevy, company, covert.**
Examples: covey of coxcombes, 1590; of new doctrines, 1641; of fiddlers, 1616; of girls; of grouse; of mathematicians, 1616; of partridges, 1440; of ptarmigan, 1835; of sage hens, 1868; of trumps [playing cards], 1839; of victims, 1827.

covin   a number of persons banded together; a combination or union. See also **band, confederacy, coven.**
Examples: covin of heathen, 1415; of masons and carpenters, 1361; of wicked men, 1374; of witches.

cow   a bunch of twigs; a birch or besom of twigs.
Examples: cow of heather, 1651; of birch; of broom; of twigs.

cowardice   of curs —*Bk. of St. Albans,* 1486.

cracker   a bundle of small wood; a small parcel of sweets.

crackery   crackers *collectively.*

craft   vessels *collectively,* 1671; a brotherhood of freemasons, 1430; those engaged in a craft or trade, 1362.

cram   a dense crowd; a crush; a squeeze, 1858.

cran   a measure of fish, about 750 herrings, 1797.

crash   of rhinoceroses —*Lipton,* 1970.

crate   a measure of glass, 1823; *loosely,* a large load.

creaght   a herd of cattle driven from place to place for pasturage, 1596. See also **booly, bow.**

creche   a public nursery for infants, *hence,* a group of infants, 1882.

credence   of sewers, 1486 [from *sewer* 'a servant in charge of serving fingerbowls at the table'].

crew   a company, squad, gang, or complement, 1694; a body of soldiers, 1455.
Examples: crew of airmen; atoms, 1674; of banditti, 1768; of critics; of foxes, 1607; of gipsies, 1832; courtly crew of gentlewomen, 1579; crew of jobbers and promoters, 1884; of painters, 1581; of pirates, 1608; of sailors, 1694; of soldiers, 1455.

crockery   earthen crocks or china *collectively*, 1755.

crocodile   a long line of persons or things, *c.* 1870.
Example: a crocodile of schoolgirls.

crop   the product or yield of anything growing; something resembling a crop; the offspring of animals and birds.
Examples: crop of beardless youths, 1830; of corn, 1440; of crystals; of petty discussions, 1862; of geese, 1825; of goose pimples; of lambs, 1825; of lies; of logs, 1879; of turkeys, 1825; of ulcers; of wheat, 1530.

crowd   a number of persons or things closely pressed together, 1567; a company. See also **lot**.
Examples: crowd of advertisements, 1728; of distinguished men, 1848; of islands; of names, 1868; of people, 1567; of redwing; of rivals, 1712; of sail, 1803; of sins, 1627; of new thoughts, 1855.

crunch   of wrestlers —*Lipton,* 1970.

crush   a vast crowd of persons or things, 1806; a crowded social gathering, 1832.
Example: a crush of carts and chairs and coaches, 1840.

cry   of players: actors *collectively* —*Lipton.* Also, a cry of hounds.

cuddle   of teddy bears.

cull·   a selection; those beasts taken out of a herd for a special purpose.
Examples: cull of fat cows, 1858; of sheep, 1880.

cumulation   a heap or pile; an accumulation.
Examples: cumulation of evidence, 1794; of prosperity, 1625.

curney   a company; a host, 1823.

curse   of painters: painters _collectively_, 1486; a curse of creditors —_Lipton_, 1970.

cutting   of cobblers: cobblers or shoemakers _collectively_ —_Lipton_, 1970.

cycle   a set or series: a collection of miracle plays; a long indefinite period.
Examples: cycle of champions, 1829; of changes; of epics; of miracle plays; of morality, 1837; of poems; of metrical romances, 1837; of seasons; of songs; of sonnets, 1870; of years.

D

dairy   milking cows *collectively,* 1779.

damned   the souls in hell, 1393.

damning   of jurors: a panel of jurors, in reference to their power to condemn the accused —*Bk. of St. Albans,* 1486.

darg   a specific quantity of work, usually,the product of a day's work.
Examples: darg of hay, 1605; a darg of marl [the amount dug in a day], 1794.

dash   a small quantity thrown in or mingled with a larger mass or amount.
Examples: dash of good blood in their veins, 1712; of brandy, 1697; of commuters —*Lipton,* 1970; of eccentricity, 1820; of evil, 1678; of my former life, 1611; of light, 1713; of the ocean, 1784; of rain, 1700; of water, 1677.

deaconhood, deaconry   deacons of the church *collectively,* 1679.

debacle   a confused rush or route; a violent rush of water.
Example: a debacle of water, 1823.

debauchery   of bachelors —*Hare.*

debris   the remains of anything broken down; ruins, etc.; the accumulation of loose material or of rock, vegetable, or animal matter.
Examples: debris of the Alps, 1802; of an army, 1708; of an Empire, 1778; of ancient rocks, 1849.

decadarchy   a ruling body of ten, 1849.

decadary   period of ten days, 1801.

decade   an assemblage, group, set, or series of ten, usually, a period of ten years.
Examples: of caveats, 1679; of propositions, 1830; of soldiers; of years, 1605.

decanter   of deans: a company of deans. See also **decorum.**

deceit   of lapwing: a flock of lapwing —_Lipton,_ 1970.

decemvir   a body of ten men acting as a commission, 1579.

deck   a heap or store: a pile of things laid flat one upon the other.
Example: deck of cards, 1593.

decorum   of deans: deans _collectively._ See also **decanter.**

decury   a division, company, or body of ten, 1533.

degree   a rank or class of persons in society.

delegation, delegacy   a group of persons appointed to represent others; a body or committee of delegates.

delicatesse   of gourmets: a company of lovers of good food and wine —_Lipton,_ 1970.

delirium   of debutantes: an excited company of girls who are coming out into Society —_Lipton,_ 1970.

democracy   the population of a democratic state; the common people; the members of the U. S. Democratic Party _collectively,_ 1868.

den   a wild beasts' lair, _hence,_ the beasts themselves.
Examples: den of foxes, 1300; of lemur; of lions, 1380; of robbers, 1860; of snakes; of thieves, 1719; of tigers, 1400; of vice.

denomination   a set of the same persons, called by the same name and therefore of the same views. See also **communion, confession.**

Examples: denomination of Bapists; of Christians; of Epicureans, 1716; of the faithful, 1746; of malefactors, 1814; of methodists; of peripateticks, 1716; of Stoics, 1716.

deploy   a body of troops spread out to cover various points of defence, 1786.

deputation   a group of persons appointed to act on behalf of others, 1732. See also **delegation**.
Example: deputation of the Houses [of Parliment], 1828.

derry   a ballad or set of verses, 1553 [from the repetitive use of "Hey derry, derry" in folk songs].

descent   of woodpeckers: a flock of woodpeckers —*Lipton, 1970*; also descendants *collectively*.

desert   of lapwing: flock of lapwing —*Bk. of St. Albans,* 1486.

destruction   of wildcats: a group of wildcats. See also **dout**.

detachment   a body of troops; part of a fleet. See also **detail**.
Examples: detachment of actors, 1739; of cavalry, 1781; of ships; of troops, 1678; of witnesses, 1681.

detail   a small body of men detailed for special duties, 1780. See also **detachment**.

detritus   an accumulation of debris; any waste or disintegrated material. See also **debris**.
Examples: detritus of languages, 1851; of ruins, 1866; of loose stones, 1851; loose detritus of thought, 1849.

dicker   a lot of ten hides or skin, 1307; a package or lot of ten; a considerable number.
Examples: dicker of gloves, 1307; of hides [ten], 1307; of horseshoes, 1307; of kisses, 1602; of knives, 1553; of news, 1641; of wit, 1598.

dictature   dictators *collectively,* 1709.

diet   a formal public assembly, e.g., Diet of Worms, 1521. See also **assembly**.

digest a condensed or digested collection of fiction or of statements or information.
Examples: digest of laws, 1626; of scriptural text, 1825.

dignity persons of high rank, _collectively_.
Examples: dignity of the army, 1548; of a great kingdom, 1793; of canons —_Bk. of St. Albans,_ 1486.

dilation of pupils: schoolchildren _collectively_ —_Lipton,_ 1970.

diligence of messengers: messengers _collectively_ —_Bk. of St. Albans,_ 1486.

disagreement of statesmen: statesmen _collectivley_ —_Lipton,_ 1970.

discretion of priests: priests _collectively_ —_Bk. of St. Albans,_ 1486.

disguising of tailors: a company of tailors —_Bk. of St. Albans,_ 1486.

display a series of things on show; a group of persons participating in some kind of gymnastic, military, or entertainment display. See also **array.**

dissimulation of birds: a flock —_Bk. of St. Albans,_ 1486.

disworship of Scots. Scots _collectively. Derogatory._ —_Bk. of St. Albans,_ 1486.

divan an oriental council of state; a collection of sheets, _hence,_ a collection of poems; a register of accounts; an assembly —_Johnson,_ 1775.

diversity a variety.
Examples: _Diversity of Plants_ [book title by P. M. Synge]; of trees, 1382; of sounds, 1610.

doctrine a body or set of principles or tenets; doctors _collectively._
Examples: doctrine of comets, 1754; of instruments [laws], 1594; of doctors —_Bk. of St. Albans,_ 1486.

dodecarchy   a ruling body of twelve.

doggery   a company of dogs, 1843.

doit   a small piece of money; a trifling sum; a small part of anything; a bit; a jot —*Johnson,* 1755.

dole[1]   a portion; a share.

dole[2]   of doves; a company of doves —*Bk. of St. Albans,* 1486. Also called **dule.**

dollop   a clump of grass or weed, 1573; a large quantity, 1812.

dopping   of sheldrake: a flock.

dossier   a bundle of papers in reference to some matter or relating to a person, 1880.

dout   of wildcats: a company of wildcats. See also **destruction.**

douth   men *collectively,* 1340; a company, army, or retinue, 1205.

dovercourt   a noisy assembly —*Slang Dictionary,* 1874.

down   a flock of sheep, etc.
Examples: down of hares; of sheep.

dower   a burrow of rabbits or the like, 1490.

dowry   a portion given with a bride; a gift of nature or fortune; a lot, a great deal —*Slang Dictionary,* 1874.
Example: dowry of parny [rain or water], 1874.

dozen   a collection of twelve objects; also an indefinite small number.
Examples: dozen of ale, 1677; of beer, 1893; of bread, 1574; of wine; of wonders, 1340.

doylt   of swine: swine *collectively.*

draff   anything thrown away —*Johnson,* 1755; sweepings; refuse; lees; dregs, 1205.
Examples: draff of filthy errors, 1555; of stories, 1385.

draft, draught   a load; the quantity drawn forward; a chosen detachment of men. See also **detachment, detail.**
Examples: draft of bottlers, 1486; of calves, 1830; of cars; of cattle [culled from the herd], 1800; of eels [20 pounds]; of fish; of men, 1813; of sailors, 1890; of soldiers, 1756.

dram   a minute quantity; a small draught of cordial or liqueur.
Examples: dram of constancy, 1566; of gin; of learning, 1709; of mercy, 1646; of poison, 1592; of saffron, 1741; of well-doing.

drave   a haul or shoal of fish.
Example: drave of herring, 1854.

dray   of squirrels: the nest of a squirrel, *hence,* squirrels *collectively,* 1607.

dreadful   of Dragons [book title by P. Blakely].

dregs   refuse; rubbish; lowest form of human life; anything thrown away —*Johnson, 1755.*
Examples: dregs of conscience, 1597; of disease, 1639; of noble doctrines, 1531; of fanatics, 1761; of the measles, 1824; of nature, 1675; of ancient night, 1719; of oil, 1440; of the population, 1867; of refuse, 1531; of Romish superstition, 1789; of tar, 1752; of time, 1685; of wine, 1870; of the world, 1546.

drift   a number of animals driven or moving along in a body; a mass of matter driven forward. See also **creaght, drive.**
Examples: drift of anglers; of bees; of birds; of cattle, 1613; of dust, 1725; of fishers —*Bk. of St. Albans,* 1486; of fishing nets, 1834; of gold, 1645; of hogs; of ice; of lace, 1889; of leaves of trees, 1600; of men, 1450; of oxen, 1552; of piles, 1721; of quailes, 1613; of rain, 1300; of sand, 1634; of sheep, 1816; of smoke, 1842; of snow, 1300; of swans; of swine [tame] —*Bk. of St. Albans,* 1486; of wood [floating in the sea], 1627.

drive   collection of objects or animals driven. See also **drift, drove.**

Examples: drive of cattle; of logs [downstream], 1878; a deer drive, 1880; a grouse drive, 1880.

dronkship   of cobblers: cobblers *collectively* —*Bk. of St. Albans,* 1486.

drop   a small quantity of liquid; a minute quantity, portion, or particle.
Examples: drops of bounty, 1597; of consolation, 1576; of kindness, 1413; of light, 1687; of modesty, 1596; of my riches, 1398; of time, 1813; of words, 1607.

drove   a crowd of people moving in one direction; a number of cattle or other animals driven in a body. See also **concourse, drift, flock.**
Examples: drove of asses; of beasts, 1350; of bullocks; of cab-drivers —*Lipton,* 1970; of cattle, 1555; of heresies, 1692; of horses, 1764; of immoralities, 1692; of kine ['cattle']; of oxen; of young shoat ['pigs'], 1707; of sheep, 1837; of swine.

druggery   drugs *collectively,* 1535.

drum   a small party sent with a drum to parley with the enemy, 1745; a noisy assembly of society in a private house.
Example: a squeeze, a fuss, a drum, a route, and finally a hurricane when the whole house is full from top to bottom, 1779.

dryft   of tame swine: a herd of swine —*Bk. of St. Albans,* 1486.

duarchy   government by a body of two, 1586.

duet   two or more birds; a musical arrangement for two performers, *hence,* the collective term for the performers; two matching items.
Examples: duet of doves; of gowns [same colour], 1890; of turtles, 1486.

dule   of doves: See **dole.**

dump   a pile or heap of rubbish, 1871.

dunciad   a world of fools, 1728.

dunnage   baggage; clothes *collectively* —*Slang Dictionary,* 1874.

duodecade, duodecennial   a period of twelve years, 1656.

duodene   a group of twelve; a dozen.

E

earth   all people on the globe, 1549; a group of foxes, 1575.

echelle   a set of items in ladder form.
Example: echelle of ribbons, 1690.

echelon   an arrangement of troops drawn up in parallel lines in step formation, 1796; vessels advancing in line at an angle to the direction of sailing.

edition   the number of copies of a book or paper printed at the one time, 1555.

eelfare   the brood or fry of young eels, 1721.

eight   a rowing crew, 1847; the number of leaves in a section or gathering of an early printed book, 1858.

eisteddfod   a company of druids; a congress of bards, 1822.

elephantry   a troop mounted on elephants, 1747.

eleven   the members of a cricket or football team, 1800.

eloquence   of lawyers: company of lawyers —*Bk. of St. Albans,* 1486.

embracing   of carvers: 15th century.

embroidery   a diversity or exaggeration.
Examples: an embroidery of courtesy, 1858; of poetic dreams, 1781; of fame, 1648; of wild flowers, 1820; of humour, 1848; of lies.

emigration   emigrants *collectively,* 1863.

entente national agreements *collectively,* as in the *Triple Entente,* 1894–1907; the *Entente Cordiale,* 1844, 1904.

entrance of actresses —*Lipton,* 1970.

episcopate bishops *collectively,* 1842.

erst the first swarm of bees. See also **cast.**

erudition of editors —*Hare.*

escadrille a squadron of war vessels, usually eight in number —*Webster.*

escalade a series of terraces, one above the other as in a staircase.
Example: escalade of melted snow, 1853.

escargatoire a nursery for snails, 1705, *hence,* a large number of snails.

escheat of lawyers —*Lipton,* 1970.

escort a number of persons or a single person who accompanies another on a journey for protection, guidance, or courtesy, 1745; a body of armed men who accompany somebody or something on a journey, the troops who on ceremonial occasions escort the Queen in procession, 1579.
Example: escort of strangers, 1867.

establishment the civil, military (1689), or political body or organization in a country; a household, 1803.

exaggeration of fishermen —*Hare.*

exaltation of larks: a flock of larks —*Lydgate.*

example of masters: a company of masters —*Bk. of St. Albans,* 1486.

execution of officials: company of officers —*Bk. of St. Albans,* 1486.

expanse something spread out; a wide expanse or extent of anything.

Examples: expanse of black cloth [mourning], 1858; of wavy corn, 1781; of forest; of heaven, 1667; of crystal lakes, 1711; of life, 1758; of sand, 1869.

expedition   a body of persons, or a fleet, sent out for a specific purpose, 1693; an expeditionary force.
Example: a polar expedition.

explosion   a violent outburst; a loud noise.
Examples: explosion of anger; of fire and smoke, 1796; of merriment, 1844; of passion, 1827; of voices, 1804; of wrath.

extreme unction   of undertakers —*Lipton,* 1970.

exuberance   an overflowing amount; an outburst; an abundance.
Examples: exuberance of content, 1781; of fancy,1768; of foliage; of happiness, 1827; of imagination, 1875; of joy; of animal spirits, 1823; of water, 1786.

eye, nye   a brood of pheasants.

eyrar   a brood of swans, 1551; a nest of young birds, 1715.

eyrie, eyry   See **aerie.**

F

faction a company of people acting together, often a contentious group; a set or class of people. See also **cabal, clique, junta.**
Examples: factions of collegians, monks, and canons, 1530; of evil, 1614; of fools, 1606.

factorage the whole body or assembly of factors, i.e., agents in a manufactory, 1849.

factory a body of factors, or workers, 1702.

faculty members of a particular profession regarded as a body; a group of persons entrusted with the government and tuition in a college or university.
Examples: faculty of advocates, 1711; of physicians and surgeons, 1511.

fadge a bundle or bale of leather, sticks, wool, etc.; a bale of goods, 1588.

faggot a bundle or bunch of anything; also a bundle of material, *esp.* wood, used for fuel. See also **fascine.**
Examples: faggot of compliments, 1742; of herbs, 1741; of iron or steel rods, 1640; of reeds, 1489; of rushes, 1545; of selections, 1854; of sticks; of thorns, 1398; of twigs; of utter improbabilities, 1782.

faith of merchants: company of merchants —*Bk. of St. Albans,* 1486.

fall   the quantity born or produced at one time or within a certain period. See also **brood, cast, clutch.**
Examples: fall of hail; of lambs, 1796; of meteors; of rain; of snow; of spawn; of woodcocks, 1430.

family   an assembly of objects with some common feature; a body of servants in a house; the members of a family. See also **clan, set.**
Examples: family of curves, 1741; of gladiators; of languages, 1875; of legends; of myths; of servants, 1722; of thieves, 1749; of yews, 1731.

fangot   a bundle or faggot; a quantity of goods, *esp.* silk.
Example: fangot of white Cyprus silk, 1673.

fardage   the baggage of an army, 1578. See also **dunnage, impedimenta.**

fardel   a bundle or pack —*Johnson,* 1755; the baggage of a company of men *collectively*; also called **fardellage,** 1489; **fardlet,** a small bundle, 1413.
Examples: fardel of faults, 1644; of foolish impossibilities, 1614; of linen, 1600; of myths, 1873; of papers, 1681; of sin, 1483; of sorrow; of traditions, 1703; of troubles, 1576; of wickedness, 1381.

fare   a company ready to travel, 1562; a troop; a multitude or swarm; a catch of fish; a load of animals, 1600; the cargo of a vessel, 1884.
Examples: fare of fish; of flatterers, 1634; of flies; of fools and cheaters; of pigs ['a litter']; of travellers, 1562.

farm   the body of "farmers" of public revenue, 1786, i.e., those who undertake the collection of taxes and revenues.

farnet   a band, company, or train of attendants, 1300.

farrago   mixed fodder for cattle, *hence,* a confused mixture or hotchpotch of things or persons.
Examples: farrago of cant; of cowardice, 1827; of cunning; of doubts; of fears; of hope; of lies; of popery, Arminianism, and what not, 1637; of wishes.

fasces bundle of twigs, 1598; the birch rod, 1799 — *Wilkes.* See also **fascicle.**

fascicle small bundle or bunch; a tuft or cluster of leaves, etc. *Examples*: fascicle of fibres, 1738; of flowers; of hair, 1792; of leaves [pages of a book]; of roots; of virtues, 1622.

fascicule a handful, 1699. See also **fascicle.**

fascine long cylindrical bundle of wood bound together for use in construction of dams, jetties, etc., 1688.

fashion fashionable people; the fashionable world, 1807; the current styles of clothing.

fathom a quantity of wood, six feet square in elevation, 1577.

fawning of courtiers, 15th century.

feast the company at a feast, *collectively.* *Examples*: feast of brewers; of quests, 1400.

feck the bulk; the greater part; a quantity, 1470. *Examples*: feck of books, 1887; of work, 1876.

federation a league or confederacy; a parent organization formed by the linking of several states, countries, companies, or societies, each retaining the control of much of its own affairs.

fellowred a company of fellows or comrades, 1326. *Example*: Blithe was the Christian fellowred of King Richard, 1326.

fellowship a company of equals or friends; a union or association; habitual companions; the crew of a vessel, 1466; members of a corporation or guild; the body of fellows of a college. *Examples*: fellowship of the apostles; of friends; of holy men, 1541; of prophets, 1549; of vessels [boats], 1827; of yeomen, 1486.

ferment a tumult of agitation; an assembly of people affected by such a tumult, 1672.

fern   a huge quantity or number, 1300.

fernery   a collection of ferns, 1863.

fesnyng   of ferrets: a pack of ferrets, 15th century —*Brewer*.

festival   a series of performances of music, plays, and dances —*Wilkes*.

festoon   a chain or garland of things suspended. See also **catena, chain.**
Examples: festoon of banners, 1852; of cobwebs; of flowers, 1732; of ivy; of ribbons, 1870; of vines, 1792.

festoonery   a group of items hung in festoons.
Examples: festoonery of silver, 1836; of trees, 1881.

festschrift   a collection of writings forming a volume for presentation to a well-known scholar on the occasion of his attaining a certain age, pinnacle of his career, retirement, etc.

field   competitors in a sporting event; the runners in a horse race; a stretch or expanse.
Examples: field of benefits, 1577; of clouds, 1860; of cricketers, 1850; of hounds [hunting], 1806; of horses [racing], 1771; of huntsmen, 1806; of ignorance, 1847; of miracles, 1712; of raillery; of runners [in races]; of stars, 1608; of woes, 1590.

fifteen   a rugby team, 1880.

fighting   of beggars; a company of beggars —*Bk. of St. Albans,* 1486.

file   a collection of papers arranged in order; a line, queue, or row of people; animals or things standing or placed one behind each other; a small number of soldiers.
Examples: file of letters, 1666; of slanderous lies, 1581; of newspapers, 1806; of papers, 1525; of soldiers [two deep], 1598.

finery   best clothes; rich wearing apparel, 1680.

firkin   a measure of quantity; half a kilderkin, 1465; as a small cask for liquids, fish, butter, etc.
Examples: firkin of ale [8 gallons], 1465; of beer [9 gallons],

1600; of butter [9 gallons], 1745; of eels [10 1/2 gallons], 1600; of herrings [8 gallons], 1600; of marlvoisie ['malmsey wine'], 1828; of mead, 1713; of salmon, [10 1/2 gallons], 1600.

firlot a measure of corn; fourth part of a boll [6 Imperial bushels]; a great quantity.
Examples: firlot of butter, 1549; of corn, 15873; of gold, 1832; of grain, 1842; of meal, 1484; of oats, 1540; of partridge, 1883; of rye, 1708; of wheat, 1708.

fishery a collection of fish of different kinds, 1828; a group of fishermen, 1710.

five a basketball team.

flake a bundle of parallel fibres or threads, 1635.
Example: flake of ice, 1555.

flap of nuns —*Lipton,* 1970.

flare-up a noisy dance; a jovial social gathering —*Slang Dictionary,* 1874.

flashes of merriment: sudden bursts, 1603

flaw turfs *collectively,* 1811.

fleet the naval force of a country; a number of ships belonging to a company; a number of persons; birds or other objects moving in company; a group of lorries or trucks.
Examples: fleet of aircraft; of barges, 1840; of birds, 1884; of colliers, 1865; of wild ducks, 1810; of knights, 1450; of lanthorns, 1675; of lorries; of motor vehicles; of mudhens; of ships.

flick rabbits or hares *collectively,* 1887.

flight a number of birds or objects flying through the air together; anything resembling a flight of stairs; a flock flying in company. See also **bevy, covey, skein.**
Examples: flight of academicians; of aeroplanes; of airmen; of angels, 1602; of arrows, 1545; of bees, 1823; of birds [young birds taking first flight together]; of butterflies, 1832; of clouds,

1886; of cormorants, 1430; of doves, 1430; of dunbirds, 1875; of eloquence, 1760; of fish-hooks [used in spinning trace]; of flies, 1486; of fowls, 1688; of goshawks, 1430; of hurdles, 1486; of larks; of locks [canals]. 1861; of mallard, 1486; of pigeons, 1605; of plover; of rails, 1852; of stairs; of steps, 1820; of storks, 1720; of swallows, 1486; of terraces, 1855; of widgeon; of woodcock.

fling   a number of oxbirds flying in company; a flock of dunlin or other sandpipers.
Examples: fling of dunbirds; of oxbirds, 1859.

flit   of dancers: a company of male dancers —_Lipton,_ 1970.

float   of dancers: a company of female dancers —_Lipton,_ 1970.

flock   a company of people, birds, or animals; a group of Christians who worship together. See also **bevy, drove.**
Examples: flock of acquaintances; of affections, 1601; of auks [at sea]; of bats; of birds; of bitterns; of bustards; of camels, 1839; of Christians; of coots; of cotton, 1756; of cranes; of ducks [flying in a line]; of elephants, 1614; of fish, 1480; of friends; of geese [on the ground], 1596; of goats; of hens, 1690; of interpreters, 1581; of lice; of pamphlets, 1642; of parrots; of prophets; of seals; of sheep, 1340; of ships [book title by B. Callison]; of swifts; of wool, 1440.

floe   a field or pack of ice or similar substance.
Examples: cloud floes, 1886; ice floe, 1817.

flood   a large body of water; a great flow or stream of any fluid; any great overwhelming quantity.
Examples: flood of banknotes; of eloquence, 1599; of fire, 1711; of joy, 1719; of laughter, 1611; of lava; of golden light, 1680; of mutiny, 1710; of silver, 1894; of tears, 1589; of unbelief and carelessness, 1833; of visitors, 1607; of water; of fiery words, 1877.

floretry   something ornamented with flowers, 1615.

florilegium, florilegia   a collection of flowers, 1711; of poetic passages. See also **anthology.**
Example: florilegia of celestial stories, 1647.

flote   a fleet or flotilla; a company or troop; a herd of cattle; a shoal of fish.
Examples: flotes of people, 1647; great flote of dolphins, 1603.

flotilla   a small fleet, 1711; a fleet of small vessels. See also **armada, flote.**
Examples: flotilla of boats; of fishing boats, 1826; of destroyers; of proverbs.

flotsam   parts of wreckage of a ship or cargo found floating on the sea, 1607; of odds and ends, 1861. See also **jetsam.**

flourish   of strumpets: a company of prostitutes —*Lipton,* 1970

flowerage   flowers *collectively,* 1831.
Examples: flowerage of architectural fancy, 1887; flowerage is the setting of sorts of flowers together in husks and so to hang them up with strings, 1688.

flurry   a fluttering assembly of things.
Examples: flurry of birds [fluttering around before settling down on a lake or marsh]; of passions, 1710; of petals, 1884; of rain, 1892; of ruffles, 1882; of snow, 1836; of snowbirds, 1868; of snowflakes, 1883; of tempest, 1880; of wind.

flush   a flock of startled birds; a hand of cards of the same suit; a sudden growth of emotion.
Examples: flush of cards of the same suit; of emotion; of malard [rising from the water]; of plumbers —*Lipton,* 1970; of Wing Commanders.

fluther   of jellyfish.

flutter   of cardiologists —*Mensa.*

foison   a great quantity or number; a plentiful crop or harvest, 1587.
Examples: foison of arrows, 1489; of all being, 1303; of fat,

1545; of harvest, 1587; of our best phantasies, 1607; of happiness, 1848.

folk   people in general; members of a family. See also **kinsfolk.**

folkmoot, folkmote   a general meeting of people belonging to a town or city, 1000.

fold   a flock enclosed within a fence or shelter; a congregation or group of Christians.
Examples: fold of Christ, 1541; of sheep, 1697.

following   followers, 1450; adherents *collectively*.

fond   a stock of money or of goods. See also **store.**
Examples: fond of appreciation, 1872; of money, 1673; of physick, 1707; of wit, 1704.

font   See **fount.**

folliaminy   a body of fools, 1607; fooldom, 1886; foolery, 1843.

force   a body of men prepared for action, 1375; a body of police; policemen *collectively*, 1851. See also **army, host, troop.**

foresight   of housekeepers: company of housekeepers, 15th century.

forest   an extensive wood; the trees of a forest *collectively;* any dense collection or number of things.
Examples: forest of verbal arguments, 1875; of darts, 1669; of feathers, 1602; of people, 1645; of posts; of scaffolding; of spires, 1867; of telegraph poles; of trees.

formation   a formal assembly of troops; arrangement of rocks in a geological setting, 1815.
Examples: formation of clouds, 1808; of troop, 1796.

forum   of Greeks —*Safire* in *N. Y. Times,* 1983.

fount   a complete assortment of type of the same size and style; a spring or source. Also called **font.** See also **fountain.**

Examples: fount of fire, 1833; of inspiration, 1842; of italics, 1862; of life, 1667; of new heresies, 1874; of type, 1878.

fountain   a jet or stream of liquid. See also **spring.**
Example: fountains of blood, 1526.

four   a polo team; a rowing team; a hit at cricket in which four runs are scored, 1836.

foursome   two pairs of golfers —*Wilkes,* 1867.

fourth estate   the complete body of journalists; the profession of journalism —*Slang Dictionary,* 1874.

frail   a rush basket, *hence,* the quantity it could contain, ranging from 30 to 76 lbs.
Examples: frail of currants, 1836; of figs, 1382; of raisins, 1420; of sprats, 1618.

frame   a number of vehicles travelling together; a scaffold or framework, usually used figuratively.
Examples: the heavy frame of the forest, 1848; frame of mind, 1711; of our monarchy, 1844; of society, 1825; of the spirit, 1665; of sticks, 1577; of timber, 1545; of waggons [number travelling together]; of the world, 1561.

frape   a crowd, 1330; an unruly mob. See also **rabble.**

frary   a brotherhood; a fraternity, 1430.

fraternity   a group of men joined by a common interest or organized for religious purposes, 1330. See also **brotherhood, fellowship, guild.**
Examples: fraternity of couriers, 1838; of free masons, 1851; of goldsmiths, 1870; of mercers, 1483; of vagabonds, 1561.

fratry   a fraternity; a convent of friars, 1532.

frauch   of milliners: a company of milliners —*Bk. of St. Albans,* 1486 [from *frauch* 'eat ravenously'].

friary   a convent or brotherhood of friars, 1538.

frippery   tawdry finery, 1681; old clothes —*Johnson,* 1755.

frith   woods or wooded country *collectively*. See also **forest.**

froggery   a gathering of frogs; frogs *collectively*, 1785.

frondage   fronds *collectively;* leafy foliage, 1842.

frost   of dowagers —*Lipton,* 1970.

fruitage, fruitery   fruit *collectively*, 1610.

frush   fragments; splinters *collectively*, 1583.
Example: all the frush and leavings of the Greeks, 1583.

fry   the young or brood of fishes or other animals or insects, including oysters and bees; people held in contempt *collectively* —*Johnson,* 1755. See also **brood, swarm.**
Examples: fry of authors, 1641; of bees [young bees], 1577; of Christmas books, 1861; of Catholics, 1607; of ditches, 1600; of eel spawn; of fish [young], 1389; of foul decays; of gnats, 1613; of islands, 1652; of oysters [young].

fullage   refuse *collectively;* street sweepings, 1689.

furore   of bandsmen: noise or outcry [modern].

furrow   of brows —*Madden.*

fusillade   simultaneous discharge of firearms.
Examples: fusillade of bullets; of personalities, 1884; of swearing, 1881; of terror, 1863.

fusion   union or blending of things. See also **coalition.**
Examples: fusion of law and equity, 1875; of nations, 1841; of parties [political], 1845.

fuzz   a mass of light, fine fluffy particles; *U. S. Slang.* the police *collectively*.
Examples: fuzz of hair, 1720; of paper-lace, 1881.

G

gage   a small quantity —*Slang Dictionary*, 1874.
Examples: gage of gin, 1874; of tobacco, 1834.

gaggle   a flock of geese; a company of women. See also
giggle.
Examples: gaggle of geese, 1470; of gossips; of more than average chattering women, 1827; of women —*Bk. of St. Albans,*
1486.

galaxy   an assembly of brillant or noted persons or things.
See also **constellation.**
Examples: galaxy of ability, 1887; of astronomers —*Lipton,*
1970; of beauty, 1704; of brightness, 1762; of fame, 1649; of
governesses; of joy, 1842; of stars; of wax candles, 1862.

gale   a wind of considerable strength, 1527; a state of current
or passing emotions; the perfume or aroma of similar intangi-
ble things.
Examples: gale of animal spirits, 1663; of doubts and apprehensions, 1800; of fancy, 1675; of fragrance, 1820; of laughter; of
merriment, 1894; of opportunity, 1669; of perfume, 1711; of
praise, 1827; of wind, 1547.

galere   a group of persons; a clique.

gallery   the audience in the gallery, 1649, used in relation to
a theatre or the political arena, e.g., 'playing to the gallery'.
See also **audience.**

gallimaufry   a dish made up of hashed-up odds and ends of food, 1607; *hence,* a medley or hotchpotch of things or people; a confused jumble.

Examples: gallimaufry of nuts, 1591; of prophecies, 1668.

gam   a herd or school of whales; also whaling ships in company.

Examples: gam of porpoises; of whales; of whaling ships, 1850.

game   a flock of herd or animals raised and kept for sport or pleasure; wild animals or birds pursued, caught, or killed in the chase; *technically,* game under the Game Act of 1862 includes hares, pheasants, partridges, woodcocks, snipes, rabbits, grouse, and black or moor game.

Examples: game of bees, 1577; of conies, 1576; of partridges, 1762; of red deer, 1788; of swans, 1482.

gamut   a range or scale of musical notes.

Examples: gamut of colours, 1824; of crime, 1859; of emotions; of Latin metre, 1864; of notes of music.

gang   a full set of things; a quantity or amount carried at one time; a group of persons doing the same work; a group of people or things connected to one another. See also **company, set, team.**

Examples: gang of ale, 1590; of beer, 1590; of buffaloes, 1807; of captives, 1883; of cartwheels [set of four]; a chain gang; of chronographers, 1677; of clerks, 1668; of convicts; of coopers, 1863; of criminals, 1883; of dogs, 1740; of elk; of heretics, 1848; of light harrows [set], 1806; of horseshoes [set], 1590; of housebreakers, 1701; of labourers; of milk, 1827; of oars, 1726; of peat [amount brought by ponies on one trip], 1808; of ploughs, 1874; of porters, 1700; of ruffians; of saws [set], 1883; of shrouds [suit of sails], 1690; of slaves, 1790; of teeth, 1674; of thieves, 1782; of varlets, 1632; of water, 1858; of women [of silly women], 1645; of workmen.

gangland   gangsters *collectively.*

garb   a bundle, 1502. See also **gavel, glean, sheaf.**

Examples: garb of oats; of steel rods; of wheat.

garbage   refuse in general; worthless literary matter.
Example: the garbage of any circulating library.

garland   a wreath made of flowers or ribbons; a collection of extracts, songs, etc. See also **chaplet.**
Examples: garland of ballads, 1765; of flowers, 1756; of golden roses, 1612; of goodwill, 1631; of ribbons; of riddles, 1710; of rose leaves, 1385; of songs, 1663.

garlandry   a collection of garlands.
Example: garlandry of woven brown hair, 1853.

garnish   a set of dishes, etc., for the table.
Example: garnish of vessels, 1440.

garniture   the furniture or appurtenances of a table; a kitchen or its apparatus; the harness of a horse or mule.
Examples: garniture of a boiler, 1878; of the kitchen, 1532; of mules, 1670; of sapphires, 1753; of vases —BBC-TV programme, 1983; of violets, 1897.

garrison   a body of soldiers stationed at a town or place; a store or treasure.
Examples: garrisons of gold, 1450; of knights, 1526.

gate   the number of people attending a sporting event, usually football matches, 1888.

gathering   a crowd; an assembly; a collection.
Example: *Gathering of Ghosts* [book title by Roy Lewis], 1982.

gavel   the quantity of grain to make a sheaf; a bundle of hay, rushes, or similar grasses, 1611. See also **math.**

gear   property in general; person's belongings, as clothes, *collectively;* equipment required for a particular task or procedure.

gemote   a judicial meeting or assembly in England before the Norman Conquest —*Wilkes.*

generalcy   generals *collectively,* 1864.

generality   the majority; the main body; people in general; the generals of an army _collectively_.

gendarmery, gendarmerie   a corps or squadron of cavalry in England in the reign of Edward VI; a body of soldiers employed as police, as in France.
Example: the gendarmery of our great writers, 1670.

generation   all of the individuals born at about the same time, 1340; a race; family, offspring, or descendants.

gentry   persons of the upper class _collectively_, 1585.

genus   a class, order, or type of thing, esp. of plants or animals.

gerontocracy   a government ruled by old men, 1830.

giggle   a group of silly young girls. See also **gaggle.**
Examples: giggle of girls; of typists.

ging   a gang; a troop; a crew; the retinue, servants, or people in a household.
Examples: gings of mariners, 1594; of words and phrases, 1642.

gipsydom   collective body of gipsies, 1860.

girdle   something that encircles or confines. See also **chain, circle.**
Examples: girdle of din [noises], 1879; of eminences, 1875; of forest, 1836; of perfection, 1879; of snow, 1860.

girlery, girlhood   girls _collectively_, 1805.

glaring   of cats; a company of cats very uncertain of each other.

glean   a sheaf or bundle of a commodity which has been gleaned. See also **garb.**
Examples: glean of corn, 1602; of faith, 1654; of grain; of hemp, 1664; of herrings; of teasles, 1794; of yellow thyme, 1697; of wheat, 1430.

gloat   of examiners.

globe   a body of people or soldiers drawn up in a circle. See also **ball, crew, orb.**

gnomology   a collection of *gnomes,* i.e., 'maxims and adages, aphorisms or old saws.'

gob   a large sum of money; a small quantity —*Johnson,* 1755. *Examples:* gob of gold, 1566; of mercy, 1542; of money, 1542.

good advice   of burgesses, 15th century.

goosery   geese *collectively,* 1828.

goring   of butchers: a company of butchers —*Bk. of St. Albans,* 1486.

gossiping   an assemblage where this is the chief occupation, 1630; gossipdom, 1892; gossiphood, 1856.

gown   the students of a university *collectively;* the members of certain professions, as the magistracy, the legal profession, and those in Holy orders, *collectively.*

graft   of tree surgeons —*Lipton,* 1970.

grail   small particles of any kind —*Johnson,* 1755.

great bevy   twelve head of roe deer.

grece   steps or stairs *collectively* —*Johnson,* 1755.

grind   a school of blackfish or bottle-nosed whales, 1885.

grist   a lot; a number; a quantity; a supply for an occasion; the grain which is to be ground at the mill.
Examples: grist of bees, 1848; of corn [awaiting grinding], 1483; of flies; of grain [amount carried to the mill at one time]; of hope, 1623; of meal; of rain, 1840.

group   a set of things collected as a unit. See also **gathering.**
Examples: group of columns [three or four columns joined together on the same pedestal], 1731; of company, 1748; of crystals, 1830; of islands; of musicians; of partisans, 1809; of rocks, 1859; of singers; of trees; of woes, 1729; of words, 1748.

grove   a small wood or group of trees for providing shade, forming avenues, etc. See also **bosk.**
Examples: grove of bayonets, 1889; of ears of wheat, 1667; of fruit trees, 1838; of their own kindred, 1793; of Athenian literature, 1849; of olives, 1667; of majestic palms, 1856; of spears, 1667; of trees.

grue   a shivering or shaking as from fear.
Example: *Grue of Ice* [book title by Geoffrey Jenkin].

grummet, grommet   a ring of rope or metal resembling an eyelet, as in a sail.
Example: grummet of sooty vapour, 1881.

gry   the smallest unit of measurement; a collection of anything of little value, as the parings of nails —*Johnson,* 1755.

guard   a body of men positioned to protect or control, 1494. See also **convoy, escort.**
Examples: guard of angels, 1834; of patience, 1606.

guess   of diagnosticians —*Mensa.*

guild   an association of men or women belonging to the same class or engaged in the same industry, profession, interested in the same leisure, literary, or other pursuit, etc. See also **association, fraternity.** Used also in such forms as Townwomen's Guild, Guild of Woodworkers. etc.
Examples: guild of the learned, 1817; of Sibyls, 1871.

gulp   a mouthful; a small amount; few in number.
Examples: gulp of air, 1700; of cormorants; of swallows; of tea, 1865; of cold water, 1755; of wine, 1862.

gunnery   guns *collectively,* 1497.

gush   a sudden outflowing. See also **abundance, outburst.**
Examples: blue gush of violets, 1849; gush of bloom, 1892; of bugle-notes, 1851; of ill humour, 1836; of cheerful lights, 1840; of peaches, 1859; of praise, 1878; of sustained rhetoric, 1874; of fresh smells, 1859; of spring, 1885; of tears, 1712; of

tobacco, 1838; of water; of wind, 1704; of woe, 1715; of youth, 1812.

gust   sudden outburst. See also **rack.**
Examples: gust of fire, 1674; of grace, 1807; of grief, 1715; of hope, 1705; of joy, 1789; of passion, 1783; of pleasure, 1704; of sin, 1639; of smoke, 1811; of sound, 1849; of tears, 1870; of unholy passion, 1852; of temptation, 1681; of water, 1610; of weather, 1697; of wind, 1694.

guzzle   of Aldermen.

gynarchy   government by women, 1577.

gynocracy   women as the ruling class, 1728.

H

hack   of smokers —*Lipton,* 1970.

hagging   a meeting of witches or old hags, 1584.

haggle   of vendors: shopkeepers *collectively* —*Lipton,* 1970.

hagiocracy   groups or government by holy men or persons, 1846.

hail   a storm or shower of anything similar to hail. See also **fusillade.**
Examples: hail of bullets; of farewells; of iron globes, 1667; of ice; of peas, 1728; of round shot, 1893; of shots.

halt   a stand of armed men.

hand   a round of applause, 1590; something resembling a hand in appearance or function. See also **bunch.**
Examples: hand of applause, 1590; of bananas, 1881; of bridge; of cards, 1630; of herrings [five], 1861; of oranges [five], 1851; of tobacco, 1726; of whist, 1771.

handful   a quantity that would fill a hand; a small company or number — *Wilkes.*
Examples: handful of days, 1633; of men, 1525; of straw, 1489; of wit, 1536; of words, 1876.

hank   circular coil of anything flexible; a skein or coil of thread.
Examples: hank of cotton [840 yds.], 1788; of gut [angling], 1834; of hair, 1859; of rope, 1788; of silk, 1674; of gold wire,

1560; of wool; of words, 1745; or worsted yarn [560 yds.], 1776.

haras, harras   a stud, 1887; a breed or herd of horses.
Examples: haras of horses [stud], 1486; of wicked colts, 1300; of wild horses; of breeding mares, 1594.

hardware   computer machinery and equipment *collectively,* excepting the programs. See also **software.**

harem   a family of wives or concubines, female relatives, and servants, 1781; the occupants of a harem *collectively.*
Examples: harem of dear friendships, 1855; a literary harem ['library'], 1872.

harl   a leash of three hounds; a small quantity, sometimes termed a couple and a half. See also **leash.**
Examples: harl of greyhounds, 1847; of hounds, 1827.

harvest   one season's yield of any natural product.
Examples: harvest of bark, 1880; of captives, 1613; of grouse, 1881; of hate; of honey, 1697; of mice, 1607; of perpetual peace, 1594; of souls.

hash   a medley; a spoiled mixture; a meat dish.
Examples: hash of absurdity, 1795; of plain repetition, 1672; of tongues, 1735; of my own words, 1860.

hastiness   of cooks: cooks *collectively* —*Lydgate.*

hatch   a brood of young; a sitting of eggs —*Wilkes.*
Examples: hatch of eggs; of mayfly, 1894; of time, 1597.

haul   a single draft of fish; anything caught or taken at one time. See also **cast, catch.**
Examples: haul of fish, 1885; of salmon, 1780.

head   A collection of animals; an indefinite number; a bundle of flax or silk.
Examples: head of blackmen, 1856; of cattle, 1667; of flax; of lambs, 1533; of pheasants, 1862; of rabbits, 1894; of sheep, 1533; of silk; of wolves, 1601.

heap   a pile or mass; a collection of things thrown together; a crowd; a large number.
Examples: a heap of castles, 1661; of confessors, 1340; of fowls, 1290; of gravel, 1398; of hard names, 1741; of hounds, 1377; of good ideas; of islands, 1697; of learned men; of old papers and parchments, 1574; of people, 1590; of servants, 1867; of sheep, 1477; of sins; of trouble.

heathenry   the heathens of the world, *collectively,* 1577; heathendom, 1860; heathenesse, 1205.

heaven   the assembly of the blessed, *collectively;* an archway or canopy.
Examples: heaven of cedar boughs, of brass, 1600; of delight, 1883; of heavens, 1885; of joy, 1596; of heavenware [angels *collectively*], 1000.

helotry   slaves or bondsmen *collectively.*
Example: helotry of mammon, 1829.

herbarium   a collection of dried plants or herbs, 1700.

herbary   a garden of herbs or vegetables, 1634; a collection of herbs or dried plants, 1591.

herd   a number of animals assembled together, chiefly large animals; a crowd of common people. See also **flock, rabble.**
Examples: herd of antelopes; of asses; of attributes; of bison; of boars, 1735; of buffalo; of camels; of caribou, 1577; of cattle; of chamois, 1860; of cranes, 1470; of curlew; of deer, 1470; of elephants, 1875; of fallow beasts, 1576; of giraffes; of goats, 1700; of harlots, 1486; of harts, 1486; of coaches, 1618; of ibex; of mankind, 1665; of moose; of oxen; of parasites, 1818; of ponies; of porpoises, 1675; of seals, 1897; of swans, 1470; of swine, 1526; of sycophants; of whales, 1839; of wolves, 1697; of wrens, 1470.

heritage   heirs *collectively,* 1390.

hierarchy   a body of officials arranged in ranks; each of three groups of angels; ecclesiastics, priests, or clergy, *collectively.*

Examples: hierarchy of angels, 1398; of being, 1875; of clergy, 1563; of concepts, 1864; of intelligence, 1875; of priests.

higgledy-piggeldy a confused mass, as higglers will carry a huddle of provisions together —*Johnson, 1755.*

hill a heap of earth raised about the root of crops, *hence,* the crops themselves; an enormous mass or quantity.
Examples: hill of corn, 1817; of fire, 1320; of guilt, 1644; of knowledge, 1851; of dead men, 1450; of potatoes, 1799; of proud and rich folk, 1440; of ruffs [bird of the sandpiper family], 1875; of snow, 1784; of heavenly truth, 1644.

hive a beehive; an extremely busy place.
Examples: hive of bees, 1583; of Roman liars, 1864; of mankind, 1839; of oysters, 1882.

hoard a stock or store; something accumulated.
Examples: hoard of human bliss, 1764; of coins, 1851; of facts, 1847; of grace, 1805; of money; of nuts; of provisions; of savings; of secrets.

hodgepodge See **hotchpotch.**

hoggery hogs *collectively,* 1856.

hoi polloi the masses; the common people. See also **commonalty.**

hopping of frogs: company of frogs —*New York Times,* 1983.

horde a great company, *esp.* of savage or uncivilized people. See also **gang, rabble, troop.**
Examples: horde of barbarians; of Gauls, 1838; of gnats; of Goths, 1695; of insects, 1834; of misers —*Lipton,* 1970; of pirates, 1837; of regicides, 1796; of savages —*Brewer*; Tartars, 1594; of wolves, 1864; of young readers, 1888.

host an army; a large number of men; a great multitude of people, animals, birds, insects, or things.
Examples: host of angels; of arguments; of books, 1875; of golden daffodils; of debaters, 1773; of facts; of heaven [angels], 1382; of hoteliers [modern]; of imagery, 1862; of images,

1845; of men, 1486; of monks, 1797; of odds and ends; of parasites —*Madden*; of questions; of sparrows, 1486; of thoughts, 1845; of tongues, 1606; of trunks [piles of luggage], 1840.

hosting   a muster of armed men, 1422.

hotchpotch, hodgepodge   a confused mixture.
Examples: hotchpotch of errors, 1728; of garlic and cheese, 1591; of ideas; of many meats, 1530; of all sorts of men, 1652; of many nations, 1652; of true religion and popery, 1888; of songs, 1835; of tastes; of words, 1386.

house   the inmates of a house *collectively*; a household or family; an assembly of legislative or deliberative persons; the members of a family, including ancestors and descendants. See also **assembly.**
Examples: House of Commons, 1548; of congregation [Oxford], 1831; of convocation, 1705; of David, 1382; of Lancaster, 1548; of Lords, 1635; of Parliament, 1545; of piety, 1599; of religion, 1419; of Representatives; of ill repute, 1726; of Stuart, 1789; of water [a cavity filled with water, Cornish mining term], 1881.

household   the inmates of a house, including the servants and attendants — *Wilkes*.
Example: household of faith, 1526.

hover   of trout: a school of trout —*Lipton,* 1970; of crows.

hubbub   a multitude of speakers.
Examples: hubbub of parliamentary discussion, 1878; of all languages, 1849.

huddle   a number of persons or things crowded together; a confused mass —*Johnson,* 1755. See also **conglomeration, jumble.**

hug   of teddy bears: [book by Peter Ball, 1984].

humanity   human beings *collectively,* 1579.

hurry   a small load of hay or corn; a confused crowd; a mob, 1620.

hurtle   a flock of sheep.

husk   a down or group of hares —*Strutt,* 1801.

hutting   huts *collectively.*

I

iamb   of poets —*Lipton,* 1970.

idolatry   idols and other similar things and objects *collectively*.
Example: idolatries of the heathen, 1671.

illusion   of painters: group of painters, 15th century.

imbroglio   a confused heap of things, 1750.
Example: imbroglio of torn boughs, 1850.

impatience   of wives: company of wives.

impedimenta   the equipment and baggage of an army; the sum total of burdens or other things that weigh or slow one down. See also **dunnage, fardage.**

impertinence   of pedlars —*Lipton,* 1970.

incredibility   of cockolds —*Bk. of St. Albans,* 1486.

indifference   of waiters —*Lipton,* 1970.

ingathering   the result of gathering, i.e., a collection, e.g., the harvest, 1555 —*Wilkes.*
Examples: ingathering of his corn, 1668; of hops, 1861.

ingratitude   of children.

institute   an organization for the promotion of learning. See also **institution, society.** [First use in England appears to have been 1829.]

institution   an established or organized society, usually with its own premises.

intrusion of cockroaches —*Lipton,* 1970.

J

jam a crush or squeeze; a mass of things or persons tightly crowded.
Examples: jam of carriages, 1858; of humankind, 1807; of people, 1860; of tarts —*Lipton*, 1970; of trees, 1838; traffic jam.

jetsam cargo, equipment, or waste thrown overboard from a vessel at sea. See also **flotsam.**

Jewry Jews *collectively*, 1330.

jobbery gobs; small pieces of work *collectively*.

joint of osteopaths —*Mensa*.

jorum a large quantity; a large drinking vessel and its contents.
Examples: jorum of gossip, 1872; of mulled port, 1823; of punch, 1868.

jot the least amount, as in *jot or tittle*, 1526.
Example: jot of blood, 1596.

journey a load or amount carried on one journey; a batch minted together; a military expedition; a meeting held on a particular day for public business; a diet; 720 ounces or 2,000 gold coins.
Examples: journey of coins; of corn, 1859; of silver; of spurs, 1529.

judicature a body of judges, 1593; the judges of a country *collectively;* legal tribunal *collectively*.

jug   to nestle or collect in a covey; the covey itself.
Examples: jug of grouse; of partridge; of quail.

jumble   a confused mixture. See also **hotchpotch, huddle.**
Examples: jumble of atoms, 1706; of hills and rocks, 1882; of intentions, 1767; of disagreeable things, 1711; of words, 1757.

jungle   land overgrown with tangled vegetation containing the dwelling places of wild beasts.
Examples: jungle of disconnected precedents [legal], 1879; of information, 1897; of red tape, 1850; of sea weed, 1853.

junta, junto   a group of men united together for some secret intrigue. See also **cabal, conspiracy.**
Examples: junto of divines, 1641; of gods, 1659; of wise men; of ministers, [political]; of shrubs, 1671; of wits.

jury   a group of people empaneled to reach a verdict in a trial or to award prizes in a competitive event; a dozen people.
Example: jury of the apostles, 1649.

K

kelp   seaweeds to be burnt or processed, *collectively*, 1387.

kendle   See **kindle.**

kennel   a pack of hounds, dogs or other animals; *Contemptuous.* a set or class of persons. See also **crew, gang.**
Examples: kennel of atheists, 1649; of hounds, 1526; of leopards, 1641; lions, 1844; stock-jobbers, 1720; wolves, 1641.

kibbutz   a collective settlement in Israel — *Wilkes.*

kilderkin   a measured capacity, usually the fourth part of a tun.
Examples: kilderkin of corn, 1600; of drink, 1670; of herrings, 1423; of knowledge, 1593; of wit, 1682.

kill   the carcasses of birds or animals killed by a sportsman. See also **bag.**

kindle, kendle, kindling, kyndyll   a litter or brood. [from the German *Kinder* 'children, offspring'?]
Examples: kindle of young cats —*Bk. of St. Albans,* 1486; of elephants, 1220; of hares; of kittens, —*Brewer*; of leverets; of rabbits.

kindred   kinsfolk or relatives, *collectively*, 1225.

kinsfolk   persons of the same kin; relations by blood, 1450 —*Wilkes.*

kip   a set or bundles of hides of young or small beasts, e.g., calves or lambs.

Examples: kip of chamois skins [30 skins], 1890; of goatskin [50 skins], 1612; of lambs skins [30 skins], 1525.

kippage   a ship's crew or company; the company sailing on board a ship, passengers and crew, 1578.

kist   a chest of money, *hence,* a store or cache of money, 1619. *Example*: kist of silver, 1816.

kit   the items forming a soldier's equipment; 'articles of kit', 1785; a number, set, lot, or contents of a vessel, *hence,* a soldier's or traveller's or workman's kit —*Gepp*; a person's baggage or a collection of anything —*Slang Dictionary,* 1874. *Examples*: kit of pigeons, 1880; of tools, 1881.

kitchenry   a group of servants engaged in the kitchen, 1609; kitchen utensils *collectively* —*Century Dictionary,* 1890.

kith   persons who are known and familiar *collectively*, 1325; acquaintances, 1825; *kith and kin*: 'friends and relations' —*Wilkes.*

knighthood   knights *collectively*; a military force or host, 1377; knightage, 1840. *Examples*: knighthood of the battle, 1382; multitude of heavenly knighthood [angels], 1382.

knitch, knitchel (1500), **knitchet** (1602) a bundle of wood, hay, corn, or flax tied together. See also **bundle, cluster, faggot, sheaf.** *Examples*: knitch of fern, 1823; of flax; of hay, 1300; of reeds, 1882; of straw, 1535; of wood, 1552.

knob   a small collection of widgeons, dunbirds, teals, or the like; fewer than thirty, 1878. *Examples*: knob of dunbirds, 1878; pochard; teal, 1878; widgeon, 1878.

knot   a small cluster or group of persons or things. *Examples*: knot of astrologers; booksellers; clubs [social], 1853; of idioms, 1875; of islands, 1698; of men, 1601; of mountains [where mountain chains meet]; of palm trees, 1825; of people;

of politicians, 1874; roots [personal links]; of separatists, 1849; of small stairs, 1607; of talk; of thread or yarn; of toads; of windsors [chairs]; of witches; of young snakes.

kolkhoz   a collective farm in the USSR.

kyndyll   See **kindle.**

L

labyrinth   an intricate, complicated, or tortuous arrangement.
Examples: labyrinth of islands, 1778; of peristyles and pediments, 1873; of rivulets and canals, 1777; of scattered suburbs, 1843; of small veins and arteries, 1615.

labour   of moles: a company of moles —*Bk. of St. Albans,* 1486.

lac   a great number; specifically, 100,000.
Examples: lac of islands, 1881; of pagodas, 1692; of rupees, 1613; of years, 1613.

ladyhood   ladies *collectively*; the realm of ladies, 1821.

laity   laymen *collectively,* 1616; non-professional in contrast with professionals in certain areas of work.

landlordry   landlords *collectively,* 1598.

lap   a bundle; the amount a thing overlaps.
Example: lap of beaver skins, 1673.

lash   of carters: a company of carters —*Bk. of St. Albans,* 1486.

last   a load or burden; an amount of cod or herrings [12 barrels]; a measure of grain or malt [80 bushels], *hence,* a large, indefinite number.
Examples: last of beer, 1390; of cod; of devils, 1712; of falcons, *c.* 1620; of goshawks, *c.* 1620; of grain; of herrings, 1469; of

111

kisses, 1581; of leather, 1750; of malt, 1893; of pitch or tar, 1483.

latrociny   a band of robbers, 1478.

laughter   a clutch of eggs; a group of ostlers —*Bk. of St. Albans,* 1486.

layer   a substance or things grouped together and lying between two other horizontal strata. See also **pocket.**

layette   an outfit and toilet materials for a baby or young child, 1874.

lea   a measure of yarn which varies according to type, i.e., worsted [80 yards] or cotton [120 yards], 1399.

leafage   leaves *collectively,* 1599.

league   a group of persons, states, or other organizations with a common interest.

leap   of leopards: a company of leopards —*Bk. of St. Albans,* 1486; of bandilleros —*Lipton,* 1970.

lease, lece   three; a quantity of thread.
Examples: lease of fish; of hares; of thread, 1391.

leash   *Sporting.* a brace and a half; a tierce, i.e., 'three'. See also **harl.**
Examples: leash of armies, 1705; of bucks, 1624; of days, 1609; of deer; of foxes, 1838; of greyhound, 1450; of hares, 1750; of hawks, 1486; of hounds, 1320; of kings, 1859; of languages, 1663; of partridges; of ratches, 1526; of snipe; of teal, 1826; of trout, 1882.

lede   persons *collectively* —*Beowulf,* 971; one's own people, race, nation, or countrymen; vassals.

leer   of boys —*Lipton,* 1970.

lees   dregs; anything thrown away —*Johnson,* 1755.

legation   a group of diplomats sent on a mission or stationed in a foreign country, 1603; a legacy; a body of delegates or papal legates.

legendry   legends *collectively,* 1513; legends of the lives of the saints.

legion   a multitude; a great number; a unit of Roman troops; a host of armed men.
Examples: legion of angels, 1380; of appetites and passions, 1751; of devils; of horrid hell, 1605; of knights, 1400; of reproaches, 1634; of Rome, 1387; of troops; of whelps, 1824.

legislature   a body of persons elected or invested with the power to make laws, 1676.

lek   a gathering or congregating, as in sport; as many as fifty birds gathered together.
Example: lek of black grouse, 1884.

levee   a reception often held in the morning; any miscellaneous gathering of guests, 1672.
Example: levees of ministers, 1874.

levesel   a bower of leaves; a canopy or lattice, 1386.

levet   leavings; fragments, 1528.

levy   a collection together of things levied; a meeting of scholars on some matter relating to the school; a body of men assembled or enrolled.
Examples: levy of horse, 1888; of money; of school, 1857.

library   a collection of books, 1540; therefore a collection of knowledge.
Examples: library of God's law, 1703; of opinions, 1570; of reason, 1485; of my understanding, 1549.

line   a series or rank of objects or persons, usually of the same kind; a series of persons in chronological order, usually of family descent.
Examples: long line of ancestors, 1809; of authorities (legal), 1895; line of barriers; of blood royal, 1513; of bricks, 1557; of

geese, 1802; of heroes, 1705; of trading posts, 1836; of type (printing), 1659.

lingerie   linen articles *collectively*; now chiefly the underclothes of women, 1835.

lingot, linget   a small mass of metal —*Johnson,* 1755.
Examples: lingots of ripe Indian corn, 1856; of gold, 1488; of silver, 1653.

list   a number of names, words, or figures written together.

litter   the young brought forth at one time by a sow or similar animal; a disorderly cumulation of papers; rubbish, 1730.
Examples: litter of children, 1704; of constitutions, 1796; of kittens; of lions, 1734; of opinions, 1662; of pamphlets, 1688; of pigs, 1604 —*Brewer*; of rabbits, 1802; of sins, 1639; of whelps, 1486; of women, 1860.

little herd   20 head of deer.

livery   retainers *collectively,* 1413.

load   a great amount; quantity. See also **burden, charge.**
Examples: load of public abhorrence, 1855; of care, 1791; of drunks —*Lipton,* 1970; of guilt; of sorrow, 1799; of troubles; of waters, 1698; of woes, 1593.

lobby   those who try to influence legislators, *collectively*; a body of lobbyists.

lock   a handful, armful, or small bundle; locks of hair on the head, *collectively.*
Examples: lock of bacon, 1843; of cover, 1847; of corn, 1629; of cotton, 1849; of flax, 1673; of grass, 1661; of hair, 1526; of ham; of hay, 1575; of lightning, 1850; of money, 1804; of straw, 1563; of tar, 1823; of wheat, 1827; of wool, 1463.

locket   group or set of jewels.
Example: locket of diamonds, 1664.

lodge   a collection of objects lodged or close together; a fam-

ily unit of four to six persons; the body of members of a masonic or other society.
Examples: lodge of beavers, 1744; of islands, 1720; of masons, 1686; of otters.

loft   a flock of pigeons, 1899.

lot   a number of persons or things, *collectively*; a group of items sold at an auction or for sale in set quantities. See also **break, sort.**

lump   a great quantity; the majority.
Examples: lumps of fables, 1875; of figs, 1611; of honey, 1713; of mankind, 1674; of money, 1869; of pain, 1841; of English papists, 1650; of people, 1880; of raisins, 1611; of ships, 1781; of sorrows, 1549; of swearers, 1709.

lurch   of buses —*Lipton,* 1970.

lurry   a confused group or sound of voices. See also **hubbub.**
Examples: lurry of friars, 1607; of lawyers, 1607; of superstitious opinions, 1664; of people, c. 1800.

lute   a flock of mallard.

lying   of pardoners; company of pardoners, i.e., those who pardon or forgive sins —*Bk. of St. Albans,* 1486.

M

macaroni   a medley; poetic selections.
Example: political songs in Latin or in a maccaroni of Latin and English, 1884.

madder   of painters.

magazine   a place where goods are stored; a warehouse or depot, 1583; a building in which arms, ammunition, or provision for an army are kept for use in time of war, 1596; in modern times it is a periodical publication which contains a wide range of articles, pictures, and advertisements, aimed at a class, age group, or other category of readers interested in a specific subject or place.
Examples: magazine of arms, 1810; of bliss, 1599; of chaises, 1786; of coal, 1771; of darts and arrow, 1781; of flesh, milk, butter, and cheese, 1719; of knowledge, 1836; of law, 1760; of learning, 1610; of malice, 1750; of nourishment, 1615; of petitions, 1817; of powder (gunpowder), 1613; of power, 1836; of provisions, 1589; of sin, 1709; of topics, 1795; of good words, 1638; cloudy magazine of storms, 1644.

malapertness   of pedlars: 1486.

manhood   men *collectively*.
Example: manhood of Lancaster, 1588.

maniple   a handful; a small band of soldiers —*Johnson*, 1755.
Examples: maniple of papers and petitions, 1632; of people, 1829; of soldiers, 1755.

mantle   a covering; a quantity of furs of 30 to 100, depending on the size of the skins.
Examples: mantle of darkness; of fox skins, 1545; of furs, 1490; of ivy, 1829; of meekness, 1526; of deep obscurity, 1526; of prudence, 1430; of silence; of skins; of snow; of white kid, 1549.

many   a large number; a company; multitude of people: the many, 1688.

mass   a large quantity; the whole quantity or the larger amount; a dense collection of objects seeming to form one body; the populace of the lower orders: the masses, 1837. See also **bulk.**
Examples: mass of abuses, 1867; of bruises; of bullion, 1630; of colours, 1716; of confusion, 1647; of evidence, 1865; of evil, 1855; of faults; of folly, 1616; of fountains, 1626; of heresies, 1623; of letters, 1879; of mankind, 1713; of mistakes; of money, 1568; of people, 1837; of prejudice, 1855; of priests; of sand; of seeds, 1766; of stones, 1660; of treasures; of violets, 1845; of water; solid mass of living, 1875.

math   an amount of mown grass, 1585; one of a number of mowings possible in a year or season.

maze   a complexity of winding paths or passages.
Examples: maze of arteries, 1615; of bracken and briar, 1872; of history, 1781; of metaphor and music, 1837; of dirty traditions and foolish ceremonies, 1542.

medley   a mixture, jumble, hotchpotch; a mixed literary or musical composition.
Examples: medley of astrology and homely reciepts, 1897; of houses, 1885; of mirth with sadness, 1529; of music; of many nations, 1652; of philosophy and rhetoric, 1865; of sounds; of tunes; of voices; of sense and madness, 1755.

meet   the persons or group of men or women who gather for a fox hunt or other sporting event.
Examples: a meet of cyclists; of huntsmen.

meeting   a public gathering, 1513; a race meeting, 1764; an assembly for worship, 1593.

meiny, meine   a family; a body of attendants; a company of people employed together; a great number; the multitude, 1609. See also **flock, retinue, train.**
Examples: meiny of attendants; of brooks; of chessmen (a set); of cranes, 1484; of geese, 1484; of male foals, 1522; of oxen, 1530; of people, 1609; of pilgrims, 1442; of plants, 1530; of discontented puritans, 1670; of rascals, 1529; of sheep, 1522; of sparrows, 1556; of villains, 1529.

mêlée   a lively contention or debate; a mixed fight between two parties; a skirmish.
Example: mêlée of battle, 1871.

mellay   a mixture, usually of coloured items, e.g., cloth, 1381.

melleficium   a collection of quotations. See also **miscellany.**
Example: melleficium of quotations.

melody   of harpers: harpists *collectively* —*Bk. of St. Albans,* 1486.

ménage   members of a household, 1297; members of a club or benefit society, 1829; staff or company of a theatre.
Example: ménage of the opera, 1746.

menagerie   a collection of wild or foreign animals; an aviary, 1712.
Examples: menageries of live peers in Parliament, 1850; of pheasants, 1830.

merchantry   merchants *collectively,* 1862.

merdaille   a dirty crew; rabble; scum, 1375.

mess   a confused mixture; a group of four; a group of people who regularly eat together; the quantity of milk at one milking; a quantity of food; a haul of fish. Also, **officers' mess, sergeants' mess, etc.**
Examples: mess of beans; of cream, 1633; of eggs, 1888; of fish,

1854; of food, 1841; of guests, 1671; of judges and barristers; of kingdoms, 1603; of mackerel, 1901; of marines; of milk, 1533; of officers; of peas, 1870; of pooridge, 1598; of potage, 1456; of sons (four); of strawberries; of suitors, 1625; of tongues, 1617; of verse, 1764; of victuals; of vinegar, 1597.

meute   pack of hounds, alternative for *meuse* or *mews*.

mews   stable for horses, 1394; collection of hawks moulting, or hens and capons fattening. [From the cage for hawks when mewing or moulting, 1386.]

mickle   a large amount —*SOED*; **mickle folk** 'many people,' 1275. The expression, 'Many a pickle makes a muckle' is used in 1905; 'Many a pickle makes a mickle' is in the *Oxford English Dictionary*.

midden   an accumulation of refuse, especially from a prehistoric kitchen fire; a dunghill, manure heap, 1375.
Example: midden of ashes, 1667.

middle bevy   ten head of roe deer; forty head of deer in general.

migration   the persons, mammals, or birds that take part in migratory movements abroad, *collectively*.
Examples: migration of birds, 1704; of salmon, 1704; of souls of men, 1727.

militia   a military force or 'citizen army,' 1590.

mine   of egoists —*Madden*.

mingle   a mingled mass; a mixture, 1548.
Examples: mingle of divers sorts, 1621; of thankfulness and dread, 1811.

ministry   a group of ministers of state, 1710; the clergy, 1566.

mint   a vast sum of money or something of equal value.
Examples: mint of bravery, 1869; of money, 1655; of phrases; of questions, 1598; of reasons.

minstrelsy   body of minstrels, *collectively,* 1350; of musicians; musical instruments *collectively*; a body or collection of minstrel poetry.
Examples: minstrelsy of heaven (angels), 1667; of the Scottish Border, 1802.

misbelief   of painters; painters *collectively* —*Bk. of St. Albans,* 1486.

miscarriage   of justices: company of judges of magistrates —*Daily Telegraph,* 28 June, 1984.

miscellanea   a collection of miscellaneous materials or matter.
Example: a literary miscellanea, 1571.

miscellany   a mixture of various things; a medley, 1617; a collection of writings on various subjects.
Examples: miscellany of Christians and Turks together, 1703; of deformities, 1620; of humours, 1668; of prose; of irreconcilable theorists, 1833; of trees, 1703.

mishmash   a confused mixture, c. 1450; a mingle or hotchpotch; "a low word" —*Johnson,* 1755. See also **jumble, medley.**
Examples: mishmash of conceits and practices, 1676; of superannuated customs, 1876; of vile and wretched persons, 1600; of worshipping, 1860.

mission   a body of persons sent to a foreign country to conduct negotiations, 1626; such a body sent by a religious community for the conversion of the heathen, 1622 —*Wilkes.*

mizmaze   a labyrinth; a state of confusion —*Johnson,* 1755.
Examples: mizmaze of glory, 1814; of variety of opinions.

mob   a rabble, 1688; a crowd or collection of things. See also **canaille, flock, herd.**
Examples: swell mob of authors, 1846; of books, 1892; of boys, 1784; of cobblers, 1700; of ducks; of horses, 1906; of kangaroos, 1846; of mankind, 1795; of metaphors, 1728; of natures, 1830; of peasants, 1813; of people; of quality, 1704; of sheep,

1875; of snobs, 1883; of theives, 1843; of thoughts, 1742; of whales, 1898.

mobble, moble   moveable goods, property, *c.* 1300.

mobocracy   mob-rule; rule by the lowest classes, 1754.

mobile   the populace; the route; the mob —*Johnson,* 1755.
Example: the mobile were fast gathering, 1830.

mobility   the populace; the great unwashed —*Slang Dictionary,* 1874.

moiety   a half; the better half; a small part; a lease; a share, portion, or quantity.
Examples: the moiety of the human species; of a scruple, 1641.

monkery   monks *collectively,* 1549; **monkdom,** 1883; **monkship,** 1620.

montage   a musical composed of fragments of music; a quick succession or burst of dialogue or of music and sound effects used to fill the gap in time of a play, opera, etc.

monte, monty   the pile of cards left after each player has taken his share.

mop   a bundle of coarse yarn fastened to the end of a stick, 1496; something likened to a mop.
Examples: mop of leaves, 1887; of powdered hair, 1847.

morris   a group of morris dancers, *collectively,* 1500.

morsel   a small quantity —*Johnson,* 1755.
Examples: morsel of feeling, 1860; of quicksilver ore, 1839; of territory, 1860.

mort   a great quantity.
Examples: mort of luck, 1821; of merrymaking, 1775; of money, 1887; of prisoners, 1694; of talk, 1850; of wit, 1708.

motorcade   a procession of motor vehicles. See also **cavalcade.**

mow   a stack or heap of grain or hay in a barn; a heap or pile.
Examples: mow of earth, 1424; of grain, 1573; of hay, 1539; of peas, 1718; of wheat, 1398.

muckle   See **mickle**.

muddle   a confused collection; a confused assemblage. See also **jumble, mess.**
Examples: muddle of objects, 1865; of paint, 1891.

muid   a dry measure for corn, meat, salt, etc.
Examples: muid of coals, 1727; of corn, 1692; of land, 1674; of gold rings, 1547; of rye, 1771; of bay salt, 1703; of wine, 1491.

mulada   a drove of mules.

multiplying   of husbands —*Bk. of St. Albans,* 1486.

multitude   a great number; a host of persons or things. See also **army.**
Examples: multitude of actions, 1651; of barnacles, 1875; of cares; of favours, 1586; of mercy, 1450; of misery, 1777; of money, 1529; of peace, 1560; of people, 1470; of questions, 1773; of riches, 1325; of serpents, 1375; of sins; of stars; of waters, 1604; of words, 1683.

murder   of crows: a flock —*Brewer.*

murmuration   of starlings: a flock —*Lydgate,* 1470.

musketry   muskets *collectively,* 1646.

muster, mustering   a number of things or persons assembled on a particular occasion; a collection, as a muster of peacocks —*Johnson,* 1755. See also **levy.**
Examples: mustering of horses, 1835; muster of peacocks, 1470; mustering of storks; muster of troops.

mutation   of thrushes: group of moulting birds.

mute   pack of hounds —*Bk. of St. Albans,* 1486.

myriad   a countless mumber of persons, animals, or things; _specifically,_ a group of 10,000.
Examples: myriad eyes, 1830; of horses, 1803; of lambs, 1817; of lives, 1800; of men, 1555; of people, 1660; of precedent, 1860; of sundry cases, 1570.

N

nabobery   nabobs (of India) *collectively,* 1777.

nation   inhabitants of a country; a community of men or animals; the people of the earth, *collectively,* 1667. See also **people, race.**
Examples: nation of field and wood, 1733; of hedges and copses, 1726; of herbs, 1768; of sea, 1697; of unfortunate birds, 1590.

navy   a fleet of ships, 1330; the sailors or crew, *collectively,* 1648.

neddy   a considerable quantity —*Slang Dictionary,* 1874.
Examples: neddy of fish, 1874; of fruit, 1874.

nerve   of neighbors —*Lipton,* 1970.

nest   a number or collection of people; a number of birds or insects gathered in the same place; an accumulation of similar objects; a number of buildings or streets; a set of objects. See also **aerie, bike, brood, swarm.**
Examples: nest of alleys, 1875; of ants, 1818; of arguments, 1874; of boxes (which fit inside each other), 1658; of low bushes, 1845; of caterpillars, 1760; of chicken, 1562; of coffins (set inside each other, e.g., as in as Egyptian burial), 1834; of crocodiles; of dormice, 1774; of drawers, 1704; of eagles, 1484; of evils, 1666; of fish, 1835; of flowerpots, 1849; of fools, 1721; of foxes, 1470; of goblets, 1524; of hedgehogs; of hornets, 1727; of hummocks, 1756; of kittens, 1881; of mice; of miracles, 1642; of nightcaps, 1689; of outlaws, 1861; of partridge, 1593; of pirates; of profaneness; of quiet streets, 1861; of rab-

bits, 1470; of robbers; of rumours; of salmon, 1899; of scorpions, 1593; of seraphim, 1652; of shelves, 1785; of tables; of toads, 1589; of traitors; of trotters; of tyranny, 1586; of vipers; of wasps, 1486; of wharfs and warehouses, 1796.

network collection or arrangement of items to resemble a net; anything reticulated or decussated —*Johnson, 1755.*
Examples: network of brass, 1560; of spider's broods, 1781; of bundles, 1884; of canals; of fictions, 1856; of islands, 1839; of leaves, 1816; of lines; of pearls, 1881; of property, 1816; of railways; of ribbons, 1712; of rivers; of roads; of ropes, 1748; of trenches, 1871; of veins, 1729; of waters, 1857; of wrinkles.

never-thriving of jugglers: a company of jugglers —*Bk. of St. Albans,* 1486.

nexus a connected group or series, 1850.
Example: nexus of matrimonial excesses. —*BBC,* 23 April 1983.

nide a nest or brood of young birds. See also **bike.**
Examples: nide of eggs, 1896; of geese; of pheasants, 1679.

nieveful a handful, 1375.
Examples: nieveful of dominoes, 1839; of oatmeal, 1839; of prunes, 1686.

nine a set of nine persons, players, etc.; a baseball team, 1866; the nine muses, 1600.

nobility the body of persons forming the noble class of a country or state —*Wilkes.*
Example: nobility of the realm, 1530.

non-patience of wives: company of wives —*Bk. of St. Albans,* 1486.

nosegay bunch of fragrant flowers or herbs. See also **bouquet.**
Examples: nosegay from the drains, 1889; of the elect, 1626; of flowers, 1578; of gold, 1704; of herbs, 1853; of wit and politeness, 1731; of yellow hair.

nucleus   a central mass or number; a collection of persons or items to which addition will be made.
Examples: nucleus of epic cycles, 1835; of a library, 1875; of pain and pleasure, 1876; of physicists —*Lipton,* 1970; of fine thoughts, 1820.

nunnery   a community of nuns; a convent, 1275.
Examples: nunnery of eyes, 1651; of lively black-ey'd vestals, 1715.

nursery   place where people are fostered or developed; a collection of plants.
Examples: nursery of evil, 1606; of kernels and stones, 1664; of racoons; of soldiers, 1839; of ungodliness, 1583; of vices, 1604; of blooming youth, 1820.

nurserydom   nurseries *collectively,* 1892.

nye   a brood of pheasants —*Bk. of St. Albans,* 1486. See also **eye.**

O

obeisance   of servants: company of servants —*Bk. of St. Albans,* 1486.

obscuration   of dons: academics *collectively.*

observance   of hermits: a company of hermits; a religious order, as the Franciscans, who observe and follow a rule —*Bk. of St. Albans,* 1486.

obstinacy   of buffaloes: a herd —*Hare,* 1939.

ochlocracy   rule by the mob, 1584.

odium   of politicians —*Lipton,* 1970.

olio, oglio   a collection of miscellaneous pieces; a hotchpotch; a mixture; medley —*Johnson,* 1755.
Examples: olio of affairs, 1700; of all ages, 1847; of musical pieces; of partisan opinions, 1880; of pictures; of various religions, 1648; of verse.

omlah   a body of native officials, 1778.

omnibus   a group of a large number and great variety of objects, persons, or societies.

omnium gatherum   an indiscriminate collection of articles; a numerous but by no means select assemblage —*Slang Dictionary,* 1874.

oncome   a heavy fall of rain or snow. See also **outburst.**

onomasticon   a vocabulary or a collection of names.
Example: onomasticon of the Christian World, 1877.

oodles   a superabundance of anything; a mass of things; a
heap; a great quantity.
Examples: oodles of food; of money; of time.

optience   a group of spectators, as at a cinema.

opulence   a wealth or abundance.
Examples: opulence of hair, 1878; of flesh, 1896.

opus   a musical composition; a collection of compositions,
1809.

orb   a collective whole; a circle of things or people. See also
ball, globe, sphere.
Examples: orb of order and form, 1603; of soldiers; of witnesses,
1866.

orchestra   a group of performers on various instruments,
1720; the collective sound which is reminiscent of an orchestra
playing, as the sound of the sea or the wind.

order   a body or society of persons united by a common rule;
a monastic society; any of the nine grades of angels; a body of
persons of the same profession, occupation, or pursuit; a category of architectural design, e.g., Doric Order. See also **rank,
row, series.**
Examples: order of architecture, 1782; of beggars, 1380; of
laity, 1597; of mouldings; of pillars, 1563; of the Round Table,
1568; of Templars, 1387.

ostentation   of peacocks; a spectacular show or exhibition,
1388.

outburst   an outbreak; explosion; volcanic eruption. See
also **outgush.**
Examples: outburst of emotion; of rage; of muscular vigour,
1855; of weeping.

outfit   articles forming the equipment or clothing for a particular purpose, e.g., a bridal outfit; persons forming a party

engaged in herding, mining, etc.; any group of persons in a particular industry or pursuit.

Examples: outfit of clothes; of sails.

outgush   a flooding forth.

Example: outgush of emotion.

P

pace   a company or herd of asses —*Bk. of St. Albans,* 1486.

pack   a bundle of things enclosed or tied together; a company or set of persons; a large collection or set of things; a number of animals. See also **bolt, bundle.**
Examples: pack of books; of coal (3 Winchester bushels); of complaints, 1862; of dogs, 1648; of fish (set out in piles to dry), 1800; of fools; of grouse, 1688; of heresies, 1638; of hounds, 1735; of ice, 1791; of icebergs; of Jews, 1548; of knaves, 1693; of lies, 1763; of mules; of nonsense, 1880; of perch; of playing cards, 1597; of ptarmigans, 1862; of rebels, 1562; of school-boys, 1885; of sorrows, 1591; of stars, 1633; of stoats; of super-stitions; of thieves, 1698; of weasels; of witches; of wolves, 1795.

package   a bundle of things packed together, 1722. See also **cargo.**
Example: package of dispatches, 1897.

packald   a pack; bundle; load; packet, 1440.
Example: packald of letters, 1516.

packery   a collection of packs or packages, 1891.

packet   a small pack, package, or parcel; a small collection, set, or lot —*Wilkes.*
Examples: packet of friends, 1766; of letters, 1530; of lies; of miracles, 1613; of photographs, 1871; of plants, 1803; of rumour, 1828.

pad   a bunch or package; a mass of anything soft, e.g., a cushion.
Examples: pad of forms, 1876; of mackerel (measure of sixty mackerel); of straw, 1554; of wool; of writing paper, 1865; of yarn.

paddling   of ducks: a company of ducks on water —_Lipton,_ 1970.

pair   two things, persons, or animals.
Examples: pair of open lips, 1647; of mules (about thirty, for carrying tin); of oars (pair of rowers), 1598; of organs (music), 1493; of playing cards, 1530; of spurs, 1375; of stairs (a flight), 1530; of tinminers (ten men).

pair-royal   a set of three of the same kind; a set of three persons or three cards.
Examples: pair-royal of armies, 1650; of kings (playing cards), 1803; of pamphleteers, 1592; of playing cards, 1608; in dice to throw a pair-royal (three), 1880.

palisade   anything resembling or likened to a row of stakes.
Examples: palisade of cliffs, 1850; of ice-pinnacles, 1871; of mountains, 1865; of shrubs; of stakes, 1832; of stiff hairs, 1713; of teeth, 1796; of trees.

pallor   of nightwatchmen —_Lipton,_ 1970.

pandemonium   a place or gathering of wild persons; originally denoted hell [from _Paradise Lost_].
Examples: pandemonium of dancing and whooping, 1865; of devils; of iniquity, 1800.

panel   a list of people; the people on such a list.
Examples: panel of experts; of interviewers; of judges; of jurymen; of patients.

panoply   the equipment of a warrior.

pantheon   the assemblage of all the gods; the deities of a people, _collectively_.
Examples: pantheon of gods; of all religions, 1639.

parade   a procession of animals or people; an assembly of people, especially of promenaders. See also **cortège, procession.**
Examples: parade of coaches, 1673; of elephants; of firemen; of promenaders; of soldiers, 1656.

parcel   a small amount; a small party; a company or collection of persons, animals, or things; articles for sale, See also **bundle.**
Examples: parcel of bachelors; of blockheads, 1702; of blood, 1548; of books, 1562; of brutes, 1778; of cocoa, 1897; of crows, 1712; of fair dames, 1588; of diamonds; of wry faces, 1818; of fire, 1864; of hay, 1863; of hens and chickens, 1775; of horses, 1689; of ideas, 1785; of land, 1642; of lies, 1758; of linnets, 1895; of liquor, 1757; of mathematicians; of matter, 1834; of money, 1586; of observations, 1822; of penguins (when walking together), 1615; of people, 1449; of riff-raff, 1811; of sheep, 1780; of soldiers, 1598; of sugar, 1882; of tobacco, 1648; of weather, 1734; of woes.

pare   parings *collectively*; the amount pared or cut off, 1430.
Example: pare of men.

parel   an army; body of troops; clothing; apparel.
Examples: parel of a pilgrim (i.e., clothing), 1393; commonalty and parel of the Realm, 1511; parel of troops.

parentage   parents *collectively,* 1513.

park   a space occupied by parked vehicles, stores, etc.; *hence,* the objects themselves, *collectively*; an enclosed area in which game beasts such as deer are bred; a place for breeding oysters.
Examples: park of artillery, 1755; a vast park of carriages, 1827; of deer, 1781; of oyster culture, 1883; of oysters; of wild fish, 1607; of young oysterlings, 1851; a park of waggons, 1859.

parliament   a legislative body and consultative assembly. Also, **cricket parliament** at Lords, 1903; **Pimlico parliament** (i.e., the mob), 1799.
Examples: parliament of bees, 1640; of brides, 1400; of fools,

1727; of fowls; of men, 1842; of owls; of religions, 1893; of tinners, 1686; of women, 1741.

partnership   an association of two or more persons for carrying on business; the persons *collectively* — *Wilkes.*

party   a company or body of persons; a detachment of troops; a group of people travelling together; a gathering for social entertainment; an assemblage or society of persons of the same political opinion. See also **clique, set.**
Examples: party of birds, 1773; of gentlemen, 1860; of jays; of Jesus Christ, 1502; of order, 1781; of pleasures, 1728; of politicians; of prisoners, 1896; of quadrille, 1726; of whales, 1840.

pash   a heavy fall of rain or snow; a great number of fragments; a collection; a medley; a great quantity or number. See also **fall, oncome.**
Examples: pash of heraldry, 1894; of people (a great many), 1790; of rain (a heavy fall), 1770; of snow.

passage   herons in flight ('on passage'); the migration or migratory flight of birds.
Examples: passage of herons, 1879; of migrating birds, 1774.

passel   alternative for **parcel.**
Examples: passel of brats; of hogs; of young ones.

pastiche, pasticcio   a medley, potpourri or hotchpotch; an opera made up of various pieces; a picture based on another's design or style.
Examples: pasticcio of gauzes, pins and ribbons, 1785; our operas begin tomorrow with a pasticcio full of my favourite songs — *Walpole, 1752.*

pastry   articles of food made of paste, as pies, tarts, etc., *collectively,* 1539.

pat   a small mass of soft substance, formed or shaped by patting.
Examples: pat of butter, 1754; of water, 1888.

patch   a collection or mass of floating ice floes; a patch or small amount of something; a scrap or remnant.
Examples: patch of earth, 1684; of ice floes, 1820; of philosophy, 1529; of poetry, 1633; of potatoes, 1894; of snow, 1807; of sunlight.

patrol   detachment of troops or police. See also **guard.**
Examples: patrol of cavalry, 1827; of soldiers, 1670.

pavanne   of matadors —*Lipton,* 1970.

peal   succession of loud sounds.
Examples: peal of artillery; of bells, 1511; of guns, 1515; of laughter, 1711; of musket, 1855; of ordnance, 1577; of praise, 1596; of thunder, 1649; of vultures, 1670; of war, 1535; of words, 1671.

peasantry   peasants *collectively*; a body of peasants, 1553.

peck   a measured quantity of either dry or wet substance; a fourth part of a bushel; more generally, a considerable quantity or number.
Examples: peck of ashes, 1710; of bees, 1713; of corn, 1386; of dirt, 1710; of kisses; of lies, 1539; of luck; of malt, 1789; of oatmeal, 1464; of oats, 1485; of pepper; of salt, 1603; of troubles, 1535.

pedigree   a race or line; lineage; a long series; a string of people.
Examples: pedigree of dogs; of Popes, 1532.

peep   of chicken; a brood of chicken —*Bk. of St. Albans,* 1486.

peerage   the body of peers, 1454.

pelage   term for the fur, hair, or wool of wild animals, *collectively*, 1828.

peltry   pelts or skins, *collectively*, 1436; refuse; rubbish; trash.
Example: peltry of hares, rabbits, dogs, and other small animals, 1861.

pencil   a small tuft; a slender cylinder of articles formed into the shape of a pencil.
Examples: pencil of feathers; of hairs, 1776; of lines (a group term in mathematics); of light rain, 1705.

pennyworth   a small quantity —*Johnson, 1755.*
Example: pennyworth of apples, 1573.

pentad   a group of five, *especially* five years, 1880.

pentarchy   government by a group of five persons, 1587.

people   human beings *collectively,* 1374.

persistence   of parents —*Lipton,* 1970.

peter   a bundle —*Slang Dictionary,* 1874.

pewage, pewing   church pews *collectively,* 1684; the money charged for pews.

phalanstery   a group or association of people or persons, especially those following the plan of Fourierism of socialist groups of 1800; people living together as one family.
Example: phalanstery of all the fiends, 1850.

phalanx   a line or array of battle; a compact group of people or animals prepared for attack or defence; a body of persons or things drawn up together in a common purpose.
Examples: phalanx of cavaliers and dames, 1837; of elms, 1891; of Greeks, 1983; of infantry; of lawyers, 1817; of sheep, 1785; of soldiers, 1553; of migrating storks, 1733.

phantasmagoria   a series of phantoms or imagined figures.
Examples: phantasmagoria of contending angels, 1875; of terrible bright colours, 1880; of feathers, spangles, etc., 1822; of figures of ghosts and phantoms; of more prodigal and wild imaginations, 1880; of the sky, 1853.

phantomry   phantoms or ghosts, *collectively,* 1835.

phraseology   a collection or handbook of the phrases or idioms of a language, 1558.

picket   a small detached body of troops, 1761. See also **detachment, detail.**
Examples: picket of cavalry and infantry, 1844; of soldiers; of the spirit host, 1866; of strikers.

pickle   a small amount. See **mickle.**

pie   a collection of things made up into a heap; a confused mass; a collection of rules.
Examples: pie of coals, 1526; of green fodder, 1887; of mangolds, 1848; of manure; of potatoes, 1791; of unsorted type (as when a printing forme has been broken down).

piece   a portion or quantity; a length.
Examples: piece of calico (ten yards); of muslin (twelve yards).

pile   a disordered heap of things; a large clump or collection of things; a heap of wood or faggots; a lofty mass of buildings.
Examples: pile of dead carcasses, 1656; of clothes, 1440; of clouds, 1812; of conjectures, 1835; of faggots, 1902; of islands; of justice, 1770; of letters and packages, 1891; of money, 1876; of shot; of stones; of trees, 1854; of wealth, 1613; of weapons, 1608; of wood, 1744.

pillar   an upright pillar-like mass or column of air. See also **column.**
Examples: pillar of air; of cloud, 1382; of fire, 1382; of heaven bright, 1340; of sand, 1813; of smoke, 1611; of printing type; of vapour; of water, 1702.

pillaring   pillars *collectively.*

pinch   a very small quantity.
Examples: pinch of pleasure, 1583; of salt; of snuff, 1712; of fresh tea, 1840.

pipage   pipes *collectively,* 1897.

pinery   plantation of pine trees, 1831.

pinetum   collection of pine trees, 1842.

pittance   a small portion; a small number or amount.

Examples: pittance of food; of grace, 1561; of instruction, 1841; of learning; of money; of reason and truth, 1561; of wages, 1749.

pity   of prisoners: a gang or group of prisoners —*Lydgate,* 1476.

pitying   of turtledoves: modern version of a **dole of doves** —*Bk. of St. Albans,* 1486.

plagiary   of printers: printers *collectively*.

plague   a group which, by their size, number, or nature, cause devastation or irritation.
Examples: plague of confessors, 1604; of gnats, 1847; of hail, 1382; of infidels, 1596; of locusts, 1774; of brass money, 1855; of rain and water, 1548; of fell (foul) tempest, 1513.

plaquet   an ornamental inscribed tablet.
Example: plaquet of advices, 1680.

plash   a heavy fall of rain or similar outpouring.
Examples: plash of rain, 1887; of sunlight, 1848; of water, 1851; of waterfowl, 1882.

plate   tableware *collectively*.

platoon   a squad; a company or set of people, 1711; a small body of soldiers; a burst of gunfire or the like.
Examples: platoon of arguments, 1775; of gunfire (a volley), 1747; of musketeers, 1637; of people, 1841; of troops, 1727.

plebs   plebeians; the common people; the mob, 1647.
Example: plebs of the Ancient Forum, 1835.

pleiad   a close group or cluster of stars in the constellation Taurus, 1388; *hence,* a group of brilliant persons or outstanding things.
Examples: pleiad of French poets, 1838; of stars, 1388; of writers, 1882.

plethora   an overfullness; repetition or excess.

Examples: plethora of capital, 1835; of Greeks, 1983; of words, 1868; of work.

pluck   of shawmers: a company of shawm players —*Bk. of St. Albans,* 1486; (a *shawm* is a medieval stringed musical instrument).
Examples: shawmer, a player of the shawm, 1505; a flourish of shawms, 1641.

plume   anything resembling a plume of feathers or a tuft of waving hair.
Examples: plume of distinction, 1848; of feathers, 1711; curling plumes of hair, 1870; of smoke, 1878; plumes of the woodland, 1859.

plump   a knot; a tuft; a cluster; a number joined together in one mass —*Johnson,* 1755; a compact body of persons, animals, or things. See also **bunch, clump, company, flock,** etc.
Examples: plump of coleworts; of conjectures and great presumptions, 1553; of green corn, 1575; of deeps (the oceans), 1535; of ducks, 1854; of folk, 1489; of hazelnuts; of moorhens; of pains, 1568; of resolution, 1659; of seals, 1591; of spearmen, 1548; of trees, 1615; of orchard trees, 1868; of whales, 1834; of wild fowl, 1697; of wood (a copse), 1470; of yachts (at anchor), 1893.

pocket   a collection or small quantity, as of ore. See also
layer.
Examples: pocket of air; of clay crops, 1872; of earth; of gold, 1850; of hops, 1767; of nuggets of gold, 1896; of red soil, 1893; of water, 1852; of wool (half a sack), 1706.

pod   a small herd or school of birds or mammals; a small herd of seal or whales.
Examples: pod of birds; of coots, 1832; of porpoises; of seals, 1897; of sperm whales, 1840; of whales, 1898; of whiting.

poesy   poems *collectively, c.* 1300; a bunch of flowers; a nose-gay, 1572.
Example: poesy of flowers, 1629.

poke   a bag containing a definite amount which varied according to the commodity.
Examples: poke of bran, 1875; of corn, 1648; of hops, 1883; of madder (20 cwt), 1347; of silver, 1733; of pardon, 1377; of pence, 1575; of plums, 1581; of wool, *c.* 1500.

pomp   a procession or pageant; a splendid display.
Examples: pomp of clothing, 1483; of flowers, 1750; of godliness, 1709; of winning graces, 1667; of mourning, 1651; of pekingese —*Hare,* 1939; of powers, 1750; of riches, 1535; of terror, 1633; of waters, 1595.

pontificality   prelates *collectively* —*Bk. of St. Albans,* 1486.
Examples: pontificality of Aaron, 1727; of these truckling Sadducees, 1879.

pook   a heap, 1718; a roughly thrown up heap of hay; a tall stack of corn nine to ten feet high. See also **cock, stack.**
Examples: pook of barley; of corn; of hay, 1853; of oats, 1718; of turves, 1868; of wheat, 1722.

pool   a small body of liquid; a reservoir of persons or things.
Examples: pool of blood, 1843; of memory, 1903; of sunlight, 1875; of typists; of water, 1622.

populace   the majority; the common people, 1572; the multitude, crowd or throng, 1871. See also **mob.**
Example: rural populace (the birds of the country), 1807.

port   a train or retinue of servants.
Examples: port of nobility, 1570; of pensioners, 1621; of stately phrases and pithy precepts, 1570; of servants.

portfolio   a large recepticle or case; a list of securities held by a financial institution, company, or individual.
Examples: portfolio of brokers —*Lipton,* 1970; of choice original designs, 1794; of drawings, 1807; of stocks and shares.

pose   a hoard or secret store.
Examples: pose of English nobles (coins), 1549; of silver and treasure, 1816; of treasure, 1637.

posse   a company or force with legal authority; a strong band of persons, animals, etc.
Examples: posse of articles (literary), 1728; of constables, 1753; of enthusiasts; of hell, 1645; of mechanisation, 1797; of silent people, 1872; of policemen, 1884; of the rabble, 1678; of ranters; of sheriffs; of cock turkeys, 1841; of silly women.

posse comitatus   the body of men over the age of fifteen which the sheriff of an English county could raise as a force in a crisis, 1285.

post   a batch or pile; letters or mail, *collectively.*
Examples: post of ore (for smelting at one time); of paper (a pile of four to eight quires of handmade paper).

postil   collection of homilies, 1566.

posy   a collection or bouquet of flowers; of poetry or rhetoric, 1569. See also **bouquet, nosegay, poesy.**
Examples: posy of flowers, 1565; of hyssop, 1866; of marjorum, 1742; of literary pieces, 1612; of poetry; of rhetoric, 1569; of roses, 1593.

pot   a mass-like material filling a pot-hole; a large sum of money; a conventional quantity or measure; a gallon measure, 1545.
Examples: pot of ale, 1724; of apples (five pecks), 1681; of butter (14 lb.), 1662; of coins, 1886; of jelly, 1587; of money, 1621; of mutiny, 1858; of porter, 1833; of sugar (70 lb.), 1775; of tea, 1773; of wine, 1535.

potpourri   a medley or collection of musical or literary extracts; a dish of different meats stewed together, 1611; a medley.
Examples: potpourri of meat, 1611; of flower perfumes, 1749; of literary pieces, 1864; of musical pieces, 1864; of sounds.

pounding   a mass or quantity pounded by natural or human means.
Examples: pounding of cider (a years supply), 1893; of pianists —*Lipton,* 1970; of rocks (the sea bottom), 1872.

poverty   the poor *collectively*, 1433; a company of pipers.
Examples: poverty of paupers; of pipers, 1486; multitude of the poverty of the town, 1537.

power   an abundance; a body of armed men; a fighting force; a large quantity, a great number —*Johnson, 1755.*
Examples: power of angels; of followers; of good, 1770; of goods (provisions); of horsemen, 1553; of fine ladies, 1706; of laymen, 1641; of men of war, 1523; of money, 1680; of poor people, 1661; of servants, 1801; of good things, 1755; of troops; of years.

prance   of equestrians —*Lipton, 1970.*

preen   of creative directors —*Ruffner, 1983.*

prelacy   body of prelates or bishops, *collectively*, 1300.
Example: the prelacy of the Lord, 1494.

presbytery   a body of elders of the church, 1611; ministers and elders of the Presbyterian Church, *collectively*, 1628.

press   a crush of people, 1400; the newspapers; journalists *collectively*; as much sail as the wind will allow on a ship; urgency; a large cupboard, closet, or container.
Examples: press of books, 1709; of canvas; of colthes, 1440; of engagements; of people, 1400; a great press was at the procession, 1400; of sail, 1860; of suspects.

pride   a group, band, or flock of animals.
Examples: pride of lions, 1486; of peacocks (a peacock with feathers outspread is said to be 'in his pride'), 1530.

priesthood   the body of priests, 1400.

priorate   the inmates of a priory as a community, 1762.

procession   a group of people moving in an orderly state; a regular series; sequence or succession of things resembling a procession. See also **cortège.**
Examples: procession of stately aqueducts; of boats, 1839; of tradesman's tools, 1688.

profession   a body of persons engaged in a craft or trade, *collectively*.
Examples: the profession (actors *collectively*); profession of divinity, 1682; of husbandry, 1557; legal profession (lawyers *collectively*), medical profession, 1541; the three great professions of divinity, law, and physick, 1771.

profusion   an abundance; a large number.
Examples: profusion of ancestors, 1709; of blood, 1743; of commodities; of gifts, 1546; of ideas; of promises; of tomes, 1752.

programme   a written or printed list of pieces, items, or musical numbers to be performed at an entertainment; *hence,* the items themselves *collectively* — *Wilkes*.

promise   of tapsters: barmen *collectively*.

proudshowing   of tailors: from the common name for the showy plumage of the goldfish, 'the Proud Tailor,' in use up to 1770 — *Bk. of St. Albans,* 1486.

provisions   a supply of necessaries or materials; a stock or store.
Examples: provision of bread, 1535; of nuts and acorns, 1796; of stewards, 1486; of words, 1690.

prudence   of vicars: vicars *collectively* — *Bk. of St. Albans,* 1486.

psalter   of bishops: bishops *collectively*.

psittosis   of parrots: a company of parrots — *Lipton,* 1970.

public   the community; the people, 1611.

pudder   a tumult; a turbulent and irregular bustle; a disturbance — *Johnson,* 1755.

pudding   of mallard: a company of mallard on water.

puff   a small quantity emitted in a blast.
Examples: puff of breath, 1667; of smoke, 1839; of vapour, 1869; of wind, 1400.

pummel   of masseurs — *Lipton,* 1970.

purl   a small rill in which waters are in a whirl of agitation.
Examples: purl of her sweet breath, 1850; of lace; of water, 1552; of youthful blood, 1650; purls flowering from the fountain of life, 1650.

push   a press; a throng; a crowd; a moving school or shoal of fish, 1878.
Examples: push of convicts (Australian), 1890; of Larrikins (Australian for convicts), 1890; of men, 1866; of people, 1718; of water, 1886.

pursuing   of stewards of the house: stewards _collectively_ —_Bk. of St. Albans,_ 1486.

pyramid   any material thing or group of objects in the shape of a pyramid.
Examples: pyramid of ambition, 1826; of white blossom, 1886; of bones, 1756; of books; of fame, 1670; of flame, 1651; of inference, 1882; of lawbooks, 1727; of men, 1831; of power, 1628.

Q

quadragesimal   consisting of forty, 1662; pertaining to Lent, a forty-day fast.

quadrille   a meeting of four or more persons; a band, troop, or company; a dance performed by four couples, 1773; a group of four horsemen, 1738; a square dance.

quality   people of good social position, 1693; actors as a body, 1603.

quantity   an amount or sum of people, things, or animals.
Examples: quantity of the offence, 1647; of sorrowful remembrance, 1485.

quarry   a heap of deer killed at a hunt, 1400; a heap of dead men, 1589.
Examples: quarry of the dead, 1603; quarry of piled vanities, 1633.

quaternary   four things *collectively*; a group of four facts or circumstances. Also **quaternion.**
Examples: quaternion of earth, air, water, and fire, 1695; of English writers—Shakespeare, Hooker, Bacon, Jeremy Taylor, 1868; of topics, 1648.

quaver   of coloraturas —*Lipton,* 1970.

quest   a body of persons appointed to hold an enquiry; a collection or donation; a jury, 1549.
Examples: quest of alms; of clerks, 1440; of cutpurses, 1612; of

faces, 1589; of gentlewomen, 1661; of mermen, 1845; of thieves, 1612; of thoughts, 1600; of yeomen, 1661.

questionary   a collection of questions, 1541. Also, **questionnaire.**

queue   a number of persons or things in a line.
Examples: queue of carriages, 1862; of people, 1837; of theatre-goers, 1862.

quick   those who are alive; live plants *collectively,* especially hawthorne; often used in the phrase **the quick and the dead.**

quill   a roll of something resembling the shape of a quill; used in the phrase **in a quill,** i.e., in a body, in combination, or in concert.
Examples: quill of dried bark, 1797; of cinnamon leaves; of females, 1690; of ropes, 1588.

quinary   a set of five things.

quintet, quintette   any set of five; things arranged for five people; a set of five people who play or sing five-part music.
Example: quintette of strings, 1880.

quintuplet(s)   a collection of five; five children born at the same time to the same woman.
Examples: quintuplet of rays, 1885; the Dionne quintuplets, 1934.

quire   any collection or gathering of leaves in a book or manuscript; a collection of 24 or 25 sheets of paper.

quiver   a sheath for arrows; *hence,* the arrows themselves.
Examples: quiver of arguments, 1641; of arrows, 1300; of darts, 1632; of ghosts (book title by R. Chetwynd-Hayes); quiver of slander, 1641.

quodlibet   a musical medley; a collection of several airs, 1377.

quorum   the number of members of a body or committee who together are authorised to transact business; justices *collectively*; a select company.

Examples: quorum of the Shire (justices *collectively*), 1455; of peers; of surgeons, 1747.

quota   part of a share that is due or ought to be contributed.

quotity   a collection, group, or a certain number of individuals.

Example: quotity of persons, 1837.

R

rabbinate   rabbis as a body, *collectively,* 1702.

rabbitry   a collection of hutches for tame rabbits; *hence,* a collection of rabbits, 1838.

rabble   a pack, string, or swarm of animals or insects; a crowd or array of disorderly people, 1513; the low or disorderly part of the populace; a disorderly collection; a confused medley.
Examples: rabble of appetites, passions and opinions, 1768; of bees; of books, 1803; of butterflies; of ceremonies, 1562; of licentious deities, 1741; of discourse, 1656; of dishes; of flies, 1847; of friars, 1560; of gnats; of insects; of monks, 1560; of murderers, 1792; of opinions, 1768; of passions, 1861; of people, 1635; of mean and light persons, 1568; of pictures, 1581; of scholastic precepts, 1589; of priests, 1529; of readers, 1691; of reasons, 1641; of remedies, 1633; of schoolmen, 1671; of strangers, 1840; of uncommanded traditions, 1545; of womenhood, 1847; of words, 1388.

race   a breed or class of individuals similar in appearance; a company; a row or series.
Examples: race of beasts, 1819; of birds; of youthful and unhandled colts, 1596; of cows, 1822; of coxcombs, 1712; of demi-gods, 1697; of doctors; of fishes, 1819; of grasses, 1802; of heavens (angels), 1667; of horses, 1781; of learned men, 1748; of plants, 1712; of poets, 1875; of serpents, 1774; of sheep, 1745; of stud of mares, 1547; of trains (a couple or set, or trains coupled together).

rack   a rush or shock.
Examples: rack of clouds (thin-flying, broken clouds), 1626; of water (a sudden rush), 1513.

racket, racquet, racquette, roquet or racker   an assembly of high society at a private house, 1745; a popular, noisy or confused group; also the noise made by such a group.
Examples: racquet of mirth and war, 1822; racket of society, 1886.

rafale   a burst of several rounds of artillery. See also **fusillade.**

raff   a promiscuous pile; a jumble; a rabble. See also **mob, riff-raff.**
Examples: raff of errors, 1677; of fellows, 1826; the raff or refuse of the river, 1838.

raffle   a jangle or tangle; a rabble, raff, or riff-raff of persons or things.
Examples: raffle of conversation, 1891; of cords; of intorted cordage, 1892; of flying drapery; of knaves, 1486; of priests and friars, 1670; of spars.

raft   a large collection of people or things taken indiscriminately; a dense flock of swimming birds; a collection of logs; fallen trees.
Examples: raft of auks (at sea); of swimming birds; of books; of crocodiles, 1774; of fellows, 1833; of folk; of logs; of masts, 1497; of people; of reporters; of tamarisk, 1822; of timber, 1745; of trees, 1806; of fallen trees; of verdure, 1876.

rafter   a large and often motley collection of people and things.
Example: rafter of turkeys.

rag   a small scrap of cloth; colts *collectively.*
Examples: rag of canvas, 1823; a flying rag of cloud, 1873; of colts, 1470; no rag of evidence, 1893; of land, 1650; of other languages, 1597; not a rag of money, 1590; lowest rag of the human race (the rabble), 1649; of rhetoric, 1529.

ragabash   a rabble; riff-raff.
Examples: the ragabash of the Sultan's following, 1891; this
scum of frantic knavery and ragabash, 1859.

rag-bag   a motley collection.
Examples: rag-bag of dissent, 1864; of dwellings, 1885.

rag-tag   the rabble or dregs of the community; usually in the
phrase **rag-tag and bobtail.**
Examples: the rag-tag and bobtail of the great Artic Army,
1882; rag-tag and bobtail of the faction, 1820.

rage   a violent passion; sometimes used collectively.
Examples: rage of maidens, 1486; of teeth —*Bk. of St. Albans,*
1486.

rain   the falling or driving of numerous particles; the particles themselves, *collectively.*
Examples: rain of frogs, 1593; of kisses, 1893; of melody, 1820;
of calm moonbeams, 1821; of pearls, 1847; of snow, 1388; of
sparks; of tears, 1541.

rainbow   a rainbow as a symbol of a past storm.
Examples: rainbow of hope, 1876; of the storms of life, 1813.

raise   things collected; a heap of stones. See also **cairn.**
Example: such rising as are caused by the burial of the dead . . .
are called raises, 1695.

raisin   a bunch or cluster of grapes, 1382.

rake   colts or mules, *collectively*; a row or series.
Examples: rake of colts —*Bk. of St. Albans,* 1486; rake of hutches
(a string of horses), 1901.

rakeage   a collection of things made by raking or scouring,
1851.

rally   a group of persons gathered together with a common
purpose, as a political rally, U.S., 1878; a scramble or chase; a
series of strokes in tennis; a series of comments, criticisms or
humorous banter between two or more participants.
Example: rally of stirring springs, 1674.

ramage   branches _collectively_, 1656.

ramification   branches of a tree, _collectively_, 1821.
Example: ramification of commercial intercourse, 1800.

rancho   _Spanish._ a company who eat together; a collection of huts, 1860.

rangale   rank and file; camp followers; rabble, 1375.
Example: rangale of common herd of deer, 1513.

range   a series of things; a row, line, or file.
Examples: range of beehives, 1836; of books, 1863; of buildings, 1618; of campfires, 1677; of cliffs, 1859; of colours; of emotions; of hunters; of islands, 1748; of ladies,1760; of morasses, 1791; of mountains, 1705; of oars, 1652; of outbuildings; of ovens; of pillars, 1511; of piles; of pupils, 1847; of soldiers; of trees, 1695; of vases, 1786.

rank   row or line, 1570; series or tier; a social group.
Examples: rank of baskets, 1693; of carriages; of criminals, 1585; of death, 1813; of geese and ganders, 1577; of nobles, 1596; of opposition, 1855; of organ pipes, 1811; of osiers, 1600; of poor, lame and impotent persons, 1597; of prejudices, 1725; of the priesthood, 1874; of soldiers, 1668; of swelling streams, 1697; of taxi-cabs; of teeth, 1590; of trees; of poetic tribe, 1781; of war, 1738; of wretched youths, 1697.

rant   fanatics _collectively_.

rascal   the rabble _collectively_; a mob, as of camp followers; ill-conditioned beasts, as deer. See also **rascality.**
Examples: rascal of boys, 1470; of the city, 1494; of the people, 1561.

rascaldom   the world or body of rascals, 1837.

rascality   the low mean people, 1577; —_Johnson_, 1755.

rash   a splashing shower of rain; an unwelcome or unsightly outburst.
Examples: rash of dermatologists _(modern)_ —_Mensa Society_; of rain, 1470.

ravel   a tangle or complication.
Examples: ravel of waters (book title by G. Jenkins); political ravels, 1853.

ray(s)   an order or array of soldiers, 1470.
Examples: rays of chastity, 1634; of comfort, 1781; of divinity, 1674; of genius, 1856; of gold, 1729; of hope, 1838; of horsemen, 1542; of truth, 1732.

readership   readers *collectively*, 1923; used chiefly by periodical publishers.

realm   an alternative for *ream*; an abstract state, domain, or collective body.
Examples: realm of death, 1725; of fancy, 1873; of hell, 1816; of night, 1667; of nonsense, 1682; of paper, 1589; of pleasance, 1830; of rest, 1812.

ream   a bale or bundle of clothes or paper; specifically, today, 500 sheets; a large amount of paper, 1392.
Examples: ream of ballads, 1630; of bloom, 1699; of modern plays, 1814; of nonsense; of rhyme, 1839; of writing paper, 1689.

reap   reapers *collectively*; a handful or sheaf of grain, 1388; a set of reapers, 1826.
Examples: reap of beans, 1523; of grain, 1388; of peas, 1523.

recession   of economists —*Lipton,* 1970.

recrement   superfluous waste, 1599; refuse; dross of metallic substances, 1611. See also **colluvies.**
Examples: recrement of ancient traditions, 1882; of iron, 1678.

reek   a pile of corn or hay —*Johnson,* 1755.
Examples: the snow was reek up, 1886; reek of corn, 1780.

regiment   a body of soldiers, 1579; a large number of things.
Examples: regiment of old vellum books, 1860; of dogs, 1656; of mice, 1849; of secret motives, 1768; of soldiers, 1579; of watermills, 1960; of waters, 1623; monstrous regiment of women.

register   a list or catalogue — *Wilkes.*
Examples: register of my belief, 1817; of fate, 1726.

repertory   provincial theatres *collectively*; a treasury or book in which anything is to be found —*Johnson,* 1755; a storehouse of knowledge; repertoire.
Examples: repertory of unconnected criticism, 1839; of all histories, 1593; of German lyric stage, 1845; of statutes and usages, 1868.

repertorium   a catalogue; a storehouse; a repository.
Examples: repertorium of the laws, 1818; the Bible is not a great repertorium of quotations, 1866.

reservoir   a store; a collection; a reserve.
Examples: reservoir of important facts, 1837; of means, 1784; of nourishment, 1813; of water, 1708.

resort   people who resort or go together to a place. See also **concourse.**
Examples: resort of ladies and damoyles, 1470; of learned men, 1817; of men of talents, 1806; of abundance of merchants, 1630; of politicians, 1768; of swordsmen, 1768.

retinue   a body of retainers, followers, or attendants, 1375. See also **servantry, staff.**
Examples: retinue of horses, 1667; of men, 1592; of nymphs, 1595; of officers and servants, 1878; of retainers, 1375; of servants, 1770.

reunion   a meeting or social gathering of persons acquainted with each other through some former event or connection.

revelrout   a mob; an unlawful assembly of the rabble —*Johnson,* 1755; a lively crowd of revellers or merrymakers, 1655.

review   a formal inspection of military men or naval forces, 1585; *hence,* the men who are reviewed, *collectively* — *Wilkes.*
Examples: review of cavalry, 1683; of the Fleet; of ships; a naval review, 1878.

rhapsody   a collection of persons; notes; miscellaneous collections; any number of parts joined together —*Johnson,* 1755.
Examples: rhapsody of errors and calumnies, 1639; of freebooters, 1689; of condemned heresies, 1580; of impertinence, 1765; of nonsense, 1711; of evening tales, 1755; of wild theory, 1837; of words, 1602.

ribbon   a group or length of things in a form suggestive of a length of ribbon.
Examples: ribbons of bark, 1872; of beach, 1857; of iron, 1843; of lightning, 1889; of sky, 1893.

richesse, richness   wealth or opulence; martins *collectively,* 1486.
Examples: richesse of glory, 1382; of all heavenly grace, 1590; of virtues and comfort of the Holy Ghost, 1400; of good works, 1539.

rick   a heap or pile; a stack of hay, corn, peas, etc., especially one built and thatched. See also **mow.**
Examples: rick of bricks, 1703; of coal, 1881; of corn, 1382; of grain; of peas; of snow, 1886; of straw, 1589; of wheat, 1557; hay rick, 1895.

riff-raff   a rabble; a mob; persons of the lowest class in the community. See also **raff.**
Examples: riff-raff of knaves, 1486; of the parish, 1686; of the people, 1619; of the scribbling rascality, 1593; of the world, 1545.

rigging   ropes or chains employed to support masts, 1594.

rigmarole   a succession of incoherent statements.
Examples: rigmarole of grannies; of nonsense.

ring   a circular arrangement or group. See also **circle.**
Examples: ring of disciples, 1732; of branching elms, 1784; of forts; of all iniquity, 1578; of jewellers —*Lipton,* 1970; of fair ladies, 1450; of mushrooms; of oaks, 1820.

riot   an unrestrained outburst; an uncontrollable company or assemblage of persons, 1400.

Examples: riot of laughter; of Romans, 1400; of students —*Madden*; of words.

riotry   rioters *collectively*.
Example: the electioneering riotry, 1780.

river   an abundant flow of water or other liquid.
Examples: river of bood, 1588; of fire, 1767; of mist, 1855; of oil, 1382; of thy pleasure, 1538; of socialism, 1892; of talk; of tears; of water, 1611; of waters of life, 1526.

robes   a loose outer garment; the legal profession *collectively*, as 'the robe'.
Examples: robes of jasmine, 1864; of light, 1849; of night, 1623; of vapours, 1857.

roll   a succession of sounds.
Examples: roll of drums (drum beats), 1842; of language, 1858; of thunder, 1818; of breaking waves, 1889.

rookery   a collection of rooks' nests; the breeding place or large colony of sea birds or other marine mammals; *hence,* the birds themselves, as herons or penguins; a cluster of dilapidated buildings. See also **building.**
Examples: rookery of albatross, 1838; of buildings; of crows, 1822; of herons; of penguins, 1840; of prostitutes, 1851; of rooks, 1725; of sea bears, 1881; of sea elephants, 1860; of seals, 1847; of volcanoes.

roost   a collection of fowls roosting together.
Examples: roost of bats hanging from trees —*David Attenborough*; of fowls; of small birds, 1827.

rope   a row or string of items or people similar to a rope; a long series.
Examples: rope of hair, 1891; of hay, 1610; of onions, 1469; of pearls, 1632; of popes, 1621; of sand, 1624; of turf, 1759; of water, 1843.

rosary   a bed of roses; a string of beads; a chaplet, garland or collection of poems or quotations.
Examples: rosary of fragrant flowers, 1533; of kisses, 1616; of

poems; of prayers, 1649; of quotations; of roses; of faithful souls, 1533; of good works, 1667.

roster   a roll or list.
Examples: roster of diplomats, 1892; of duties; of honours.

rot   a file of six soldiers.
Examples: rot of musketeers, 1635; of pikemen, 1637.

rota   a rotation of persons undertaking some duty or form of work; a list of such persons.
Examples: rota of qualified jurors, 1878; of people.

rouleau   a roll of coins; a coil.
Examples: rouleau of coins; of gold, 1884; of grey hair, 1876; of cheap repository poetry, 1795; of wire, 1825.

round   a circle; a group or series of events. See also **knot**.
Examples: round of applause, 1895; of dead bodies, 1620; of columns, 1663; of drinks; of duties; of fauns and satyrs, 1590; of knowledge; of ladyships, 1784; of memories, 1865; of peers, 1728; of pleasures; of politicians, 1711; of stools, 1700; of talks; of toasts; of visits.

rout, route   a troop, throng, company; a clamourous multitude; a rabble; a tumultuous crowd —*Johnson*, 1755.
Examples: rout or route of Black beasts, 1576; of clerks, 1430; of rural folk, 1616; of gentlemen; of knights, 1486; of lords, 1386; of nightingales, 1366; of ragged rhymers, 1579; of roiters, 1750; of ruffians and robbers, 1568; of worldly and gallant servants, 1491; of sheep, 1821; of snails, 1440; of soldiers; of strangers, 1737; of the wicked, 1561; of wolves, 1275; of words and actions, 1624.

row   a number of things or persons set out in a circle, in a string or series, or in a line —*Wilkes*.
Examples: row of answers, 1674; of beans; of grain, 1707; of houses, 1450; of onions, 1880; of piles, 1229; of pillars, 1610; of pineapples, 1779; of stakes, 1719; of theatre seats, 1710; of teeth, 1887; of words, 1510; of writers, 1576.

royalty   royal persons *collectively*, 1480.

ruck   a large number; a crowd; a heap or pile; a rick or stack of hay or corn.
Examples: ruck of coal, 1483; of corn, 1610; of fortune, 1601; of fuel, 1459; of hay, 1725; of horses, 1856; of rich pearls and sparkling diamonds, 1601; of sheep and goats, 1657; of stones, 1828; of wheat, 1570.

ruelle   a 17th-century morning social gathering in the bedroom of a fashionable lady, 1676. See also **levée.**

rug   a torn-off portion; a "haul" of something; a catch.

rumble   a commotion, tumult, or uproar; a low continuous distant sound.
Examples: rumble of basses —*Lipton,* 1970; of cannon, 1817; of carts and waggons, 1842; of traffic.

rummage   miscellaneous articles; lumber; rubbish, 1598.
Example: good riddance to bad rummage, 1880.

rumpus   a riot; uproar; disturbance.
Example: rumpus of shapes —*Dylan Thomas.*

run   an assemblage or school of fish that migrate.
Examples: run of eels, 1892; of fish; of salmon, 1887; of whales, 1820.

rush   a group formed by a moving forward with great speed; a stampede of horses or cattle.
Examples: rush of birds, 1901; of blood, 1848; of business, 1849; of dunbirds, 1875; of horses, 1881; of men, 1813; of shyness, 1883; of tears, 1873; of terror, 1865; of tide, 1789; of troops; of water; of wind.

S

sabre   a cavalry unit, 1829.
   Example: sabres and bayonets of the fields, 1829.

safari   the men, animals, and equipment involved in an expedition, 1892.

safe   of ducks: a sore of ducks; two ducks. See also **sord.**

safeguard   of porters: company of porters, 1486.

sagene   a network, as a railway complex, 1846; a number of fishing nets.
   Example: the railway sagene, 1871.

sail   sailing vessels *collectively,* 1436; sails *collectively,* 1385; windmill sails *collectively.*
   Examples: sail of ducks, 1727; of ships, 1633; of Spaniards, 1458.

sailful   enough wind to fill the sails of a ship.
   Example: sailful of wind, 1650.

sailrife   an area full of sailing ships; abounding in sails.
   Example: the sailrife seas, 1513.

salad   a cold dish composed of a variety of fruits, vegetables, meats, etc.
   Examples: salad of murder and Te Deums, of conflagration and general fasts, 1635; salad of styles (architectural), 1893; the Puritan, Anabaptists, Brownist, like a grand salad, 1635.

salariat   the body of people who receive a salary, 1687.

salon   a gathering or reception in a Parisian house, 1810; similar gatherings at other capitals; the annual exhibition in Paris of paintings, sculpture, etc., by living artists.

salvo   a salute or discharge of firearms, rockets, etc.; shouts or cheers of the crowd.
Examples: salvo of applause, 1845; of cannons, 1826; of confetti, 1860; of despair, 1875; of gunfire; of rabble, 1734; of rockets, 1799; of shot, 1591.

sample   a small quantity; an example.
Examples: sample of ingenuity, 1706; sample of salesmen —*Lipton,* 1970.

savagedom   savage people *collectively,* 1845.

savagery   savage beasts or savage people, *collectively;* wild vegetation, 1599.
Example: the savagery that roamed in that great forest, 1867.

sawt   of lions: a pride of lions.

scads   a lot of; heaps, 1869; U.S. money, 1809; a slab of peat or a tuft of grass, 1880.

scaff-raff   *Scottish.* rabble; riff-raff.

scaffolding   a framework.
Example: scaffolding of words, 1718.

scalp   an oyster colony or a mussel bed, 1521.
Examples: mussel scalp; 1557; oyster scalps, 1862.

scant   a dearth; a scarcity; a little amount.
Example: scant of squirery, 1475.

scantling   a small quantity —*Johnson,* 1755.
Examples: scantling of apples, 1849; of burgundy, 1765; of eloquence, 1704; of food 1835; of geological knowledge, 1876; of paper, 1743; of time, 1665; of wit, 1680.

scatter   a scattering; a small amount or number. See also **sprinkling.**

Examples: scatter of diamonds and pearls, 1888; of granite, 1859.

scattering   a sparse amount or number. See also **scantling.**
Examples: scattering of affections, 1662; of good and evil, 1662; of learning; of nations, 1545; of pearls, 1908; of rays, 1866; of thoughts.

scheme(s)   a body of related doctrines; a methodical list; a programme of action.
Examples: scheme of questions, 1780; of times, 1677; schemes of blood, 1646; of saddest evils, 1701.

schemozzle   of monkeys.

school   the body of pupils in a school; a group of painters or musicians; the disciples of a teacher; a collective body of teachers; a company of thieves; a set of persons who agree on certain philosophical, scientific, or other opinions; a herd of sea mammals or fish.
Examples: school of abuse, 1579; of beggars; of bream, 1552; of card players, 1812; of clerks, 1486; of dolphins, 1615; of ducks, 1858; of experience, 1671; of fish, 1486; of gladiators, 1863; of gulls, 1894; of haddock, 1819; of hell, 1390; of herrings, 1578; of hippopotami, 1861; of oysters, 1665; of painters; of pamphlets, 1567; of patience, 1583; of patterers (thieves), 1859; of pheasants, 1592; of pickpockets; of pigeons, 1880; of pilchards, 1769; of politics, 1690; of porpoises, 1863; of scolds, 1589; of shallow coves (thieves), 1851; of smolt, 1863; of thieves, 1856; of troop of the Imperial Guard; of whales, 1585.

scolding   of kempsters: 15th-century seamstresses —*Bk. of St. Albans,* 1486; scolding of seamstresses —*Lipton,* 1970.

scoop   an amount of some items obtained in a large quantity, as with a scoop; a piece of luck; an exclusive newspaper story.
Example: scoop of penance, 1440.

score   a group or set of twenty; a weight of 20 or 21 pounds used in weighing pigs, oxen, and other commodities.

Examples: score of bachelors (from the phrase 'to score')
—*Lipton,* 1970; flour (20 lb.), 1858; of people.

scotship   a party or group of people paying "scot and lot", a
communal fine or tax.

scourge   a load or burden. See also **plague.**
Examples: scourge of adversity, 1386; or mosquitoes; of priests,
1560; of Turks, 1596.

scramble   a confused or disorderly event.
Examples: scramble of the world, 1839; a scramble of Tories,
1839; motorcycle scramble (race meeting).

scran   a collection of things to eat; the provisions for a picnic;
food carried by labourers to the field, 1887; broken or unpleasant food.

scrap(s)   a bit or fragment.
Examples: scrap of a thunderous epic, 1847; of evidence, 1868;
of knowledge, 1879; of learning; of news; of paper, 1726; of
supper, 1761; of time, 1767; of other folks' wit, 1700.

screech   of gulls.

screed   a lengthy piece of writing; a discourse or harangue.
Examples: screed of cribbing, 1884; of doctrine, 1816; of malevolence, 1902; of notes; of poetry, 1812.

screen   a line or belt of trees; the cinema and its films,
collectively, 1928; a small body of troops detached to cover the
movements of other soldiers.
Examples: screen of oak and sycamore trees, 1894; of privet,
beech, holly and yew, 1882; of troops, 1894.

scroll   a roll of parchment, *hence,* its contents; a list of names;
a schedule.
Examples: scroll of actors, 1590; of pearly clouds 1862; of eternal counsels, 1649; of the fallen; of fame, 1820; of fate, 1891;
of heaven, 1656; of honour; of mortal mystery, 1817; of sins,
1621; of smoke, 1886; of tragedies, 1903.

scrum   of rugby players: 1896.

scry   a flock of wild birds; a shouting, clamorous group.
Example: scry of fowls (wild fowl), 1450.

sea   a great quanitity; a flood; anything resembling the seas.
Examples: sea of acclamations, 1632; of blood, 1598; of cares, 1574; of carpets, 1654; of claret, 1821; of clouds, 1644; of discussions, 1816; of examples, 1586; of eager faces, 1862; of forces and passion, 1667; of glory, 1613; of heads, 1849; of sand 1770; of seaweed; of white tents, 1898; of troubles, 1602; of green vegetation, 1869; of wine, 1646; of wrath, 1692; of seas of time, 1822.

seam   a horse-load; a load or burden; *specifically,* eight bushels of grain; three hundredweight of hay or manure; two hundredweight of straw (a cartload).
Examples: seam of apples (9 pecks); of corn (a quarter), 1440; of dung, 1726; of glass (120 lb.), 1325; of grain (8 bushels); of hay (3 ctw), 1880; of lime, 1536; of manure, (3 cwt); of oats (8 bushels), 1377; of sand (6-8 pecks); of straw (3 cwt); of wood, 1545.

seat   a setting or clutch of eggs, 1892; a sitting of a court; a collection of guests at a banquet or wedding reception.
Examples: seat at bride's reception, *c.*1200; of ducks' eggs, 1892; of justices; the Forest seat at Chelmsford 1635 (court of justices); Lords of the Seat (Supreme Court of Scotland), 1532.

seating   See **sitting.**

secession   a body of seceders, 1600; secessionists *collectively,* 1862. Also, **secesh.**

secretariat   a body of secretaries, 1811.

sect   the group of people who follow a particular creed or embrace a certain set of opinions or rituals.
Examples: sect of astronomers, 1837; of atheists, 1692; of flatterers and Hostlers, 1515; of Lollards, 1390; of men of letters, 1776; of old maids, 1788; of pathologists and theorists, 1843; of philosophers; of physicians, 1628; of thieves and murderers, 1568; of writers, 1609.

section   a separated portion of any collection or people, 1832; a fourth part of a military company, 1863.

sederunt   a list of people present at a meeting, 1701; a sitting for discussion or talk, 1825.

sedge, sege   a collection of rush-like marsh plants, *hence,* a group of sea or marsh birds that use it as a nesting place. Also, **siege.**
Examples: sedge of bitterns; of cranes; of herons —*Bk. of St. Albans,* 1486.

sedila, sedile   a series of seats in a church, usually three in number, frequently set into the wall and surmounted by decorative arches, 1793.

seethe   a boiling; an extreme state of agitation, 1606.
Example: seethe of patriotic feelings.

seigniory, seignory   a body of seigniors or Lords, 1485.

select   a selection; a selected group of people or things; a part of a public house set aside.
Examples: a select of friends and acquaintances, 1733; of oysters, 1881.

selection   collection of things selected.

senary   a sequence or series of six things; frequently used for the six days of the Creation.
Examples: one senary of days, 1686; four senaries of hours, 1693.

senate   an assembly or Council of citizens; a body of the elders, 1586; the governing body of a nation, state or university.
Examples: the senate of the Gods is met, 1821; the senate of the heart, 1540.

seniority   seniors or senior Fellows of a college, 1678.

sentence   of judges —*Bk. of St. Albans,* 1486.

sept   a clan or tribe, 1517.
Example: sept of bards, 1610.

septemvirate   a group of seven leaders, a set of seven men, 1750; a body of seven.
Example: septemvirate of Christian youths (the Seven sleepers), 1859.

septenary   a group of seven; seven years.
Examples: septenary of days (a week), 1660; of planets, 1650; of years.

septet, septette   a set of seven, 1886; seven infants at a birth.
Examples: septette of watercolours, 1907; a septette (a field of seven horses in racing), 1886.

septuagint   a group of seventy, 1864.

sequel   a train of followers, 1420; a suite, 1572, a logical consequence; descendants.
Examples: sequel of hangers-on, 1552; of descendants 1572; of followers, 1420; of heirs and sequels, 1533; a sequel and route of worldly and gallant servants, 1491; of songs and rhapsodies, 1713.

sequence   a continuous or connected series, 1575.
Examples: sequence of causes, 1829; of chambers, 1668; of reflections, 1823; of saints, 1589.

seraglio   the inmates of a harem, 1634; a house of women kept for debauchery —*Johnson, 1755.*
Examples: seraglio of the godly (i.e., a nunnery), 1672; of flattering lusts, 1711; of maids of honour, 1860; a cock and a seraglio of seven hens, 1773.

sergeancy, serjeancy   a body of sergeants, 1330.

serial   items in a row or series.
Examples: serial of concerts, 1864; of pictures, 1854.

series   a number of things or events linked by some factor. See also **chain.**
Examples: series of abuses, 1656; of calamities; of experiments,

1864; of facts, 1837; of landscapes, 1812; of reasons, 1656; of divine revelations, 1871; of revolutions; of good successes, 1646; of barren times, 1709; of triumphs; of words, 1765; of years, 1886.
Examples:

serfage   a body of serfs, 1864; serfhood, 1841.

serge   of herons. See **sedge.**

seron   a bale or package, especially of spices or special commodities.
Examples: seron of almonds, 1706; of medical barks, 1890; of cohineal, 1833; of cocoa, 1745; of dollars, 1748; of soap, 1545.

serpentry   serpents or serpentine-like creatures as a body, 1818; a place where serpents are kept and reared, 1864.

serra   a series of mountains; a saw-like ridge, 1830.

serry   a crowd or massed bunch of people.
Examples: serry of pikemen, 1581; of warriors, 1843; serried ranks of soldiers, 1821.

servantry   a body of servants, 1860. See also **retinue.**

service   the settings for a table; sets of dishes, etc.
Examples: service of china, 1788; of gilt plate, 1669; of plate; of tableware.

servitude   slaves or servants, _collectively,_ 1667.

session   a group of judges, administrators, or other persons in session.

set   a number of items of a similar nature usually used together; a group of persons who habitually meet socially or through some other contact.
Examples: set of acquaintances, 1779; of artisans, 1705; of bells, 1771; of books, 1596; of booksellers; of bowls —_Brewer_; of chairs; of china; of customers, 1866; of eggs; of games; of golfclubs —_Brewer_; of fishing hooks, 1867; of horses, 1687; of motives, 1897; of oysters (crop of young oysters in any local-

ity), 1881; of pains,1742; of punches, 1683; of shuttlecocks, 1711; of smugglers, 1815; of ushers.

settlement   a community settled in a locality, 1697.

sewerage   sewers *collectively,* 1834.

shaft   a missle or beam. See also **ray.**
Examples: shaft of lightning, 1878; of love, 1600; of malice; of ridicule, 1779; of gentle satire, 1847; of sunlight; of wit.

shaw   a thicket or small wood; a tuft of trees —*Johnson,* 1755.
Examples: shaws of coral and pearly sands, 1721; a shaw of wood, 1462.

sheaf, *plural* **sheaves**   a collection of things bound together; a large bundle; a cluster of flowers; leaves. See also **garb, gavel.**
Examples: sheaf of arrows, 1318; of banners, 1863; of barley, 1796; of beans, 1862; of blooms, 1882; of painting brushes, 1855; of columns (of liquid), 1857; of corn, 1717; of fire, 1811; of telegraph forms, 1888; of glass (bundle of six plates), 1402; of grain; of hemp; of jets of flame; of jets of water; of letters, 1865; of librarians; of lines (geometry); of rain, 1888; of rays (light rays); of reeds, 1846; of rye; of snakes, 1631; of spears, 1805; of steel (30 pieces), 1495; of timber, 1534.

sheltron   a band or army; a battalion, 1205; a compact body of ships, 1400.
Example: the sheltron of Christ (the army of Christians), 1425.

shelving   shelves *collectively,* 1844.

shindig   *U.S.* a dance or party, *hence,* the people present, 1892.

shindy   a row; a commotion; a spree, 1821.

shingle   pebbles *collectively,* 1598 —*Wilkes.*

shive, shove   fragments or splinters, *collectively;* a cluster of splinters of raw fibres in papermaking, 1483.

shivoo   *Australian.* social gathering.

shoal   a great number; a crowd; a throng: especially of fish.
Examples: shoal of bass; of boats, 1839; of crows, 1759; of eagles, 1801; of fish, 1579; of frogs, 1692; of goslings, 1584; of herrings, 1774; of martyrs, 1610; of minnows; of miracles, 1639; of novelties, 1900; of injured people, 1901; of perch; of pilchards; of quails, 1659; of seals, 1835; of shepherds, 1579; of sticklebacks; of texts, 1688; of troubles; of whales, 1836; of small troubles, 1858; shoals of actors and actresses, 1749; of letters; of people, 1881; of Scotsmen, 1791.

shock   pile or heap of sheaves of grain, wheat, rye, etc.; a bunch or bundle of things; a crowd of people; a lot of sixty pieces.
Examples: shock of actors; of beans, 1862; of corns, 1584; of folks; of grain, 1584; of hair; of wheat, 1899.

shot   pellets *collectively;* shots or discharges of missiles.
Examples: shot of cannon, 1642; of general dangers, 1662; of fish (single draught or catch), 1859; of foot soldiers; of ice, 1650; of nets (entire throw of fishing nets at one time); of noise and nastiness, 1718; of rain, 1673; of water, 1400; of words, 1567.

shote   a clump or group.

show   a body or exhibition of persons, 1889; animals or things on exhibition; the exhibiting of an emotion, etc.
Examples: show of alarm, 1841; of attention, 1872; of foxes, 1885; of gladiators, 1770; of hands, 1789; of horses, 1864; of interest; of livestock, 1840; of people, 1889; of questions, 1581; of reason, 1604; of vegetables, 1695.

shower   something resembling a fall of rain; a copious supply; *Derogatory.* a crowd of people.
Examples: shower of arrows, 1375; of ashes, 1829; of beauty, 1803; of blessings; of blood, 1643; of blows, 1852; of bullets, 1687; of clubs, 1570; of emoluments, 1817; of gifts; of gold, 1840; of eternal graces, 1616; of grief, 1638; of hailstones, 1576; of leaves 1877; of letters 1888; of light, 1781; of meteorologists —*Lipton,* 1970; of hard names, 1751; of plenty,

1748; of rain, 1618; of sleet, 1570; of snow, 1570; of sparks; of stars, 1811; of stones, 1849; of tears, 1663; of water, 1859.

shrewdness   of apes: company of apes, 1452; shrewdness was defined in 1567 as naughtiness or mischievousness.

shrivel   of critics: critics *collectively* —*Lipton,* 1970.

shrubbery   shrubs *collectively,* 1777; a plantation of shrubs. *Example*: shrubbery of birch, oak, and alders, 1791.

shush   of librarians: group of librarians —*Lipton,* 1970.

side   either team in a sporting or other competitive contest, 1698.

siege   of herons: company of herons, from the way the heron waits for its prey in the shallows at its feet, 1452. *Examples*: siege of bitterns, 1452; of cranes; of herons, 1452.

sight   a great number; a quantity; a sum; a multitude. *Examples*: sight of asses, 1577; of rare flowers, 1752; of lawyers; of money; of ships, 1449; of thanks, 1800; innumerable sight of stars, 1538; noble sight of books, 1432.

signary   a series or arrangement of signs. *Example*: signary of signs, hieroglyphs, or other alphabetical signs.

singular   of boars: a pack of boars —*Bk. of St. Albans,* 1486.

sisterhood   an association of women, or things which are considered to be feminine. *Examples*: sisterhood of canting females, 1718; of churches, 1883; of Holy nuns, 1687; of planets (seven) 1827.

sitting   the meeting together of a body of persons authorised to transact business; the number of eggs covered by a fowl in a single brood; a number of people taking a meal or sitting examination at a certain time. *Examples*: sitting of a commission; of a judicial court; of eggs, 1854; of parliament, 1700.

size   a quantity or an amount of bread, 1785.

skein   a flight of wild fowl, duck, or geese; a quantity of yarn; thread or silk taken from the reel.
Examples: skein of geese (in flight) —*Brewer*; of wild geese, 1851; of human affairs, 1797; of shadowy hair, 1874; of policy, 1884; of state politics 1831; of silk, 1628; of thread, 1440; of wool; of worsted, 1704

skelp   a heavy fall of rain.

skep, skip   a quantity of grain, 1100; of malt or charcoal (usually twelve bushels).
Examples: skep of bread, 1470; of chaff, 1846; of charcoal, 1353; of corn, 1380; of grain, *c.* 1100; of malt; of sand, 1669; of vegetables, 1824.

skill   those in a profession or occupation, *collectively;* a guild or craft.

skirl   of pipers: company of bag-pipe players —*Lipton,* 1970.

skirt   the edge of a crowd; a number of trees bordering or surrounding a place, 1617.
Examples: skirt of the enemy host, 1577; of the thickets, 1835; skirts of the cause, 1629; of congregation, 1764; of the crowd, 1894; of human nature, 1820; of the night, 1624; of power, 1839; of religion, 1648; of wood, 1617.

skulk   a furtive group; a gathering of persons or animals given to skulking, 1883.
Examples: skulk of poisoned adders, 1582; of foxes, 1450; of friars, 1450; of heretics, 1532; of thieves, 1450.

skull   a school or shoal of fish.

sky   the top row of paintings in an exhibition gallery, 1891.
Examples: sky of fame, 1597; of pictures, 1891.

slam   of cards: a number of tricks; at bridge, six or seven.

slash   a large quantity of liquid, as of soup or broth, 1614.

slate   a list of candidates prepared for nomination.

Examples: slate of candidates —*Lipton,* 1970; of horses (in a race); of officers.

slather   a large quantity.

slew, slue   a large quantity; a lot.
Example: a slew of people.

sloth   of bears: a company of bears —*Bk. of St. Albans,* 1486.

slouch   of models: —*Lipton,* 1970.

slumber   of the Old Guard: —*Lipton,* 1970.

slumdom   slums *collectively,* 1882 —*Webster.*

smack   a smattering; a taste; a small quantity.
Examples: smack of jellyfish —*Lipton,* 1970; of knowledge; of my muse, 1766; of every sort of wine, 1759; of wit.

small beer   any collection of trifles or trifling matters.

smear   of curriers: a company of men skilled in dressing and colouring tanned leather, 1476.
Examples: smear of curriers, 1486; of gynaecologists —*Mensa.*

smidgeon   a small quantity.

smuth   of jellyfish.

snail   *Military.* a D-shaped formation, 1579.

snake   a term applied to things or a formation resembling a snake — *Wilkes.*
Examples: a black snake of men winding across the plain, 1891; snakes of ribbon, 1894.

snatch   of robbers —*Lipton,* 1970.

sneer   of butlers —*Lipton,* 1970.

snobbery, snobdom   snobs *collectively,* 1833.

snows   of paper: piles of paper, 1728.

society   the people in the fashionable world, 1813; certain communities of animals or insects.
Examples: society of beavers, 1794; of wasps, 1826.

sodality   a fellowship or fraternity.
Examples: military sodality of musketeers, crossbowmen, archers, swordsmen in every town, 1855; the sodality of the Chaplet of Our Lady, 1628; the sodality with the Jesuits to overthrow our country, 1600; the seraphick sodality (seraphim *collectively*), 1737.

software   the collection of computer programmes that can be used with a particular computer, 1963.

soldiery   soldiers *collectively,* 1570.
Examples: the soldiery . . . all flocked unto him, 1635; full of soldiery, 1580.

solemn   of parsons —*Lipton,* 1970.

sord, sore   a flight or flock of mallard in the air, 1470. See also **safe.**
Examples: sord of mallard, 1470; of ducks.

sorites   a heap or series of propositions; a heap or pile.
Examples: sorites of flaming anthracite, 1871; sorites of facts, 1875; sorites of observances, 1664; song sorites of sciences and tongues, 1670.

sorority, sorory   a body or group of women united for some common aim, as to promote education, social welfare, or the arts, 1532.

sorosis   a women's club or society, 1868.

sort   a group having similar qualities; a crowd or flock. See also **batch, set, suit.**
Examples: sort of benefit, 1578; of doves, 1687; of ewes, 1611; of figs, 1438; of gallants, 1598; of goodly knights, 1509; of raisins; of ships, 1681; of pretty tales, 1584; of traitors; a great sort of wives, 1529.

sounder   a herd of wild swine; pigs or boars, 1410.
Example: sounder of scholars —*N. Y. Times,* 1983.

sounding   of storytellers.

soupçon   of justice, 1849; of sense, 1849.

sowarry   the mounted attendants of a person of high rank
—*Anglo-Indian,* 1776. A number of sowarrys form a cavalcade.

sownder   of swans.

sowse   of lions —*Egerton Mss.*

span   a pair, harnessed or yoked to match in colour, size, or
both.
Examples: span of elephants, 1860; of mules; of oxen, 1893; of
printing houses, 1884.

spanges   a spangle; a glittering cluster.
Examples: spanges of glory, 1625; of gold, 1616 of stars, 1616.

spangle   a star-like cluster or ornamentation.
Examples: spangles of beauty, 1647; of happiness, 1652; of
stars, 1893.

species   a group of individuals of common parentage; a sort,
kind, or variety.

sphere   the persons with whom one is normally in contact,
1839; a group of persons of a certain rank, standing, or interest, 1601.
Examples: sphere of sweet affections, 1602; of fortunes, 1671; of
the theatre; of the world of music.

spiling   pilings *collectively,* 1841.

spill   a small quantity of money —*Johnson,* 1755; a small
amount of spilt liquid.
Examples: spill of heart's blood, 1848; of money, 1707; of rain,
1888.

splother   of children.

spoils   goods acquired by confiscation or seized by force.

Examples: spoils of the city, *c.*1300; of the continent, 1774; of time, 1750; of war, 1697.

spray   a bundle of small branches and foliage or anything resembling them.
Examples: spray of branches; of flowers; of honeysuckle, 1854; of roses, 1873; of the sea, 1813; of water.

spread   an expanse or stretch of something; food *collectively*.
Examples: spread of boughs, 1701; of canvas, 1691; of knowledge, 1805; of favours; of sail, 1840.

sprinkle   a small quantity that is sprinkled.
Examples: sprinkle of common turnip cabbages, 1768; of disconnected factions, 1862; of fruit, 1825; of new growth on the market, 1890; of better instructed persons, 1844; of snow, 1888; of holy water, 1665.

spring   a group of animals or birds flushed from their covert; a flow of water or similar flow; a copse or grove of young trees; young shoots or new growth.
Examples: spring of blood, 1596; of honour, 1509; of all my joys, 1709; of oaks; of plants, 1601; of roses, 1667; of talk, 1818; of teal, 1450; of thoughts, 1892; of waters of grace, 1440; of wood, 1483.

sprinkling   a small amount falling in drops; a small number scattered here and there.
Examples: sprinkling of blood, 1835; of dung, 1760; of our gentry, 1621; of grey hairs, 1706; of mud, 1760; of people; of pepper; of rain, 1700; of salt, 1842; of foreign words, 1876.

spurt   a sudden outbreak, as of feeling or energy; a gushing of liquid; a flight of wild fowl.
Examples: spurt of activity, 1792; of business, 1791; of drink, 1859; of ducks (flying), 1874; of dust, 1868; of energy, 1858; of angry feelings, 1880; of jealousy, 1859; of prosperity, 1867; of spray, 1877; of water, 1775; of wind, 1746.

squad   a small number of individuals engaged in a common task or occupation; a small number of men in a military setting.

Examples: squad of animals, 1857; of authors, 1809; of beaters —*Brewer*; of butchers, 1797; of labourers, 1825; of people, 1818; of liveried servants, 1896; of small ships, 1676; of soldiers; of witches, 1830.

squadron   any body of men in a regular formation; a division of a fleet or air force; a force of 150 to 200 men in the army.
Examples: squadron of air craft —*Brewer*; of angels; of bees, 1713; of cardinals, 1906; of clouds, 1862; of consideration, 1680; of dissent, 1824; of galleons, 1588; of the Fathers, 1617; of blessed spirits, 1684; of ships; of soldiers, 1656.

square   a body of troops drawn up in a square formation.
Examples: square of battle, 1599; of pedestrians, 1893; of pikes, 1602.

squat   of daubers: company of plasterers, 1450.

squeeze   a crowded assembly or social gathering, 1779.
Examples: squeeze of books; of the fashionable mob, 1802.

squib   a small measure of quantity, 1766.
Examples: squib of gin, 1805; of punch, 1766.

squiry, squirary, squirarchy   a company of squires.
Examples: new tally of squiry, 1327; a scant of squirary, 1475.

stable   horses *collectively*.
Examples: stable of asses, 1576; of brave horses, 1700.

stably   a stand or halt of armed men, 1450.

stack   a large quantity; a group or set; an orderly pile or heap; bookstacks *collectively;* a unit of measure for coal or fuel (4 cubic yards).
Examples: stack of arms; of beans, 1795; of Bibles; of billets; of bills; of books; of buildings, 1698; of conventions, 1896; of cornmills, 1772; of salt fish, 1596; of letters; of money, 1894; of statutes, 1581; of wood, 1460.

staff   a body of servants, officers, nurses, or employees,

collectively; a pair of cocks, three hawks, or a bundle of teasels.
See also **retinue.**
Examples: staff of cocks (two), 1688; of hawks (three), 1688; of
nurses; of officers; of servants —_Brewer;_ of teasels, 1794.

stale   a body of armed men posted for ambush.
Examples: stale of hunters, 1425; of armed men, 1350.

stalk   of foresters: company of foresters —_Bk. of St. Albans,_
1486.

stamp   printing type or founts of type, _collectively;_ a complete
set of things.

stand   a suit or set, as of soldiers, clothes; a suit of armour; a
hive of bees; a stud of horses; an assemblage of game birds.
Examples: stand of armour (a suit); of bees; of bells, 1534; of
birds, 1881; of sugar cane, 1887; of clothes; of planted cotton,
1904; of flamingoes; of horses, 1711; of chain mail, 1896; of
needles (set of four); of pikes, 1598; of gold plover, 1882; of
plovers; of timber, 1767; of trees; of wheat, 1868.

standard   a quantity of timber, 1858; a body of troops kept in
reserve, 1297; a company of cavalry.
Examples: standard of apparel (suit of clothes), 1630; a standard
of feathers (a set of plumes), 1578; a cornet or standard of
horsemen, 1580.

starboline   men of the starboard watch, 1769.

stare   of owls.

stash   a hidden cache, 1942.

state   of princes: princes _collectively_ —_Bk. of St. Albans,_ 1486.

statuary   statues _collectively,_ 1701.

staupings   the hoof-marks of cattle, 1847.

stew   layers of oysters in an artificial oyster bed; a cooked dish
consisting of meat and other vegetables; a breeding place for
pheasants —_Wilkes._
Examples: stew of oysters, 1817; of pheasants, 1888.

stir   a collection of solid bodies or particles, especially burning coals.

stock   cattle, horses, or sheep that are bred for use or profit, *collectively*; a swarm of bees.
Examples: stock of bees, 1675; of Quakers, 1674.

stockpile   a reserve; a store of things.

stone   of drunks —*Lipton,* 1970.

stook   a heap or bundle; a truss of flax or of sheaves of grain, 1530. See also **cock.**
Examples: stook of corn, 1530; of flax; of grain, 1530; of hay, 1600; of leaves, 1892; of rocks, 1865; of straw, 1571; of good thatch, 1876.

store   a build-up of material or goods; a body of persons; a large number or quantity.
Examples: goodly store of blows, 1705; of flowers, 1853; of gypsies —*Lipton,* 1970; of horses, 1538; of knowledge; of mice, 1594; of people, 1653; of ancient poets, 1536; of provisions; of snow, 1677; of chosen soldiers, 1570; of swine, 1590; of trees growing, 1598.

storm   a shower or flight of objects; a passionate outburst.
Examples: storm of applause, 1832; of arrows, 1667; of blows, 1817; of bullets, 1615; of eloquence, 1712; of fate, 1713; of galloping hoofs, 1847; of invective, 1849; of music, 1781; of prayers, 1842; of shot, 1849; of sighs, tears, or plaints, 1602; of snow, 1681; of sobs; of thoughts, 1569; of weeping, 1891; of whistlings, 1615; of words, 1693; of wrath.

strain   a family of people or animals; a group of plants bred away from the original species.

stramash   an uproar; a state of noise and confusion, 1821.

stratum   one of a number of layers, 1902.
Examples: stratum of society, 1850; of mythological thought, 1870; the lower social stratum, 1902.

stray   a number of stray beasts; of stragglers from an army, 1717; a detached fragment, 1789.
Examples: stray of bullocks and heifers, 1717; the scattered stray, 1597.

stream   a continuous flow.
Examples: stream of abuse; of beneficence; of blood, 1225; of bubbles, 1727; of cold air; of emigrants, 1849; of fire, 1777; of ice; of people, 1639; of swifts, 1857; of tears, 1591; of wind, 1753; of words.

strength   a body of soldiers; a sufficient number.
Examples: strength of men, 1565; of people, 1500; of troops, 1400.

strew   a number of items scattered over an area, 1578.
Examples: strew of books and pamphlets, 1907; of printer's proofs, 1891; of weeping verse, 1657.

strick   a bundle of broken hemp, 1616; of flax or jute; a grain measure (one bushel), 1893. See also **strike.**
Examples: strick of barley, 1530; of coals, 1576; of corn, 1421; of flax; of malt, 1600; of silk fibres, 1887.

strike   a unit of eels; a dry measure varying from two pecks to four bushels; a bundle or hank of flax; a large catch of fish. See also **strick.**
Examples: strike of acorns, 1681; of coins (the number struck at one time), 1891; of eels, 1667; of fish; of flax, 1386; of herrings, 1894; of peas, 1523.

string   a line or series of things or animals.
Examples: string of arguments; of ballads, 1710; of barges, 1885; of beads, 1687; of coral beads, 1620; of birds (flying in a single line), 1813; of camels, 1717; of captives, 1910; of carriages, 1820; of empty carriages, 1849; of cash, 1902; of codling, 1891; of doggerel, 1870; of elephants, 1814; of error, 1685; of excuses; of facts, 1859; of flounders, 1737; of gabble, 1858; of geese, 1801; of herrings, 1732; of horses, 1686; of houses, 1843; of islands, 1788; of lies; of life, 1577; of lumber (logs fastened together to be carried down river), 1874; of

mules, 1764; of oaths, 1902; of onions, 1834; of packhorses, 1842; of pearls, 1488; of ponies; of questions, 1797; of race-horses, 1809; of rafts, 1885; of resolutions, 1772; of sausages, 1830; of schoolboys, 1830; of slaves, 1734; of stories, 1713; of teal, 1889; of violinists —*Lipton,* 1970; of visits, 1839; of waters, 1683; of words.

stringing   string *collectively,* 1722.

strut   of junior executives —*Ruffner,* 1983.

stubble   stumps of the stalks of wheat or other grain, *collectively,* 1846.

stubbornness   of rhinoceros.

stud   a collection of horses or other animals kept for breeding, racing, or riding. See also **stable, string.**
Examples: stud of colts and good mares, 1400; of dogs; of grey-hounds, 1828; of horses, 1611; of mares —*Brewer;* of motor-cars, 1907; of partridges, 1854; of poker players; of racehorses; of sows, 1813.

subjects   those under the dominion of a reigning prince, *collectively* —*Wilkes.*

subtlety   of sergeants —*Bk. of St. Albans,* 1486. (From the use of the title *sergeant* for lawyers, *hence,* lawyers *collectively.*)

succession   a series of things.
Examples: succession of all ages, 1605; of bishops, 1594; of facts; of heirs; of popes, 1579; of prophets, 1662; of rain, 1797; of worldly things, 1577; of victories, 1849.

succour   ships *collectively.*
Example: succour of galleys.

superfluity   of nuns: a company of nuns —*Bk. of St. Albans,* 1486.

suit   a number of things used together; a company of follow-ers or disciples. See also **set, stand.**
Examples: suit of armour, 1859; of beads, 1654; of biscuits (1

cwt); of clothes, 1761; of diamonds, 1782; of hair, 1893; of hangings, 1623; of hounds; of mallards (a flight), 1486; of oars, 1817; of pasturing paddocks, 1778; of pages, esquires, and chaplains, 1865; of pictures; of playing cards, 1529; of ribbons, 1762; of sails (a set), 1626; of saints and good men, 1612; of spars; of trees, 1402; of witnesses, 1647; of married women, 1799; of years, 1625.

suite a connected series of items; a retinue of attendants. See also **set, staff.**
Examples: suite of childish amusements, 1770; of apartments, 1858; English authors, 1824; of crystals, 1805; of tree sparrow's eggs, 1864; of letters, 1761; of minerals; of musical pieces; of computer programmes —*Ponton,* 1984; of rooms, 1716; of shells, 1833; of fair white teeth, 1845; of trumps, 1850; of woe, 1602.

sum a quantity of money; a number of things; a host; an assembly.
Examples: sum of conceits, 1576; of facts, 1840; of gold, 1375; of happiness, 1772; of malt, 1528; of men, 1450; of misery, 1827; of silver, 1596; of soldiers, 1400; of Muscovado sugar, 1680; of tobacco, 1872; of treasure, 1300.

surge a high, rolling swell of water.
Examples: surge of buzz of voices, 1891; of contempt, 1602; of low hills, 1863; of lava, 1869; of mishaps, 1583; of passion, 1520; of popular opinion, 1890; of popular resentment, 1834; of schismatics and heretics, 1550; of the sea, 1624; of tears, 1567; of water, 1538.

swad a thick mass, clump, or bunch; a great quantity, 1828.
Examples: swad of fine folk, 1833; of grass, 1833; of hair, 1844; of words, 1855.

swag quantity of money or goods, usually stolen; a bundle of personal belongings carried by a tramp, miner, or traveller in the bush, 1864; a decorative festoon of flowers, 1794; of fruit and flowers, 1813.

swale timber planking, 1597.

swarm   a large number of small animals or insects, usually in motion; throngs of people or things, sometimes of an irritating or annoying nature.
Examples: swarm of adders, 1569; of fair advantages, 1596; of the Anti-Christ, 1549; of ants; of bees, 1300; of bishops, 1553; of their demands, 1785; of dust, 1890; of eels; of fireflies, 1842; of flies, 1560; of folk, 1423; of footmen, 1542; of fowl, 1600; of fry, 1780; of gnats —*Brewer;* of heretics, 1581; of hornets; of horsemen, 1542; of insects; of locusts, 1684; of meteorites; of ministers of Christ, 1685; of sins, 1582; of tiger, 1600; of vessels, 1698; of wasps.

swathe   a crop mown and lying on the ground, 1325.
Examples: swathe of clover, 1834; of corn, 1766; of grass, 1614; of mist 1818; of rain, 1856; of water, 1852; of winds, 1859.

sweep, sweepage   things that are swept up, *collectively,* as the sweeping of gold or silver in a goldsmith's workshop.
Example: sweep of hay, 1672.

sweepdom   chimney sweeps *collectively.*

sweepings   a collection of persons or things, 1641; rubbish. See also **riff-raff.**
Example:

swelldom   people of distinction; swells *collectively,* 1855.

swelling   a rising emotion; an inflation by pride, etc.
Examples: swelling of the deep, 1781; of grief, 1709; of heads —*Daily Telegraph,* 1984; of vain hopes, 1750; of floating tide, 1676.

swinery   swine *collectively,* 1849.

swirl   objects that move rapidly in a circle or in a whirling motion, 1858.
Examples: swirl of rain clouds, 1853; of flame, 1861; of sea, 1871; of wood smoke, 1894.

swish   of hairdressers —*Lipton,* 1970.

syllabary   a collection or list of syllables.

sylloge   a collection; a summary, 1686.
Example: sylloge of many illustrious persons, 1697.

sylva, silva   a collection of literary pieces or poems; a thesaurus of words or phrases, 1787; the trees of a particular region or period, *collectively,* 1846.

symbolism   symbols *collectively,* 1882.

symphony   a collection of sounds; a chorus; a collection of musical sounds or attractive colours, 1874.
Examples: symphony of colour, 1874; of commendations, 1654; of laughter, 1713; of the ocean, 1849.

symposium   a collection of opinions, 1882; a conference on a specific topic, 1869; a drinking party, 1748 — *Wilkes.*

synagogue   an assembly; a congregation of Jews, 1175; of Rome, 1674; of Satan, 1565.

syndicate   a council or body of syndics, 1624; a combination of financiers or of newspapers proprietors, 1865.

synod   an assembly of the clergy; of ministers or elders.
Examples: synod of greedy caterpillars, 1580; of cooks, 1763; of peers, 1849; of prelates; of all sweets, 1649.

synonymy   synonyms *collectively,* 1683.

syntax   a connected system or order; a union of things.
Examples: syntax of being, 1661; of phantasy or imagination, 1676.

synthesis   a body of things put together, 1865.
Examples: synthesis of human belief, 1865; of divine graces, 1882; of qualities, 1870.

system   an assembly of things arranged in a series that conforms to a plan.
Examples: system of beacons, 1868; of botany; of communications; of deceit, 1781; of iniquity, 1663; of logic, 1699; of philosophy; of railways; of rocks, 1830; of truths, 1845; of telegraph wires, 1855.

T

tabagie   a group of smokers who meet as a club, 1819. Also called **tobacco parliament.**

tabernacle   of bakers: a company of bakers —*Bk. of St. Albans,* 1486.

tablature   murals or ceiling paintings, *collectively.*
Example: a tablature of splendid hues and imposing forms, 1819.

table   the company at dinner or at a meal, 1602; a company of plaes at a gambling table, 1750.

tableau   a group of persons and props used to produce a picturesque effect, 1813.

tableware   the articles used at meals, as dishes, plates, knives, forks, etc., 1832.

tag   the rabble; the lowest class of the populace, 1607. See also **rag-tag.**

tail   the inferior and often least influential members of a group, political party, etc., 1604; those who make up the end of a procession.
Examples: tail of the army, 1604; of poor followers, flappers, and flatterers, 1838; of maids, 1633; of people, 1604; of ignorant persons, 1578; of precedence, 1895; of an honest profession, 1604.

tail-end   the last portion or lowest part of something.

Examples: tail-ends of glaciers, 1874; tail end men of the Victorian Eleven, 1904.

tale   a number of things; a list or series; a tally or total.
Examples: an exact tale of the dead bodies, 1722; tale of fair children, 1864; goodly tale of folios, 1826; of lambs (the total number), 1697; tale of oysters (quantity by which they are sold), 1594; of good works, 1732.

talent   an abundance or plenty; persons of ability _collectively;_ actors _collectively;_ girls _collectively._
Examples: talent of his hatred, 1635; rising talent of the kingdom, 1838; talent of the stage, 1885.

tally   a number, group, or series, 1674; a unit of measure, sometimes, five dozen objects.
Examples: tally of cabbage, 1891; of cauliflowers, 1883; of hops, 1868; of marrows, 1891; of squirary (young squires), 1327; of turnips (five dozen bunches), 1851.

tangle   a knot of threads or other items in confused piles.
Examples: tangles of courts, 1861; of creepers, 1842; of facts and figures, 1883; of metaphysics, 1858; of low scrubby oaks, 1873; of serpent tresses, 1819; of words, 1866.

tankage   tanks _collectively,_ 1866; a provision or system of storage tanks.

tarradiddle   of ducks: team of ducks.

tass   a heap; a small cup, _hence,_ its contents; a pile.
Examples: tass of the bodies dead, 1386; of brandy, 1818; of cherry brandy, 1859; of corn, 1440; of hay, 1887; of tea, 1825; of wine, 1583.

team   family or brood of young animals; a group of animals moving together; people joined in some sporting or other competitive event.
Examples: team of athletes; of baseball; of cattle, 1840; of chicken (a brood), _c._1400; of cows, 1876; of debaters; of dogs, 1835; of dolphins; of ducks (in the air, or a brood of young ducks), 1688; of footballers, 1902; of geese, 1720; of carriage

horses; of polo horses; of oxen; of pigs (a litter), 1511; of sins, 1225; of swans (swans with cygnets), 1697; of villains, 1622; of wild ducks (flying in a line or string); cricket team, 1885.

teem   a brood of young ducks.

temperance   of cooks: a company of cooks —*Bk. of St. Albans,* 1486.

tempest   a tumultuous throng; a rushing crowd of people or things, 1746.
Examples: tempest of cheering, 1909; of wild horses, 1866; of sand, 1856; of temptations, 1606; of wind, 1250.

templary   Knights Templar *collectively,* 1661.

temple   a local group of Oddfellows.

tenantry   a body of tenants, 1628.

tendance   attendants *collectively;* a train or retinue, 1607.

tern   set of three; trio; triplet; a group of three stanzas in poetry, 1856.

ternary   set or group of three, *especially* the Holy Trinity.
Examples: ternary of stanzas, 1779; ternary of worthies, 1654; the Holy Ternary, 1662; the Almighty Ternarie, 1570.

ternery   a place where terns congregate to breed, *hence,* a flock of terns —*Century Dictionary,* 1891.

ternion   a company of three; a triad or set of three.
Examples: ternion of angel hierarchies, 1652; of triumvirs, 1600; happy ternion of brothers, 1661.

terrace   a series of things, *especially* houses.
Examples: living terrace of crippled children, 1896; terraces of gravel (geology), 1878; of houses (e.g., Adelphi Terrace), 1796.

tetrad   a group of four; four things regarded together as a single object or thought.
Example: Great Tetrad of senior wranglers, 1898.

theatre   an open stage; a series of passing scenes; an audience or "house", 1602; the dramatic work of a playwright, *collectively,* 1640.
Examples: theatre of action, 1774; of all his brutalities, 1654; of violent earthquakes, 1850; of Gods, 1634; of hills, 1818; of misery, 1640; of public life, 1855; of rising terraces, 1886; of valour, 1615; of war; of water, 1645; of the whole world, 1581.

thesaurus   a treasury or storehouse, 1491; a repository, as of words, *hence, Roget's Thesaurus,* 1852.

thicket   a clump of trees, 1440; a collection of tangled underbrush.

though   of barons —*Bk. of St. Albans,* 1486.

thrap   a crowd of people, 1814.

thrave   a bundle or handful; a herd or drove; a number of two dozen —*Johnson,* 1755.
Examples: thrave of ballads, 1825; of barley (24sheaves), 1812; of corn (24 sheaves), 1423; of flax, 1462; of gallants, 1610; of heather, 1716; of hemp, 1618; of Jews, 1656; of oats (24 sheaves), 1812; of peas (24 sheaves), 1812; of rye, 1551; of thrushes, 1486; of wheat (28 sheaves), 1551.

thread(s)   a line or string that links together actual items, episodes, or thoughts, *collectively,* and carries the theme along with it.
Examples: thread of our poor human affairs; of argumentation, 1774; of comforts, 1719; of history, 1736; of delicious melody, 1879; of patience, 1670; of rain, 1593; of sand, 1674; of truth, 1836; of his verbosity, 1588.

threat   a crowd; a multitude of people; a group of men in an attacking mood. See also **throng.**

threatening   of courtiers —*Bk. of St. Albans,* 1486.

throng(s)   a large number of persons or things that are crowded and jostled together. See also **multitude.**

Examples: throng of business, 1730; of work, 1707; throngs of gentle dreams, 1760; of thoughts, 1602.

thrum a band; a troop; a crowded area; a bundle of arrows, 1450.

thrust a large milling crowd, 1565.
Example: they were faint with the great thrust and throng of the people, 1588.

tide a stream; a current of things or emotions.
Examples: tide of blood; of emigration, 1830; of emotions; of events; of feelings; of upright freedom, 1519; of popular prejudice, 1777; of sorrows, 1738.

tiding of magpies: a flock.

tier a row or rank; a series; ships moored or at anchor, 1732.
Examples: tier of galleries; of guns; of organ pipes; of shelves; of shipping (moored), 1858; of snakes, 1646; of theatre boxes; the lower tier of society, 1882.

tierce a band or company of soldiers; a cask of wine, *hence,* a similar amount of other commodities; the third part of a thing or group of people or things.
Examples: tierce of beef (a cask), 1800; of coffee berries, 1825; of French claret (cask), 1707; of honey (a cask), 1585; of pork (a cask), 1800; of soldiers (a band or company); of tobacco, 1886; of wine (a cask).

tillage the crops growing on tilled land, 1543.

timber furs or animal skins, *especially* 40 skins of martens, ermines, or sable, and 120 skins of other animals.
Examples: timber of ermine skins, 1714; of marten skins, 1707; of mink skins, 1707; of sable skins, 1566.

tip a mound or mass of refuse or rubbish, 1863.

tirade an outburst of speech, 1801.
Examples: tirade of infamous falsehoods, 1818; of bombastic nonsense, 1858; of words, 1801.

tirocinium   a group of recruits or novices, 1651.
Example: tirocinium of genius, 1711.

tissue   a web; a framework of something.
Examples: tissue of crimes, follies, and misfortunes, 1763; of epigrams, 1711; of lies; of misfortunes; of misrepresentations, 1820.

tittering   of magpies: a flock.

toft   a small grove of trees, 1706.

toggery, togs   clothes *collectively*, 1812.

tok   the nesting place or an assembly of the great grouse.

token   a small amount; a suspicion, often called a **token amount.**
Example: a token of paper (250 printed impressions), 1683.

toll   a clump of trees, 1644.

ton   a very large amount; a measure of weight (2240 lb. in the United Kingdom, 2000 lb. in the United States); also used in the plural, e.g. "tons" of something; people of fashion, *collectively*, e.g. "the ton," 1815.

top   a tuft or handful of hair; wood fibres; a bundle of combed wool ready for spinning, 1637.

torque   of mechanics —*Lipton,* 1970.

torrent   an overflowing river, *hence,* a rapid flood.
Examples: torrent of abuse, 1784; of eloquence; of ivy, 1864; of lace, 1880; of lava, 1858; of notes, 1826; of oaths; of passions, 1647; of rain, 1806; of smoke, 1821; of vices; of wind, 1782; of words.

tow   a string of barges being towed, 1805.

towelry   a large number of towels, 1885.

tower   a raised pile of something that resembles a tower.
Examples: tower of buttered Yorkshire cake, 1840; of his conscience, 1483; of giraffes —*Hare,* 1939; of hawks (high flying

Hoby hawks), 1575; of heaven, 1240; of lace, 1852; of pikes; of state, 1605; of timber (siege tower), 1483; of waves, *c.* 1400; of wood (siege tower), 1665; secret tower of his heart, 1374.

town   the inhabitants of a town; a nest of penguins, 1839; a group of burrows of the prairie dog, 1808.

township   the inhabitants of a town, *collectively, c.* 890.

trace   of hares: hares *collectively;* a line or train of people, 1385.

track   a train or linked sequence of thoughts or events, 1681; a series of actions.
Examples: track of hills, 1687; of scripture, 1693; of fruitless impertinent thoughts, 1681; of my thoughts, 1793; of dry weather (a spell), 1851.

trackage   railway lines *collectively,* 1884.

traffic   merchandise transported from place to place; the movement of vehicles; lumber; trash; rubbish, 1628; the rabble.
Examples: traffic of faculties, 1633; of honour, 1702; of omnibuses, cabs, carriages, and carts, 1886.

trail   a train; a trailing mass of plants or ornament; a line of persons or things following behind something; a wreath or spray of flowers or leaves.
Examples: trail of bear's foot, myrtles green, and ivy pale, 1697; of tangled eglantine, 1861; of foliage, 1869; of golden hair, 1844; of ivy leaves, 1423; of roses, 1454; hurrying trails of black clouds, 1872; of light, 1697; of lightning, 1770; long trails of chanting priests, 1856.

train   a number of followers; a procession; a succession of things, persons, or animals.
Examples: camel train, 1884; funeral train; waggon train; train of admirers, 1711; of coaches, 1669; of consequences, 1871; of courtiers, of evils, 1721; of fortunate events, 1769; of wild geese, 1698; of hawks, 1698; of ideas, 1690; of listeners, 1875; of mourners, 1833; of reasoning, 1732; of happy sentiments; of

suppositions or assertions, 1740; of good things, 1833; of thoughts; of waggons, 1829; of words; long train of lost causes, ·1858.

train band   a trained band or company of citizen-soldiers, 1630.

trance   of lovers —*Lipton,* 1970.

traps   articles of dress; personal effects and belongings, 1813.

trash   rubbish; dross; worthless people *collectively;* splinters and twigs from tree or hedge cutting, 1707.
Examples: trash of straw, 1574; tobacco trash, 1763.

treasure   a store or stock of valuable things.
Examples: treasure of central fire (volcanos), 1707; of the church, 1753; of the field, 1382.

treasury   a collection of valued things, often of wit, poems, or quotations.
Examples: great treasury of language, 1879; rich treasury of God's word, 1673; treasury of divine knowledge, 1772.

treen   wooden items *collectively,* e.g., utensils, ornaments, working tools, or implements, 1300.

treillage   latticework or grille, *hence,* treillage of vines, 1830.

trek   a movement of people or animals from one place to another, 1895; an organized migration or trek of the Boers.
Example: trek of elephants, 1850.

trenle   a circle; a ring; a bundle of wool, 1493.

tress(es)   a plait; a braid or lock of hair.
Examples: tress of flowers; of hair, 1386; of rushes; of straw; leafy tresses of the wave, 1810; luxuriant tresses of the maidenhead fern, 1875; radiant tresses of the sun, 1641.

triad   a group of three.
Examples: triad of deities; of matricides (Nero, Orestes,

Alcmaeon), 1862; of lancet windows, 1898; the sacred triad (celestial graces), 1774.

triangle   a set of three.
Example: long wavering triangle of waterfowl, 1895.

tribe   a number or company of persons or animals; a social group containing a number of families.
Examples: tribe of children, 1835; of critics, 1843; of chronical diseases, 1744; of goats —*Brewer*; of medicines, 1822; of nieces, 1909; of vulgar politicians, 1796; of savages; of snails and worms, 1731; of sparrows; of whales, 1820.

tribute   a sum of money or a contribution of praise paid to another.
Examples: tribute of affection, 1850; of tears.

triennium   a period of three years, 1847.

trinary   a set of three.
Example: trinary of peers, 1654.

trine   three; triad; a favourable aspect of the planets.
Examples: trine of astrologers—*Lipton,* 1970; single trine of brass tortoises.

trinity   any combination or set of three persons; three things united into one, 1542.

trinket   of corvisors: shoemakers *collectively,* —*Bk. of St. Albans,* 1486.

trinketry   trinkets or jewellery, *collectively,* 1810.

trio   a musical composition for three performers; a group or set of three.
Examples: trio of charming cousins, 1904; of walruses, 1856.

triology   series or group of three collected dramatic or literary works, 1661.

trip   a flock or troop; a brood or litter.
Examples: trip of dotterel, 1805; of wild ducks, 1893; of wild fowl, 1859; of goats, 1470; of hares, 1470; of hippies; of lambs,

193

1470; of sheep, 1584; of stoats; of tame swine, 1410; of widgeon, 1826.

triplet(s)   a set of three; three children at a birth, 1787.

tripletrine   the nine muses.

tristich   a group of three lines of verse; a stanza of three lines, 1813.

troop, troupe   a collection of people; a company; a number of things; soldiers *collectively;* a company of actors. See also **band, party.**
Examples: troop of baboons; of bees, 1812; of children, 1833; of dogfish; of doves, 1847; of friends, 1605; of gladiators, 1863; of gypsies, 1711; of kangaroos *—Brewer;* of lions; of lovers, 1881; of monkeys *—Brewer;* of sheep, 1587; of soldiers, 1794; of stars, 1601; of tenements; of wolves, 1719; troupe of acrobats; of actors, 1779; of dancers *—Brewer;* of minstrels, 1584; of players.

triumvirate   a group, party, or association of three leaders, 1601.

triune   a group of three things united, 1635.

truckage   supply of trucks; trucks *collectively,* 1901.

truss   a pack or package; a bundle of hay or straw; a cluster of flowers or fruit.
Examples: truss of minor associations, 1878; of the most barbarous authors, 1531; of grass, 1400; of hay, 1483; of straw, 1609; of trifles.

trust   a group of people appointed as trustees to an estate or trust, 1712.

tubing   tubes *collectively,* 1845.

tuft   a small cluster; a small group of trees.
Examples: tuft of elms, 1778; of feathers, 1585; of hairs, 1386; of grass, 1523; of pines, 1611; of plants; of plumes, 1842; of

slender prisms, 1845; of rushes, 1824; of desert shrubs, 1879; of trees, 1555.

tumble   confused pile or mass. See also **jumble, tangle.**
Examples: tumble of bush and bramble, 1903; of clowns; of feathers, 1755; of rocks and trees, 1762.

tump   a heap of anything; a clump of trees; shrubs, or grass, 1802.
Examples: tump of wiry grass, 1880; of old hay, 1892; of rubbish, 1905; of trees, 1802; of whortles, 1869.

tumult   a disorderly mob; a violent commotion.
Examples: tumult of grief and indignation, 1844; of joys, 1777; of passions, 1711; of spirits.

tun   a large quantity —*Johnson,* 1755.
Examples: tun of bliss, 1603; of gold, 1603; of gracious health, 1447.

turm   troop of horsemen, specifically 30 to 32 men, 1483.
Examples: turm of horsemen, 1533; of horse and wings, 1671.

turmoil   of porpoises: [From the disturbed water where they meet and sport.]

turn   of turtles: a group of turtles.

tussock   a tuft; a small cluster.
Examples: tussock of long grass, 1607; of hair, 1550; of leaves, 1783; of thorns, 1681; of twigs.

twaddle   of public speakers —*Lipton,* 1970.

U

umpty an indefinite, fairly large number.

unction of undertakers: a company of undertakers —*Lipton,* 1970.

unemployment of graduates: a group of students —*Hare,* 1939.

unhappiness of husbands —*Hare,* 1939.

unit a group of troops; a special department; a part of a collective whole —*Wilkes.*

university a body of teachers and students; a number of creatures, persons, or things, 1677; a class of person *collectively,* 1678.
Examples: the university or common multitude, 1677; of beasts, fowls and fish, 1604; of Christians, 1659; university of all creatures, 1494; of all evils, 1526; of gentiles, 1382; of wickedness, 1382.

unkindness of ravens: a company of ravens, 1452.

untruth of sompners: a group of summoners, 1486. Also **somner.**

upsy of swings: a row of swings or swinging boats in action at a playground or fair.

V

vagabondage   vagabonds *collectively,* 1853.

valetaille   a number or retinue of valets, 1858.

valetry   valets *collectivley,* 1806.

van   a company of troops moving forward; the forward section of such a company or train of persons, 1633.
Examples: van of armies, 1879; of circumstances, 1820; of insurgents, 1816; of the Celtic migrations, 1850; of the procession, 1878; of testimonies, 1772; of the war, 1716.

variety   a number or collection of different things. See also **miscellany.**
Examples: variety of discourse, 1757; of goods, 1708; of movements, 1851; of pleasant orchards and gardens, 1680; of pleasures, 1553; of prospects, 1718; of readers, 1623; of simpler scenes, 1798; of temporary blessings, 1623; of vices, 1891.

variorum   a collection of an author's complete works with a commentary or notes, 1728.

varletry   varlets *collectively.*
Examples: the varletry of censuring Rome, 1606; of the towns, 1759.

vassalage   vassels *collectively,* 1807.

vaultage   a series of vaults, 1599.

venery   wild animals which are hunted as game, 1350.

verbiage   a large number or overuse of words, 1721.

Examples: verbiage of the parlour fireside, 1814; of pleadings, 1787; of words, 1721.

vermin   a kind or class of obnoxious animal, 1400; applied to persons of an offensive nature, 1562.
Examples: vermin of the earth, 1690; of the soul, 1621.

verse   a certain amount of poetry; the poetic output of a particular author or group of authors, 1586; poetry considered as a whole.

verticil   a number or set of organs or parts of items arranged in a circle or round an axis, 1793.
Examples: verticil of beads, 1703; of branches, 1881; of leaves, 1872.

vespiary   a group of wasps; a wasps' nest, 1817.

vestiary   a room in which clothes are kept, *hence,* a collection of clothes, 1450.

vestry   in the Church of England, the body which administers the affairs of the church or parish, *hence,* the collective body of churchwardens, 1672.

vexillation   a company of veteran soldiers in the Roman army, 1656.
Example: the vexillation of the 20th Legion, 1656.

vianage   a number of places lying near each other, *collectively;* people living in the same area, 1647.

viandry   food *collectively,* 1450.

victuals   articles of food *collectively.*

viduage   widows *collectively.*

villadom   a group of villas or their residents, 1880.

village   a small group or cluster of burrows of the prairie dog. 18008; a collection of dwelling houses and other buildings, 1386; the occupants of a village, *collectively.*

villagery   villages *collectively,* 1560.

vinery   vines *collectively,* 1883.

vintage   wine made from the grape-crop of a certain district in a certain year, 1746.
Example: vintage of divinity, 1607.

virtuosity   virtuosi *collectively,* 1831.

vivarium   a place or enclosure where living animals, especially fish, are kept, 1600.

vocabulary   a collection or list of words, 1532.
Examples: vocabulary of arms, 1862; of new denominations, 1821; of dishes, 1825; a vocabulary to the understanding, 1662.

volary, volery   a flight or flock of birds —*Johnson,* 1755; the birds kept in an aviary, 1693.

volley   a flight of missiles; a bursting forth of many things at once; a crowd of persons or things; a company of troops; a flock of birds in flight.
Examples: volley of anathemas, 1874; of angels, 1610; of archers, 1656; of arrows, 1598; of bullets; of small charms, 1749; of compliments, 1782; of darts,1788; of disgraces, 1593; of ring doves, 1601; of duns (debts, or the people trying to cover them), 1693; of grievances, 1779; of gunfire; of guns, 1839; of tumultuous hail, 1737; of love and loyalty, 1647; of merriment, 1877; of miseries, 1639; of musketry, 1817; of oaths, 1649; of praises, 1620; of scriptures, 1590; of shot, 1583; of stones, 1686; of words, 1591.

vulgarity   the common people, 1579; the commonalty.

W

wad a little amount; a tuft or bundle; a heap or swathe.
Examples: wad of banknotes, 1899; of beans, 1856; of clovergrass, 1750; of cotton (a plug), 1861; of greenbacks (U. S. money); of groans; of hay, 1596; of hemp, 1799; of linen (to carry on the head), 1752; of lupins, 1601; of money; of peas, 1620; of reeds, 1886; of straw, 1573; of tobacco; of tow; of wheat, 1763.

waggon of teetotalers —*Madden.*

wale a selection, or that chosen as the best.
Example: wale of pleasures, 1887.

walk a procession, *hence,* the group in the procession; the procession participating in the beating of parish boundaries, 1563.
Examples: walk of snails; of snipe (a flock), 1486.

wall something that represents a wall in appearance.
Examples: black wall of forest, 1859; wall of fog, 1903; of rock, 1860; of snow, 1697; of soldiers, 1797; of water, 1859.

wandering of tinkers —*Lipton.*

wap a bundle or truss of straw; a sudden storm.
Examples: wap of snow, 1818; of straw, 1828.

wappenshaw a Scottish term for a muster of men and armour, 1503; a volunteer rifle meeting, 1868 —*Wilkes.*

warble the united sound of bird song.
Examples: the general warble of the season, 1776; the warble of the grove, 1794.

ward   a body of guards or defenders, as a garrison (its use survives in *wardroom*); a body of watchmen, 1500; patients in a hospital ward, *collectively,* 1768.

ward-room   naval commissioned officers as a body on a ship, 1801.

warp   a throw or cast; a set of four items.
Examples: warp of cod, 1533; of fish, 1598; of herrings, 1894; of oysters, 1796; of salt-fish, 1436; of weeks (four weeks), 1599.

warren   a place for keeping game animals; a place in the river for keeping fish, 1377.
Examples: warren of conies, 1600; of fish, 1377; of flies, 1625; of hares, 1538; of huts, 1918; of partridge; of passages, 1919; of pheasants; of the poor, 1886; of rats, 1856; a rabbit warren, 1773.

watch   a body of watchmen or guards, 1532; a flock of birds, 1847.
Example: watch of nightingales, 1452.

wave(s)   a body of water; the forward movement of a large body of persons, animals, or things.
Examples: wave of admirals; wave after wave of the enemy, 1879; wave of enthusiasm; of error, 1781; of strong feeling, 1855; of immigrants, 1893; of materialism, 1903; of militarism, 1915; of opinion, 1870; of passion, 1781; of population, 1852; of prejudice, 1847; of snow, 1886; of tribulations; of weary wretchedness, 1590.

waywardness   of haywards: a company of haywards—*Bk. of St. Albans*. 1486; of herdsmen —*Lipton,* 1970.

wealth   a large possession; a great amount.
Examples: wealth of antiquity, 1697; of feeling; of information; of knowledge; of learning; of inarticulate speech, 1874; of wit, 1596; of words, 1850.

web   a texture; a fabrication; webbing *collectively;* a system. See also **tissue.**
Examples: web of conjecture; of crime and guilt, 1859; of glass

(a quantity), 1545; of learning, 1605; of lies; of life; of miseries, 1577; of diplomatic negotiation, 1860; of thought, 1672; of woes, 1574; of criss-cross wrinkles, 1917.

wedge　anything in the form of a wedge, e.g., a body of troops; a group of animals or birds; silver plate *collectively,* 1725.
Examples: wedge of cheese, 1835; of wild fowl, 1869; of clangorous geese, 1889; of wild geese, 1725; of horse, 1615; of men, 1614; of policemen, 1887; of standing people, 1913; of swans; of troops.

weedery　weeds *collectively,* 1642.

weight　an unidentified group, used to counter or support arguments.
Examples: weight of affection, 1587; of argument, 1787; of judgement, 1787; of opinion.

well　a source of supply.
Examples: well of all courage, 1377; of all crafts, 1377; of gentleness, 1440; of grace, *c.*1300; of mercy; of mischief, 1538; of pity, 1530; of tears, 1382; of serious thought; of wisdom, 1225.

welter　confusion or turmoil; a surging or confused mass of material things, persons, animals, etc.
Examples: welter of ruined buildings; of controversies; of miscellaneous exhibits, 1891; of inconsistencies and errors, 1880; of opinions.

were, wered, wering　a military force; a band of troops.

whack　a portion or share.
Examples: whack of booty, 1785; of gold, 1790; of prize money, 1805; of the spoils; of troubles.

wharfage　wharves *collectively,* 1807.

wheen　a few; not many; a division; a group; a small amount; a fair number.
Examples: wheen of Amazons, 1340; of knaves, 1680; of canny wise professors, 1680.

whine   of clarinettists —*Lipton,* 1970.

whirlwind   something rushing; a confused condition.
Examples: whirlwind of applause, 1837; of tempestuous fire, 1667; of horse, 1840; of passion, 1603; of town pleasure, 1855.

whisk   a bundle or tuft of twigs, hair, feathers, etc.; a small bunch of grass; a swarm of insects moving quickly. Also, **wisp.**
Examples: whisk of feathers; flowers, 1848; of mushroom fly, 1867; of hair; of insects; of straw, 1862; of twigs.

whisp   a flock of snipe. Also, **wisp.**
Examples: whisp of rushes, 1622; of snipe; of straw, 1693.

wholesale   large quantities; a large number; in abundance, 1601.

wilderness   a mingled confusion; a large number of people, animals, or things, 1588.
Examples: wilderness of interminable air, 1821; of books, 1868; of more rare conceits, 1824; of enquiry, 1664; of faults or follies, 1775; of masts on the rivers, 1857; of monkeys, 1596; of sea, 1588; of steeples, 1857; of tigers, 1588; of trees, 1613; of waves, 1865; of wretches, 1616.

wince   of dentists —*Lipton,* 1970.

wind   wind instruments in an orchestra; their players *collectively,* 1876.
Examples: wind of adulation, 1480; of doctrines, 1526; of hope, 1591; of laughter, 1859; of passions, 1665; of praise, 1634.

wing   a flock of plovers; a section of a political or other party; either of two divisions (right wing or left wing) on each side of an army or fleet in battle array; each of the divisions or regiments of an air force.

witenagemot   an assembly or council of the Witan, the Anglo-Saxon Council to the king; a modern assembly, e.g., the first select Witenagemot of the Sciences of the World, 1899; the Witenagemot at Cambridge, 1833.

wobble   of cyclists —*Hare,* 1939.

wodge, wadge   a lumpy bundle or mass, 1860.

womanhood   women *collectively;* women as a body, 1523; womenkind, 1357.

wood choir   the chorus of birds.

woodkern   Irish outlaws, 1548.

world   the inhabitants of the earth; human society; the human race; a great quantity or amount, e.g., *it makes a world of difference.*
Examples: worlds of company, 1590; of ships, 1586.

worship   of writers: authors *collectively* —*Bk. of St. Albans,* 1486.

wrangle   a noisy quarrel; a jangle.
Examples: wrangle of bells, 1873; of philosophers —*Lipton,* 1970; of the stages, 1839.

wreath   a garland or intertwined chaplet; a drift of snow or sand.
Examples: wreaths of fire, 1789; wreath of flowers; of sand; of sea, 1875; of smoke, 1859; of snow, 1725; of vapour, 1794; of worms, 1684.

wreckage   fragments of the remains of shipwrecks or damaged buildings, 1874.

writhen   something arranged in the form of coils, having folds or windings, 1542.

Y

yeomanry   yeomen *collectively,* 1375; a volunteer force.

yield   an amount or quantity yielded or grown, e.g., a yield of fruit, 1440.
Examples: yield of the country, 1577; of gold, 1863; of the olive grove, 1893.

yoke   a pair of animals, especially oxen, that are or may be coupled by a yoke, *hence,* a pair or couple of animals, things, or persons.
Examples: yoke of bulls, 1660; of cattle, 1879; of discarded men, 1598; of oxen, *c.*1200.

Z

zeal   of zebras: zebras *collectively*.

zodiac   a recurrent series; a round; a set of twelve.
Examples: zodiac of the twelve apostles, 1631; of my expectations, 1609; of feasts, 1856; of life, 1560; of learned lives, 1742; of wit, 1586.

zoo   a collection of animals; strangely acting persons. [From the Zoological Gardens, London.]

Index

Index

This Index lists, in alphabetical order, all of the "things collected" from the dictionary, i.e., those items about which a collective term is used, as taken from the text.

The Index provides a "key-word" feature: it lists phrasal items alphabetically by each significant word in the phrase. Thus, for the phrase *association of men* (from the entry **guild** in the text), a listing will be found both at *association of men* and at *men, association of*; at each, the user is referred to the entry **guild** in the text. The words considered as insignificant for the purpose of the key-word concept are: articles *a, an, the*; conjunctions *and, or*; pronouns and adjectives *I, me, we, us, you, he, she, it, him, her, they, them, this, these, that, those, who, whom, which*; prepositions *at, for, in, of, on*; verbs *is, are*; adverb *together*.

A

Aaron: **pontificality.**
abhorrence, public: **load.**
ability: **galaxy.**
ability, persons of: **talent.**
absurdity: **hash.**
abuse: **school; stream; torrent.**
abuses: **mass; series.**
academicians: **flight.**
academics: **calendar; obscuration.**
accidental knowledge: **chaos.**

accidents: **chapter; conjuncture.**
acclamations: **sea.**
accountants: **column.**
accounts: **divan.**
acorns: **strike.**
acorns, nuts and: **provisions.**
acquaintances: **circle; cohort; flock; kith; set.**
acquaintances, friends and: **select.**
acquainted with each other through some former event, persons: **reunion.**
acrobats: **acrobacy; troop.**
action: **circle; consection; theatre.**
actions: **multitude.**

215

actions, splendid: **conflux.**
actions, words and: **rout.**
activities: **aggregate.**
activity: **spurt.**
actors: **cast; clamjamphine;
company; condescension;
corps; cry; detachment;
profession; quality; scroll;
shock; talent; troop.**
actors, Greek: **chorus.**
actors and actresses: **shoal.**
actresses: **entrance.**
actresses, actors and: **shoal.**
acts, good and evil: **commixture.**
acts, many of the worst:
consociation.
acts of providence: **consociation.**
adages: **gnomology.**
adders: **bed; swarm.**
adders, poisoned: **skulk.**
adherents: **clientage; following.**
adherents to an opinion: **consent.**
administration of justice,
organisation for the: **court.**
administrators: **session.**
admirals: **wave(s).**
admirers: **circle; claque; clique;
cordon; train.**
adolescents: **acne.**
adulation: **wind.**
Adullam: **cave.**
advanced studies, school of:
conservatory.
advantages, fair: **swarm.**
adversity: **scourge.**
advertisements: **crowd.**
advices: **plaquet.**
advisors: **camarilla.**
advisors, legal: **counsel.**
advisory body: **commission.**
advocates: **faculty.**
aeroplanes: **flight.**
affairs: **conjuncture; olio.**
affairs, human: **skein; thread(s).**
affectations, domestic: **chaplet.**

affection: **tribute; weight.**
affections: **flock; scattering.**
affections, repugnant: **congeries.**
affections, sweet: **sphere.**
age: **accretion.**
ages, all: **olio; succession.**
ages and nations: **assemblage.**
agreement, party united by
common: **consent.**
agreements, national: **entente.**
air: **column; gulp; pillar; pocket;
quaternary.**
air, cold: **body; stream.**
air, interminable: **wilderness.**
aircraft: **airfleet; armada; circus;
fleet; squadron.**
airmen: **crew; flight.**
alarm: **show.**
albatross: **rookery.**
aldermen: **bench; confraternity.**
Aldermen: **guzzle.**
alders: **shrubbery.**
ale: **dozen; firkin; gang; pot.**
alive, those who are: **quick.**
all ages: **olio; succession.**
all being: **foison.**
allegations: **camp.**
alleys: **conjunction; nest.**
alloy: **amalgam.**
almonds: **bag; seron.**
alms: **quest.**
alphabetical signs: **signary.**
Alps: **debris.**
alum: **bing; cark.**
amazons: **wheen.**
ambition: **pyramid.**
amusements, childish: **suite.**
anathemas: **volley.**
anatomists: **corps.**
ancestors: **line; profusion.**
ancient night: **dregs.**
ancient records: **archive.**
ancient rocks: **debris.**
ancients: **anciety.**
ancient traditions: **recrement.**

anecdotes: **conglomerate.**

angel hierarchies: **ternion.**

angels: **charm; choir;
commonwealth; concert; flight;
guard; heaven; hierarchy;
host; legion; order; power;
squadron; volley.**

angels, contending:
phantasmagoria.

(angels), heaven: **minstrelsy.**

(angels), heavens: **race.**

anger: **explosion.**

anglers: **drift.**

angry feelings: **spurt.**

animal, obnoxious: **vermin.**

animal functions: **cabinet.**

animals: **band; breed; burrow;
clamour; game; head; herd;
myriad; pride; spring; squad;
team; yoke.**

animals, bovine: **cattle.**

animals, collection of: **zoo.**

animals, domestic: **bestial.**

animals, small: **bed.**

animals, wild: **venery.**

animals, wild or foreign:
menagerie.

animal skins: **timber.**

animal spirits: **exuberance; gale.**

answers: **row.**

antelopes: **herd.**

anthracite, flaming: **sorites.**

Anti-Christ: **swarm.**

antiques: **ancientry.**

antiquities: **ancientry.**

antiquity: **wealth..**

ants: **anthood; army; bank;
bike; colony; nest; swarm.**

ants, hill: **bank.**

anxiety: **cark.**

apartments: **suite.**

apes: **apery; shrewdness.**

aphorisms: **gnomology.**

apostles: **company; convent;
fellowship; jury.**

apostles, holy: **congregation.**

apostles, twelve: **zodiac.**

apparel: **finery; parel; standard.**

appetites: **rabble.**

appetites and passions: **legion.**

applauders, paid: **claque.**

applause: **burst; hand; round;
salvo; storm; whirlwind.**

apples: **cluster; pennyworth; pot;
scantling; seam.**

appointed as trustees, people:
trust.

appreciation: **fond.**

apprehensions, doubts and: **gale.**

aqueducts, stately: **procession.**

archdeacons: **bundle.**

archers: **archery; bow; sodality;
volley.**

(architectural), styles: **salad.**

architectural fancy: **flowerage.**

architecture: **order.**

area, crowded: **thrum.**

argument: **weight.**

argumentation: **thread(s).**

arguments: **army; camp; host;
nest; platoon; quiver; string.**

arguments, methodical: **congest.**

arguments, verbal: **forest.**

armed force: **armoury.**

armed men: **halt; hosting;
legion; stably; stale.**

armies: **leash; pair-royal; van.**

Arminianism: **farrago.**

armour: **armoury; brace;
burden; cast; stand; suit.**

armour, men and: **wappenshaw.**

arms: **magazine; stack;
vocabulary.**

army: **debris; dignity; douth;
parel; sheltron; tail.**

Army, Artic: **rag-tag.**

army, baggage of an: **fardage;
impedimenta.**

army, stragglers from an: **stray.**

army officers: **brass.**

arrow: **magazine.**
arrows: **cloud; flight; foison; quiver; sheaf; shower; storm; thrum; volley.**
art, works of: **collection.**
arteries: **maze.**
arteries, small veins and: **labyrinth.**
arteries, veins and: **convent.**
Artic Army: **rag-tag.**
articles: **catalogue; posse.**
articles, linen: **lingerie.**
articles of dress: **traps.**
articles of food: **victuals.**
articles of vertu: **bijouterie.**
artillery: **park; peal.**
artisans: **set.**
artists: **cabal; colony.**
ash, volcanic: **cascade.**
ashes: **bed; midden; peck; shower.**
ash trees: **ash-holt.**
assemblage: **gossiping.**
assembled, people: **agora.**
assembly: **althing; comitia; divan.**
assembly, educational: **chautauqua.**
assembly, formal: **congress.**
assembly, noisy: **dovercourt; drum.**
assembly, private: **conversazione.**
assembly for worship: **meeting.**
assembly or council of citizens: **senate.**
assembly or council of the Witan: **witenagemot.**
assembly place: **agora.**
assertions, suppositions or: **train.**
asses: **coffle; drove; herd; pace; sight; stable.**
association: **confluence; coterie.**
association of men: **guild.**
association of people, group or: **phalanstery.**

association of two or more persons: **partnership.**
associations, minor: **truss.**
astrologers: **knot; trine.**
astrology and homely receipts: **medley.**
astronomers: **galaxy; sect.**
atheists: **kennel; sect.**
Athenian literature: **grove.**
athletes: **team.**
atmosphere: **column; conjuncture.**
atoms: **concourse; conjugation; crew; jumble.**
atoms, fluid: **complex.**
atoms, gaseous: **congregation.**
attacking mood, men in an: **threat.**
attendants: **farnet; meiny; retinue; tendance.**
attendants, mounted: **sowarry.**
attention: **show.**
attorneys: **array.**
attributes: **herd.**
audience: **gallery.**
auks: **colony; flock; raft.**
authorised to transact business, persons: **sitting.**
authorities, local: **consortia.**
authorities (legal): **line.**
authors: **concent; consort; fry; mob; squad.**
authors, English: **suite.**
authors, most barbarous: **truss.**
author's complete works: **variorum.**
avocets: **colony.**

B

baboons: **troop.**
bachelors: **bachelory; debauchery; parcel; score.**

bed, mussel: **scalp.**
beech: **screen.**
beef: **tierce.**
beehives: **range.**
beer: **dozen; firkin; gang; last.**
beers: **batch.**
bees: **breed; cast; cattle; clew; cluster; college; colony; drift; erst; flight; fry; game; grist; hive; parliament; peck; rabble; squadron; stand; stock; swarm; troop.**
bees, bumble: **bike.**
bees, wild: **bike.**
before Christ, years: **chiliad.**
beggars: **beggary; bike; colony; fighting; order; school.**
being: **hierarchy; syntax.**
being, all: **foison.**
beings, human: **aggregation; chain; humanity; people.**
beings, self-loving: **agglomeration.**
belief: **accrescence; register.**
belief, human: **synthesis.**
belief, mystic: **branchage.**
believers: **aggregation.**
bells: **change; chime; peal; set; stand; wrangle.**
belongings: **clobber.**
belongings, personal: **swag.**
belts: **belting.**
beneficence: **stream.**
benefit: **sort.**
benefits: **field.**
berries, coffee: **tierce.**
best, citizens;: **aristocracy.**
better instructed persons: **sprinkle.**
Bibles: **stack.**
billets: **stack.**
bills: **stack.**
birch: **cow; shrubbery.**
birch rod: **fasces.**
bird calls: **consort.**

birds: **aviary; brood; caravan; charm; clamour; concent; congregation; consort; covert; dissimulation; drift; duet; fleet; flight; flock; flurry; lek; migration; nest; party; passage; pod; race; rush; spring; stand; string; volary; watch; wood choir.**
birds, flock of: **clamour.**
birds, sea or marsh: **sedge.**
birds, small: **roost.**
birds, swimming: **raft.**
birds, unfortunate: **nation.**
birds, wild: **scry.**
birds, young: **eyrar; nide.**
birds of prey: **aerie.**
bird song: **warble.**
birth, seven infants at a: **septet.**
birth, three children at a: **triplet.**
biscuits: **suit.**
bishops: **bench; bishopdom; brace; conclave; consistory; episcopate; prelacy; psalter; succession; swarm.**
bison: **herd.**
bitterns: **flock; sedge; siege.**
bitter passion: **book.**
bitter waters: **brash.**
black cloth: **expanse.**
black clouds: **brewing; trail.**
blackfish: **grind.**
blackgame: **brood.**
black grouse: **lek.**
blackmen: **head.**
black or moor game: **game.**
blessed: **heaven.**
blessed spirits: **squadron.**
blessings: **shower.**
blessings, temporary: **variety.**
bliss: **magazine; tun.**
bliss, human: **hoard.**
blockheads: **parcel.**
blocks, piled: **confusion.**
blocks of stone: **confusion.**

bowls: **set.**
bowmen: **bow.**
boxes: **nest.**
boxes, theatre: **tier.**
boys: **blush; boyhood; leer; mob; rascal.**
bracken and briar: **maze.**
brackets: **bracketing.**
bramble, bush and: **tumble.**
bran: **poke.**
branches: **branchage; ramage; spray; verticil.**
branches of a tree: **ramification.**
branching elms: **ring.**
brandy: **dash; tass.**
brandy, cherry: **tass.**
brass: **clod; heaven; network.**
brass ['debts']: **burden.**
brasses, memorial: **brass.**
brass money: **plague.**
brass tortoises: **trine.**
brats: **passel.**
brave horses: **stable.**
bravery: **mint.**
bread: **batch; cast; clump; dozen; provisions; size; skep.**
breaking waves: **roll.**
bream: **school.**
breath: **puff.**
breath, superfluous: **abundance.**
breath, sweet: **purl.**
breeding mares: **haras.**
brethren: **brace.**
brewers: **brewery; feast.**
briar, bracken and: **maze.**
briar bushes: **briar.**
briars: **brake.**
bricks: **clam; clamp; line; rick.**
brides: **parliament.**
bridge: **hand.**
briefs: **boredom.**
brigands: **brigandage; cateran.**
bright, heaven: **pillar.**
bright damsels: **bevy.**
brightness: **galaxy.**

broken beams: **concentration.**
broken or unpleasant food: **scran.**
broken sighs: **volley.**
brokers: **portfolio.**
brood: **kindle.**
broods, spider's: **network.**
brooks: **confluence; meiny.**
broom: **bush; cow.**
broth: **slash.**
brothers: **bretheren; ternion.**
brown hair, woven: **garlandry.**
brown sugar: **cargo.**
brows: **furrow.**
bruises: **mass.**
brushes, painting: **sheaf.**
brushwood: **bavin; brake; brush.**
brutalities: **theatre.**
brutes: **parcel.**
bubbles: **stream.**
bubbles, small: **aggregate.**
bubbling springs: **coil.**
buckets: **chain.**
bucks: **brace; leash.**
buffalo: **herd.**
buffaloes: **gang; obstinacy.**
bugle-notes: **gush.**
buildings: **conglomeration; range; rookery; stack.**
buildings, ruined: **welter.**
bullets: **brace; fusillade; hail; shower; storm; volley.**
bullfinches: **bellowing.**
bullion: **mass.**
bullocks: **drove.**
bullocks and heifers: **stray.**
bulls: **yoke.**
bulls, papal: **bullary.**
bumble bees: **bike.**
bundle of small wood: **cracker.**
bundles: **network.**
bungles: **concatenation.**
burdens: **impedimenta.**
burgesses: **good advice.**
burgundy: **scantling.**
burning coals: **stir.**

burrows, mole: **citadel.**
burrows of the prairie dog: **town.**
buses: **lurch.**
bush and bramble: **tumble.**
bushes: **brake; bush.**
bushes, briar: **briar.**
bushes, low: **nest.**
business: **clutter; rush; spurt; throng(s).**
business, persons authorised to transact: **sitting.**
business organizations: **cartel.**
bustards: **flock.**
butchers: **butchery; goring; squad.**
butlers: **sneer.**
butter: **firkin; firlot; magazine; pat; pot.**
buttered Yorkshire cake: **tower.**
butterflies: **flight; rabble.**
buzz of voices: **surge.**

C

cabbage: **tally.**
cabbages, common turnip: **sprinkle.**
cabdrivers: **drove.**
cabs, carriages, and carts, omnibuses: **traffic.**
cake, buttered Yorkshire: **tower.**
calamities: **catalogue; clustering; series.**
calico: **piece.**
calls, bird: **consort.**
calumnies: **bundle; rhapsody.**
calves: **draft.**
Cambridge: **witenagemot.**
camel: **train.**
camels: **band; caravan; flock; herd; string.**
campfires: **range.**
canals: **labyrinth; network.**

[canals], locks: **flight.**
candidates: **slate.**
candles, wax: **galaxy.**
cane, sugar: **stand.**
cannon: **rumble; shot.**
cannoneers: **cannonry.**
cannons: **cannonry; salvo.**
canny wise professors: **wheen.**
canons: **chapter; college; dignity; faction.**
cant: **farrago.**
canting females: **sisterhood.**
canvas: **bolt; press; rag; spread.**
capital: **accumulation; boodle; plethora.**
capons: **mews.**
captives: **gang; harvest; string.**
carcasses: **carnage; kill; pile.**
cardinals: **cabal; cardinalate; college; conclave; congregation; squadron.**
cardiologists: **flutter.**
card players: **school.**
cards: **bunch; castle; deck; hand; monte; slam.**
cards, playing: **pack; pair; pair-royal; suit.**
cards of the same suit: **flush.**
care: **load.**
carelessness: **flood.**
cares: **multitude; sea.**
caribou: **herd.**
carpenters: **covin.**
carpets: **sea.**
carriage horses: **team.**
carriages: **cavalcade; jam; park; queue; rank; string.**
carriages, and carts, omnibuses, cabs: **traffic.**
cars: **draft.**
carters: **lash.**
carts: **crush.**
carts, omnibuses, cabs, carriages, and: **traffic.**
carts and waggons: **rumble.**

cartwheels: **gang.**
carvers: **embracing.**
cases, sundry: **myriad.**
cash: **string.**
castles: **heap.**
casual writings: **accretion.**
caterpillars: **army; nest.**
caterpillars, greedy: **synod.**
catholics: **consult.**
Catholics: **fry.**
cats: **clowder; clutter; comfort; glaring.**
cats, young: **kindle.**
cattle: **armental; armentose; bow; bunch; creaght; draft; drift; drive; drove; flote; head; herd; stock; team; yoke.**
cattle, hoof-marks of: **staupings.**
cauld porridge [cold porridge]: **claut.**
cauliflowers: **tally.**
cause: **skirt.**
causes: **chain; sequence.**
causes, lost: **train.**
causes, second: **conflux.**
causes and effects: **anthology; concatenation.**
cavaliers and dames: **phalanx.**
cavalry: **detachment; gendarmery; patrol; picket; review; standard.**
cavalry unit: **sabre.**
caveats: **decade.**
cedar boughs: **heaven.**
ceiling paintings: **tablature.**
celestial graces: **triad.**
celestial stories: **florilegium.**
cellars: **cellarage.**
Celtic migrations: **van.**
central fire: **treasure.**
centre or main part of a group: **core.**
ceremonial matters: **concretion.**
ceremonies: **rabble.**
ceremonies, foolish: **maze.**

chaff: **skep.**
chaff, corn: **bike.**
chain: **catena.**
chain mail: **stand.**
chains: **rigging.**
chairs: **crush; set.**
[chairs], windsors: **knot.**
chaises: **magazine.**
chambers: **brace; congeries; sequence.**
chamois: **herd.**
chamois skins: **kip.**
champions: **cycle.**
chances: **conglomeration; huddle.**
changes: **cycle.**
chanting priests: **trail.**
chapel-goers: **chapelry.**
chaplains: **suit.**
Chaplet of Our Lady: **sodality.**
charcoal: **skep.**
chariots, warriors who fought from: **chariotry.**
charity: **bunch; chain.**
charming cousins: **trio.**
charms, small: **volley.**
charters: **chartulary.**
chastity: **ray(s).**
chattering women: **gaggle.**
cheap repository poetry: **rouleau.**
cheaters: **fare.**
cheerful lights: **gush.**
cheering: **tempest.**
cheese: **magazine; wedge.**
cheese, garlic and: **hotchpotch.**
cherries: **bob.**
cherry brandy: **tass.**
cherubim: **choir; cohort.**
cherubs: **bunch; cherubim.**
chessmen: **meiny.**
chess players: **brood.**
chestnut trees: **colonnade.**
chicken: **brood; clutch; collation; nest; peep; team.**
chickens: **cletch.**

clerks: **ana; clerkage; gang; quest; rout; school.**

clients: **clientele; connexion.**

cliffs: **array; palisade; range.**

clippings, hedge: **brash.**

cloth: **bale; bolt; cargason.**

cloth, black: **expanse.**

clothes: **chest; clobber; clothing; dunnage; finery; frippery; outfit; pile; press; ream; stand; suit; toggery; vestiary.**

clothing: **change; parel; pomp.**

cloud: **ark; cloudfield; floe; pillar; rag.**

clouds: **bank; canopy; cloud drift; cloudrack; field; flight; formation; pile; rack; sea; squadron.**

clouds, black: **brewing; trail.**

clouds, pearly: **scroll.**

clouds, rain: **swirl.**

clover: **lock; swathe.**

clovergrass: **wad.**

cloves: **complement.**

clowns: **tumble.**

club, members of a: **ménage.**

club, women's: **sorosis.**

clubs: **knot; shower.**

coaches: **crush; herd; parade; train.**

coagulated mass: **congelation.**

coal: **bed; clamp; magazine; pack; rick; ruck.**

coals: **muid; pie; strick.**

coals, burning: **stir.**

cobblers: **cutting; dronkship; mob.**

cobwebs: **festoon.**

cochineal: **seron.**

cockles: **bed.**

cockroaches: **intrusion.**

cocks: **staff.**

cock turkeys: **posse.**

cocoa: **parcel; seron.**

cod: **last; warp.**

codling: **string.**

coffee: **bale; blend; canteen.**

coffee berries: **tierce.**

coffins: **nest.**

coils: **writhen.**

coins: **hoard; journey; pot; rouleau; strike.**

coins, copper: **brass.**

(coins), English nobles: **pose.**

cold air: **body; stream.**

[cold porridge], cauld porridge: **claut.**

cold water: **gulp.**

coleworts: **plump.**

collected dramatic or literary works, three: **triology.**

collection, motley: **rag-bag.**

collection of animals: **zoo.**

collection of huts: **rancho.**

collective farm: **kolkhoz.**

collectively of a town, inhabitants: **township.**

collective settlement: **kibbutz.**

collegians: **faction.**

colliers: **fleet.**

colony, oyster: **scalp.**

coloraturas: **quaver.**

colour: **symphony.**

colours: **gamut; mass; phantasmagoria; range.**

['colours'], shades: **assortment.**

colts: **race; rag; rake.**

colts, wicked: **haras.**

colts and good mares: **stud.**

columns: **colonnade; group; round.**

columns (of liquid): **sheaf.**

combed wool: **top.**

comets: **doctrine.**

comfort: **beam; ray(s).**

comforts: **confluence; thread(s).**

Commanders, Wing: **flush.**

commendations: **symphony.**

comments, series of: **rally.**

commercial intercourse: **ramification.**

commission: **sitting.**

commissioned officers, naval: **ward-room.**

commissioners: **board.**

committee: **caucus commission.**

commodities: **profusion.**

commodity: **glean.**

common agreement, party united by: **consent.**

common community, group living together in a: **commune.**

common multitude: **university.**

common parentage: **centgener.**

common people: **commonalty; democracy; herd; hoi polloi; plebs; populace; vulgarity.**

commonplaces: **cento.**

common purpose, persons gathered together with a: **rally.**

common rule, persons united by a: **order.**

Commons: **house.**

common turnip cabbages: **sprinkle.**

communications: **system.**

communities, isolated: **archipelago.**

community: **commonalty; commonwealth; public; settlement.**

community, group living together in a common: **commune.**

community, religious: **cenoby.**

commuters: **dash.**

companions: **comitatus.**

company: **conflux; douth; group; world.**

company at a feast: **feast.**

company at dinner: **table.**

company equipped to fight: **conrey.**

company of a theatre: **ménage.**

company of citizen-soldiers: **train band.**

company of persons: **assembly.**

company of twelve: **convent.**

company who eat together: **rancho.**

competitors: **field.**

complaints: **cartload; chorus; pack.**

complete works, author's: **variorum.**

compliments: **cargason; faggot; volley.**

composition: **confection.**

composition, musical: **cento; opus.**

composition for three performers: **trio.**

compositions: **opus.**

compositors: **companionship.**

computer machinery and equipment: **hardware.**

computer programmes: **software; suite.**

computer programs: **constellation.**

comrades: **fellowred.**

conceits: **sum.**

conceits, rare: **wilderness.**

conceits and practices: **mishmash.**

concepts: **hierarchy.**

concerts: **serial.**

conclave: **areopagy.**

concubines: **harem.**

condemned heresies: **rhapsody.**

condensers: **battery.**

cones, parallel: **cone-in-cone.**

conference: **colloquium.**

confessors: **heap; plague.**

confetti: **salvo.**

confiscation, goods acquired by: **spoils.**

conflagration and general fasts: **salad.**

confused mixture: **babel.**

confusion: **mass.**
confusions and incongruities:
 aggregate.
congregation: **house; skirt.**
conies: **bevy; burrow; bury;**
 game; warren.
conjecture: **web.**
conjectures: **pile.**
conjectures and great
 presumptions: **plump.**
conscience: **dregs; tower.**
conscious observance: **catena.**
consequences: **train.**
consideration: **squadron.**
consolation: **drop.**
consonants: **clutter; collocation.**
constables: **clutch; constabulary;**
 posse.
constancy: **dram.**
constituents: **constituency.**
constitutions: **litter.**
contempt: **surge.**
contending angels:
 phantasmagoria.
content: **exuberance.**
continent: **spoils.**
contradictions: **concatenation.**
controversies: **welter.**
conventions: **stack.**
conversation: **chorus; raffle.**
convicts: **gang; push.**
convocation: **house.**
cooked dish: **stew.**
cooks: **haystiness; synod;**
 temperance.
coopers: **gang.**
cooper's wares: **coopery.**
coots: **covert; flock; pod.**
Copernicus [stars]: **circus.**
copies: **century.**
copper: **bunch.**
copper coins: **brass.**
copses, hedges and: **nation.**
coquettes: **consult.**
coral and pearly sands: **shaw.**

coral beads: **string.**
cord: **clew.**
cordage, intorted: **raffle.**
cords: **raffle.**
cormorants: **colony; flight; gulp.**
corn: **boll; burden; cast; cock;**
 congiary; crop; firlot; glean;
 grist; hill; hurry; ingathering;
 journey; kilderkin; lock;
 muid; peck; poke; pook; reek;
 rick; ruck; seam; sheaf; skep;
 stook; strick; swathe; tass;
 thrave.
corn, green: **plump.**
corn, ripe indian: **lingot.**
corn, wavy: **expanse.**
corn chaff: **bike.**
cornmills: **stack.**
corns: **shock.**
corporate body of a town or city:
 commonalty.
corrupt humours: **cargason.**
corvisors: **trinket.**
cosmical science: **choir.**
cotton: **bale; flock; hank; lock;**
 wad.
cotton, planted: **stand.**
council: **consistory.**
councillors: **camarilla.**
council of citizens, assembly or:
 senate.
council of state, oriental: **divan.**
council of the Witan, assembly or:
 witenagemot.
counsellors: **corps.**
counsels, eternal: **scroll.**
counters: **cast.**
countries: **axis.**
country: **yield.**
country, persons sent to a foreign:
 mission.
country, wooded: **frith.**
countryside, rural: **bush.**
courage: **well.**
couriers: **fraternity.**

D

daffodils, golden: **host.**
daisies: **ball.**
dames, cavaliers and: **phalanx.**
dames, fair: **parcel.**
damoyles, ladies and: **resort.**
damsels, bright: **bevy.**
dance, noisy: **flare-up.**
dancers: **choir; choir; flit; float; troop.**
dancers, morris: **morris.**
dancing and whooping: **pandemonium.**
['dandies'], men-milliners: **confraternity.**
dangers, general: **shot.**
darkness: **mantle.**
darts: **forest; magazine; quiver; volley.**
daubers: **squat.**
daughters: **brood.**
dauntless spirits: **choice.**
David: **house.**
days: **handful; leash; senary; septenary.**
days, ten: **decadary.**
deacons: **deaconhood.**
dead: **quarry.**
dead, bodies: **tass.**
dead and stupid matter: **congeries.**
dead bodies: **carnage; round; tale.**
dead men: **hill; quarry.**
deans: **decanter; decorum.**
dear friendships: **harem.**
death: **rank; realm.**
debaters: **host; team.**
debris: **brash.**
['debts'], brass: **burden.**
debutantes: **delirium.**

decaying refuse: **cagmag.**
decays, foul: **fry.**
deceit: **system.**
decorative bars or stripes: **barring.**
deductions: **chain; circuit.**
deep: **swelling.**
deep obscurity: **mantle.**
deeps (the oceans): **plump.**
deer: **brace; drive; herd; leash; little herd; middle bevy; park; quarry; rangale.**
deer, red: **game.**
deer, roe: **great bevy.**
defending, people guarding or: **ward.**
deformities: **miscellany.**
deities: **pantheon; triad.**
deities, licentious: **rabble.**
deities of Samothrace: **cabiri.**
delegates: **court; delegation; legation.**
delicious melody: **thread(s).**
delight: **heaven.**
delights, intellectual: **commixture.**
demands: **swarm.**
demi-gods: **race.**
Democratic Party, members of the U.S.: **democracy.**
democratic state, population of a: **democracy.**
denominations, new: **vocabulary.**
dentists: **wince.**
dependent plebians: **concourse.**
dermatologists: **rash.**
descendants: **descent; sequel; sequel.**
desert shrubs: **tuft.**
designs: **portfolio.**
despair: **burden; salvo.**
despots, petty: **brood.**
destroyers: **flotilla.**
detachment: **conrey.**
Deums, murder and Te: **salad.**

dragons: **dreadful.**
drains: **nosegay.**
dramatic or literary works, three collected: **triology.**
drawers: **nest.**
drawings: **portfolio.**
dread, thankfulness and: **mingle.**
dreams, gentle: **throng(s).**
dreams, poetic: **embroidery.**
dregs: **doylt; lees.**
dress, articles of: **traps.**
dried bark: **quill.**
dried plants: **herbarium; herbary.**
drink: **kilderkin; spurt.**
drink, meat and: **convoy.**
drinks: **round.**
drops: **clutter.**
drops, water: **condensation.**
dross: **recrement; trash.**
['dross; waste substance'], recrements: **colluvies.**
drugs: **druggery.**
druids: **eisteddfod.**
drum beats: **battery.**
drums: **roll.**
drunks: **load; stone.**
dry weather: **track.**
duchies: **agglomerate.**
duck: **skein.**
duckling: **breed.**
ducks: **badelyng; brace; brood; bunch; cletch; flock; mob; paddling; plump; safe; sail; school; sord; spurt; tarradiddle; team; teem.**
ducks, wild: **fleet; team; trip.**
ducks' eggs: **seat.**
dukes: **brace.**
dunbirds: **flight; fling; knob; rush.**
dunces: **confederacy.**
dung: **clamp; seam; sprinkling.**
dunghill: **midden.**
dunlin: **fling.**

duns: **volley.**
dust: **cast; cloud; drift; spurt; swarm.**
duties: **roster; round.**
dwelling houses: **village.**
dwellings: **clustering; rag-bag.**
dynamite: **cake.**
dynamos: **battery.**

E

eager faces: **sea.**
eagles: **aerie; brood; cast; convocation; nest; shoal.**
ears of wheat: **grove.**
earth: **accretion; balk; clam; clod; mow; patch; pocket; quaternary; vermin.**
earth, inhabitants of the: **world.**
earthen crocks: **crockery.**
earthquakes, violent: **theatre.**
eat, things to: **scran.**
eat together, company who: **rancho.**
eat together, people who regularly: **mess.**
eccentricity: **dash.**
ecclesiastical senate: **consistory.**
echoes: **choir.**
economists: **recession.**
editors: **erudition.**
educational assembly: **chautauqua.**
eels: **bed; bind; brood; draft; eelfare; firkin; run; strike; swarm.**
eel spawn: **fry.**
effects, causes and: **anthology; concatenation.**
effects, personal: **traps.**
effects, sound: **montage.**
eggs: **brood; cluster; clutch;**

hatch; laughter; mess; nide;
  set; sitting.
eggs, ducks': seat.
eggs, toad's: chaplet.
eggs, tree sparrow's: suite.
eglantine, tangled: trail.
egoists: mine.
elders: ana; ancientry; synod.
elders, body of the: senate.
elders of the church: presbytery.
elect: nosegay.
electricity: charge.
electric lights: bank; battery.
elegances: contesseration.
elephants: flock; herd; kindle;
  parade; span; string; trek.
elephants, sea: rookery.
elk: gang.
elms: brotherhood; colonnade;
  phalanx; tuft.
elms, branching: ring.
eloquence: flight; flood;
  scantling; storm; torrent.
elves: congregation.
emigrants: emigration; stream.
emigration: tide.
eminences: girdle.
emoluments: shower.
emotion: flush; outburst;
  outgush.
emotions: gamut; range; tide.
Empire: debris.
employees: staff.
endeavours, past: calendar.
endowments: catalogue.
ends, odds and: cagmag; host.
enemy: wave(s).
enemy host: skirt.
energy: accumulation; spurt.
engaged in the kitchen, servants:
  kitchenry.
engagements: press.
English authors: suite.
English nobles (coins): pose.
English papists: lump.

English writers: quaternary.
enlightened: clan.
enquiry: wilderness.
enthusiasm: wave(s).
enthusiasts: posse.
envy: ambush.
epic, thunderous: scrap(s).
epic cycles: nucleus.
epics: cycle.
Epicureans: denomination.
epigrams: anthology; tissue.
equestrians: prance.
equipment: gear.
equipment, computer machinery
  and: hardware.
equipment, soldier's: kit.
equipment of a warrior: panoply.
equipped to fight, company:
  conrey.
equity, law and: fusion.
ermine skins: timber.
error: ambush; string; wave(s).
errors: aviary; hotchpotch; raff;
  rhapsody.
errors, filthy: doylt.
errors, inconsistencies and:
  welter.
esquires: suit.
estates: convention.
eternal counsels: scroll.
eternal graces: shower.
eternities: conflux.
ethereal fire: confluence.
ethics: code.
Europe: concert.
evening tales: rhapsody.
event, persons acquainted with
  each other through some former:
  reunion.
events: chain; conjunction; tide.
events, fortunate: train.
evidence: cumulation; mass; rag;
  scrap(s).
evil: dash; faction; mass;
  nursery.

evil, good and: **scattering.**
evil acts, good and: **commixture.**
evil news: **cataract.**
evils: **accumulation; nest; train; university.**
evils, saddest: **scheme(s).**
ewes: **sort.**
examiners: **gloat.**
examples: **sea.**
excesses, matrimonial: **nexus.**
excuses: **string.**
executioners: **college.**
executives, junior: **strut.**
exhibits, miscellaneous: **welter.**
expectations: **zodiac.**
expedition: **safari.**
experience: **school.**
experience, past: **aggregate.**
experiments: **consection; series.**
experts: **concilium; panel.**
explosions: **concatenation.**
expression: **condensation.**
exquisite lineaments: **convention.**
eyes: **myriad; nunnery.**

F

fables: **lump.**
fabric: **bolt.**
fabulous, scoundrels, worthless and: **abundance.**
faces: **quest.**
faces, eager: **sea.**
faces, wry: **parcel.**
faction: **rag-tag.**
factions, disconnected: **sprinkle.**
factors: **factorage; factory.**
facts: **agglomerate; array; body; camp; colligation; hoard; host; reservoir; series; sorites; string; succession; sum.**
facts, observed: **colligation.**
facts and figures: **tangle.**

faculties: **traffic.**
faggots: **pile.**
fair advantages: **swarm.**
fair children: **tale.**
fair dames: **parcel.**
fairies: **bevy.**
fair ladies: **constellation; ring.**
fair maidens: **company.**
fair white teeth: **suite.**
fair women: **bevy.**
faith: **glean; household.**
faith, Christian: **compages.**
faithful: **denomination.**
faithful souls: **rosary.**
falcons: **cast; last.**
fallacy: **circle.**
fallen: **scroll.**
fallen trees: **brake; raft.**
fallow beasts: **herd.**
falsehoods, infamous: **tirade.**
false traitors: **clan.**
fame: **embroidery; galaxy; pyramid; scroll; sky.**
families: **alliance.**
family: **house; strain.**
family, members of a: **house.**
famous people: **constellation.**
fanaticism: **academy.**
fanatics: **dregs; rant.**
fancies, rich parasitic: **cluster.**
fancy: **canvas; exuberance; gale; realm.**
fancy, architectural: **flowerage.**
farewells: **hail.**
farm, collective: **kolkhoz.**
"farmers" of public revenue [tax collectors]: **farm.**
fashion, people of: **ton.**
fashionable mob: **squeeze.**
fashionable people: **fashion.**
fashionable world, people in the: **society.**
fasts, conflagration and general: **salad.**
fat: **foison.**

fishing hooks: **set.**
fishing nets: **drift; sagene.**
fist'], fives ['a clenched: **bunch.**
five: **quintet.**
five, group of: **pentad.**
five children born at the same
    time: **quintuplet.**
five dozen objects: **tally.**
five persons: **pentarchy.**
fives ['a clenched fist']: **bunch.**
five things: **quinary.**
five years: **pentad.**
flame: **cone; pyramid; swirl.**
flame, jets of: **sheaf.**
flaming anthracite: **sorites.**
flamingoes: **stand.**
flappers: **tail.**
flasks, wine: **canteen.**
flats: **block.**
flatterers: **fare; sect; tail.**
flattering lusts: **seraglio.**
flax: **beat; head; knitch; lock;**
    stook; strick; strike; thrave.
Fleet, the: **review.**
fleet of ships: **armada.**
flesh: **magazine; opulence.**
flies: **bike; business; cloud;**
    community; fare; flight; grist;
    rabble; swarm; warren.
floating tide: **swelling.**
floating vapours: **collection.**
flock of birds: **clamour.**
floes, ice: **patch.**
floods: **congest.**
flounders: **string.**
flour: **score.**
flower perfumes: **potpourri.**
flowerpots: **nest.**
flowers: **anadem; anthology;**
    anthology; bob; bosk; bouquet;
    bow; bowpot; boughpot;
    bunch; carpet; chaplet; clump;
    conglomerate; fascicle; festoon;
    florilegium; flowerage;
    garland; nosegay; poesy;

    pomp; posy; sheaf; spray;
    store; swag; tress(es); whisk;
    wreath.
flowers, festoon of: **swag.**
flowers, fragrant: **rosary.**
flowers, rare: **sight.**
flowers, wild: **embroidery.**
fluid atoms: **complex.**
flutes: **concent.**
fly, mushroom: **whisk.**
flying drapery: **raffle.**
flying machines: **aircraft.**
foals, mare: **meiny.**
fodder: **farrago; pie.**
fog: **bank; wall.**
foliage: **bush; exuberance; trail.**
foliage, leafy: **frondage.**
foliages: **circle.**
folios: **tale.**
folk: **band; break; plump; raft;**
    swarm; synagogue.
folk, fine: **swad.**
folk, proud and rich: **hill.**
folk, rural: **rout.**
folks: **shock.**
follies: **babel.**
follies, and misfortunes, crimes:
    tissue.
follies, faults or: **wilderness.**
followers: **band; clientelage;**
    following; power; retinue;
    sequel; suit; train.
followers, poor: **tail.**
following, Sultan's: **ragabash.**
following a profession, persons:
    calling.
folly: **brood; mass.**
food: **collation; mess; oodles;**
    pittance; scantling; spread;
    viandry.
food, articles of: **victuals.**
food, broken or unpleasant:
    scran.
food made of paste: **pastry.**
foolish ceremonies: **maze.**

foolish impossibilities: **fardel.**
fools: **dunciad; faction; fare; fooliaminy; nest; pack; parliament.**
footballers: **team.**
football team: **eleven.**
footmen: **swarm.**
foot (soldiers): **brigade.**
foot soldiers: **shot.**
force, armed: **armoury.**
force, military: **knighthood; militia; were.**
force, military or naval: **command.**
force, police: **constabulary.**
force, volunteer: **yeomanry.**
forces: **compages; concentration.**
forces and passion: **sea.**
foreign animals, wild or: **menagerie.**
foreign country, persons sent to a: **mission.**
foreign memoirs: **compilation.**
foreign words: **sprinkling.**
forest: **expanse; frame; girdle; wall.**
foresters: **stalk.**
forks: **tableware.**
form, order and: **orb.**
formal assembly: **congress.**
former event, persons acquainted with each other through some: **reunion.**
former life: **dash.**
forms: **pad.**
forms, telegraph: **sheaf.**
forts: **ring.**
fortunate events: **train.**
fortune: **ruck.**
fortunes: **accumulation; sphere.**
fortunes, cross: **chiliad.**
forty: **quadragesimal.**
forward section: **van.**
fought from chariots, warriors who: **chariotry.**

foul decays: **fry.**
foul disorders: **chaos.**
foul matter: **colluvies.**
(foul) tempest, fell: **plague.**
fountains: **mass.**
four, group of: **mess; tetrad.**
four or more persons: **quadrille.**
four things: **quaternary.**
fourth part of a military company: **section.**
fowl: **cattle; swarm.**
fowl, heath: **brood.**
fowl, wild: **plump; skein; trip; wedge.**
fowls: **company; flight; heap; parliament; roost; scry.**
fowls and fish, beasts: **university.**
foxes: **brace; burrow; cloud; crew; den; earth; leash; nest; show; skulk.**
fox skins: **mantle.**
fragment: **stray.**
fragments: **brash; conglomerate; frush; levet; shive.**
fragments, volcanic: **agglomerate.**
fragments of music: **montage.**
fragrance: **gale.**
fragrant flowers: **rosary.**
freebooters: **cateran; rhapsody.**
freedom, upright: **tide.**
freemasons: **craft.**
free masons: **fraternity.**
French claret: **tierce.**
French poets: **pleiad.**
fresh smells: **gush.**
freshwater: **budget.**
friars: **brotherhood; chapter; confraternity; convent; fratry; friary; lurry; rabble; raffle; skulk.**
friends: **clique; convoy; fellowship; flock; kith; packet; troop.**
friends and acquaintances: **select.**
friendship: **contesseration; cord.**

friendships, dear: **harem.**
frogs: **colony; froggery; hopping;
    rain; shoal.**
frog-spawn: **clump.**
fronds: **frondage.**
fruit: **bob; conglomerate;
    fruitage; neddy; sprinkle;
    swag; yield.**
fruitless impertinent thoughts:
    track.
fruit trees: **grove.**
fry: **swarm.**
fuel: **ruck.**
fugitives: **band.**
functions, animal: **cabinet.**
funeral: **train.**
fur: **pelage.**
furniture shops: **congeries.**
furs: **bottle; mantle; timber.**

G

gabble: **string.**
gallants: **sort; thrave.**
galleons: **squadron.**
galleries: **tier.**
galleys: **succour.**
galloping hoofs: **storm.**
gambling table, players at a:
    table.
game: **brace; brood.**
game, black or moor: **game.**
[game beaters], beaters: **bouquet.**
games: **set.**
ganders, geese and: **rank.**
gangsters: **gangland.**
gardens, pleasant orchards and:
    variety.
garlands: **garlandry.**
garlic and cheese: **hotchpotch.**
Garter, Noble Order of the:
    chapter.
gaseous atoms: **congregation.**

gathered together with a common
    purpose, persons: **rally.**
gathering, public: **meeting.**
gathering, social: **crush; ruelle;
    shivoo.**
gathering or reception in a
    Parisian house: **salon.**
gauds and baubles: **conservatory.**
Gauls: **horde.**
gauzes: **pastiche.**
geese: **alag; clutch; crop; flock;
    gaggle; goosery; line; meiny;
    nide; skein; string; team.**
geese, clangorous: **wedge.**
geese, wild: **skein; train; wedge.**
geese and ganders: **rank.**
geldings: **brace.**
General Assembly of, Iceland;:
    althing.
general dangers: **shot.**
general fasts, conflagration and:
    salad.
general knowledge: **budget.**
generals: **generalcy; generality;
    score.**
genius: **constellation; ray(s);
    tirocinium.**
gentiles: **university.**
gentile superstition: **accrescence.**
gentle dreams: **throng(s).**
gentlemen: **party; rout.**
gentlemen, young: **confluence.**
gentleness: **well.**
gentle satire: **shaft.**
gentlewomen: **crew; quest.**
gentry: **sprinkling.**
geological knowledge: **scantling.**
geologists: **conglomerate.**
German lyric stage: **repertory.**
ghosts: **gathering;
    phantasmagoria; phantomry;
    quiver.**
gift-horses: **assortment.**
gifts: **profusion; shower.**
gilt plate: **service.**

gin: **dram; gage; squib.**
ginger: **cargo; cark.**
gipsies: **crew; gipsydom.**
giraffes: **corps; herd; tower.**
girls: **bevy; bushel; covey;
   giggle; girlery; talent.**
glaciers: **tail-end.**
gladiators: **family; school; show;
   troop.**
glass: **bolt; crate; seam; sheaf;
   web.**
glasses, fine: **company.**
glass plate: **bundle.**
gleanings, literary: **analects.**
globes, iron: **hail.**
glory: **beam; circle; consection;
   mizmaze; richesse; sea;
   spanges.**
gloves: **dicker.**
gnats: **cloud; fry; horde; plague;
   rabble; swarm.**
gnomes: **gnomology.**
goats: **flock; herd; tribe; trip.**
goats, sheep and: **ruck.**
goatskin: **kip.**
goblets: **nest.**
God, sons of: **brotherhood.**
godliness: **pomp.**
godly: **seraglio.**
gods: **junta; pantheon; senate.**
Gods: **synagogue; theatre.**
God's law: **library.**
God's word: **treasury.**
gold: **burden; drift; firlot;
   garrison; gob; lingot; nosegay;
   pocket; ray(s); rouleau;
   shower; spanges; sum; tun;
   whack; yield.**
gold, sapphire and: **array.**
golden daffodils: **host.**
golden hair: **trail.**
golden light: **flood.**
golden roses: **garland.**
goldfinches: **charm.**
gold leaf: **book.**

gold plover: **stand.**
gold rings: **muid.**
goldsmiths: **fraternity.**
gold wire: **hank.**
golfclubs: **set.**
golfers: **foursome.**
good: **community; power.**
good and evil: **scattering.**
good and evil acts: **commixture.**
good ground: **balk.**
good ideas: **heap.**
goodly knights: **sort.**
good manners: **code.**
good mares, colts and: **stud.**
good men: **suit.**
goods: **clobber; congregation;
   fadge; fangot; fond; power;
   swag; variety.**
goods, moveable: **mobble.**
goods acquired by confiscation:
   spoils.
good social position, people of:
   quality.
good spirits: **consociation.**
good successes: **series.**
good things: **abundance;
   conjunction; power; train.**
goodwill: **garland.**
good words: **army; magazine.**
good works: **richesse; rosary;
   tale.**
goose pimples: **crop.**
gorillas: **band.**
goshawks: **cast; flight; last.**
goslings: **shoal.**
gossip: **jorum.**
gossip, literary: **ana.**
gossips: **gaggle.**
Goths: **horde.**
gourmets: **delicatesse.**
governesses: **galaxy.**
governing body: **council.**
governing body of a nation, state,
   or university: **senate.**

government, group forming an interim: **commune**.

government officials: **bureaucracy**.

governors: **board**.

gowns: **duet**.

grace: **assemblage; confluence; gust; hoard; pittance; well**.

grace, heavenly: **richesse**.

grace, waters of: **spring**.

graces: **conspiracy**.

graces, celestial: **triad**.

graces, divine: **synthesis**.

graces, eternal: **shower**.

graces, winning: **pomp**.

gracious health: **tun**.

graded according to quality, items or things: **class**.

graduates: **unemployment**.

grain: **boll; cast; cob; firlot; gavel; glean; grist; last; mow; reap; rick; row; seam; sheaf; shock; skep; stook; strick**.

grammarians: **conjunction**.

granite: **scatter**.

granite houses: **agglomeration**.

grannies: **rigmarole**.

grapes: **bob; bunch; cluster; raisin**.

grass: **carpet; clump; clutter; cock; dollop; lock; swad; swathe; truss; tuft**.

grass, long: **tussock**.

grass, mown: **math**.

grass, wiry: **tump**.

grasses: **alliance; gavel; race**.

grasshoppers: **cloud**.

gratitude: **burst**.

gravel: **bar; conglobation; conglomerate; heap; terrace**.

great grouse: **tok**.

great kingdom: **dignity**.

greatness, human: **colluvies**.

great presumptions, conjectures and: **plump**.

greedy caterpillars: **synod**.

Greek actors: **chorus**.

Greek poets: **corpus**.

Greeks: **attic; forum; phalanx; plethora**.

green and grey mists: **chaos**.

greenbacks: **wad**.

green boughs: **cache**.

green corn: **plump**.

green vegetation: **sea**.

grey hair: **rouleau**.

grey hairs: **sprinkling**.

greyhound: **leash**.

greyhounds: **brace; harl; stud**.

grey mists, green and: **chaos**.

grey rock: **clatter**.

greys: **cete**.

grief: **gust; shower; swelling**.

grief and indignation: **tumult**.

grievances: **cartload; volley**.

grille: **treillage**.

groans: **wad**.

ground, good: **balk**.

group, centre or main part of a: **core**.

group, religious: **cell; confession; confriary**.

group forming an interim government: **commune**.

group living together in a common community: **commune**.

group of nations: **allies**.

group of women: **sorority**.

group of five: **pentad**.

group of four: **mess; tetrad**.

group of seven: **septenary**.

group of seventy: **septuagint**.

group of 10,000: **myriad**.

group of three: **ternary; triad**.

group or association of people: **phalanstery**.

grouse: **brace; brood; covey; drive; game; harvest; jug; pack**.

grouse, black: **lek**.

grouse, great: **tok.**
grove, olive: **yield.**
growth on the market, new:
　sprinkle.
Guard, Old: **slumber.**
guardians: **board.**
guarding or defending, people:
　ward.
guards: **watch.**
guests: **feast; mess.**
guests, wedding: **convoy.**
guild: **skill.**
guilt: **hill; load.**
guilt, crime and: **web.**
guilty wishes: **brood.**
gulls: **colony; school; screech.**
gunfire: **platoon; salvo; volley.**
gunpowder: **charge.**
(gunpowder), powder: **magazine.**
guns: **battery; gunnery; peal;**
　tier; volley.
gut: **hank.**
gynaecologists: **smear.**
gypsies: **store; troop.**

H

haddock: **school.**
hags, old: **hagging.**
hail: **fall; plague.**
hail, tumultuous: **volley.**
hailstones: **shower.**
hair: **bob; bunch; bushel;**
　capillament; cascade; cob; coil;
　fascicle; fuzz; hank; lock;
　opulence; pelage; plume; rope;
　shock; suit; swad; top;
　tress(es); tussock; whisk.
hair, golden: **trail.**
hair, grey: **rouleau.**
hair, lady's: **ambush.**
hair, powdered: **mop.**
hair, shadowy: **skein.**

hair, woven brown: **garlandry.**
hair, yellow: **nosegay.**
hairdressers: **swish.**
hairs: **pencil; tuft.**
hairs, grey: **sprinkling.**
hairs, stiff: **palisade.**
half: **moiety.**
halls: **congeries.**
ham: **lock.**
handful: **fascicule.**
handmaidens: **college.**
hands: **show.**
hangers-on: **sequel.**
hangings: **suit.**
happiness: **exuberance; foison;**
　spangle; sum.
happy sentiments: **train.**
hard names: **heap; shower.**
harem, inmates of a: **seraglio.**
hares: **brace; down; flick; game;**
　husk; kindle; lease; leash;
　peltry; trace; trip; warren.
harlots: **herd.**
harpers: **melody.**
harpists: **melody.**
harrows, light: **gang.**
harts: **herd.**
harvest: **foison.**
harvest waggons, labourers and:
　cortége.
hate: **harvest.**
hawks: **aerie; brood; cast; leash;**
　mews; staff; tower; train.
hawthorn: **bob.**
hawthorne: **quick.**
hay: **bottle; cast; cob; cock; coil;**
　darg; gavel; hurry; knitch;
　lock; mow; parcel; pook; reek;
　rick; rope; ruck; seam; stook;
　sweep; tass; truss; wad.
hay, old: **tump.**
haywards: **waywardness.**
hazelnuts: **plump.**
heads: **sea; swelling.**
health, gracious: **tun.**

heap, manure: **midden.**
heap, stone: **bourock.**
heart: **senate; tower.**
heart's blood: **spill.**
heat: **beam.**
heathens: **heathenry.**
heather: **covin; cow; thrave.**
heath fowl: **brood.**
heaven: **canopy; expanse; host;**
  scroll; tower.
heaven (angels): **minstrelsy.**
heaven bright: **pillar.**
heavenly grace: **richesse.**
heavenly truth: **hill.**
heavens: **heaven.**
heavens (angels): **race.**
heavenware: **heaven.**
hedge clippings: **brash.**
hedgehogs: **array; nest.**
hedges: **brush.**
hedges and copses: **nation.**
heifers, bullocks and: **stray.**
heirs: **heritage; sequel;**
  succession.
hell: **posse; realm; school.**
hell, horrid: **legion.**
hell, souls in: **damned.**
hemp: **beat; glean; sheaf; strick;**
  thrave; wad.
hens: **battery; brood; flock;**
  mews; seraglio.
hens, sage: **covey.**
hens and chickens: **parcel.**
heraldry: **pash.**
heralds: **college.**
herbs: **bouquet; bundle; faggot;**
  herbarium; herbary; nation;
  nosegay.
herdsmen: **booly; waywardness.**
heresies: **drove; mass; pack.**
heresies, condemned: **rhapsody.**
heresies, new: **fount.**
heretics: **conciliable; gang;**
  skulk; swarm.
heretics, schismatics and: **surge.**

hermits: **observance.**
heroes: **assemblage; line.**
herons: **passage; rookery; sedge;**
  serge; siege.
herring: **drave.**
herrings: **cade; cast; firkin;**
  glean; hand; kilderkin; last;
  school; shoal; strike; string;
  warp.
hides: **dicker; dicker.**
hierarchies, angel: **ternion.**
hieroglyphics, Tuscan: **collect.**
hieroglyphs: **signary.**
Highlands, people of the: **cateran.**
high rank, persons of: **dignity.**
hill ants: **bank.**
hills: **circus; theatre; track.**
hills, crags and: **assembly.**
hills, low: **surge.**
hills and rocks: **jumble.**
hippies: **trip.**
hippopotami: **bloat; school.**
histories: **repertory.**
history: **maze; thread(s).**
history, natural: **body.**
hogs: **drift; hoggery; passel.**
holly: **bosk; screen.**
holy apostles: **congregation.**
holy maidens: **congregation.**
holy men: **communion;**
  fellowship; hagiocracy.
Holy nuns: **sisterhood.**
Holy orders: **gown.**
Holy Trinity: **ternary.**
holy water: **sprinkle.**
homely receipts, astrology and:
  medley.
homilies: **postil.**
honest profession: **tail.**
honesty: **conspiracy.**
honey: **harvest; lump; tierce.**
honeysuckle: **break; spray.**
honour: **convoy; scroll; spring;**
  traffic.

honours: **accumulation; bushel; roster.**

hoof-marks of cattle: **staupings.**

hoofs, galloping: **storm.**

hooks, fishing: **set.**

hope: **farrago; grist; gust; rainbow; ray(s); wind.**

hopes, vain: **swelling.**

hops: **bag; ingathering; pocket; poke; tally.**

hornets: **bike; nest; swarm.**

horrid hell: **legion.**

horse: **banner; body; levy; wedge; whirlwind.**

horse and wings: **turm.**

horseback, persons on: **cavalcade.**

horsemen: **cavalcade; cavalry; power; ray(s); standard; swarm; turm.**

horses: **cavalry; coffle; drove; field; haras; mews; mob; muster; myriad; parcel; race; rake; retinue; ruck; rush; set; show; slate; stable; stand; stock; store; string; stud.**

horses, brave: **stable.**

horses, carriage: **team.**

horses, polo: **team.**

horses, wild: **haras; tempest.**

horseshoes: **dicker; gang.**

horses in racing, seven: **septet.**

horse soldiers: **cavalry.**

host, enemy: **skirt.**

host, spirit: **picket.**

hostile tribes: **concentration.**

Hostlers: **sect.**

hoteliers: **host.**

hounds: **brace; clan; cry; field; harl; heap; kennel; leash; meute; mute; pack; suit.**

hours: **senary.**

house, gathering or reception in a Parisian: **salon.**

housebreakers: **gang.**

household: **establishment; house; ménage.**

housekeepers: **foresight.**

house of wits: **calling.**

house of women: **seraglio.**

houses: **block; circus; clump; cluster; medley; row; string; terrace.**

houses, dwelling: **village.**

houses, granite: **agglomeration.**

houses, printing: **span.**

Houses of Parliament: **deputation.**

human affairs: **skein; thread(s).**

human beings: **aggregation; chain; humanity; people.**

human belief: **synthesis.**

human bliss: **hoard.**

human greatness: **colluvies.**

humankind: **jam.**

human nature: **skirt.**

human race: **rag; world.**

human society: **world.**

human species: **moiety.**

hummocks: **nest.**

humour: **embroidery.**

humour, ill: **burst; gush.**

humours: **concourse; miscellany.**

humours, bad: **accretion.**

humours, corrupt: **cargason.**

humours, ill: **conflux.**

humours, remaining: **colluvies.**

humours, tough: **coacervation.**

hunters: **blast; range; stale.**

huntsmen: **field; meet.**

hurdles: **flight.**

husbandry: **profession.**

husbands: **multiplying; unhappiness.**

hutches: **rabbitry; rake.**

huts: **hutting; warren.**

huts, collection of: **rancho.**

hymns: **anthology.**

hypocrites: **congregation.**

hyssop: **brush; posy.**

I

ibex: **herd**.
ibises: **colony**.
ice: **accretion; brash; cake; cascade; conglomerate; drift; flake; floe; grue; hail; pack; shot; stream**.
ice, snow and: **conservatory**.
icebergs: **cluster; pack**.
ice floes: **patch**.
Iceland; General Assembly of: **althing**.
ice-pinnacles: **palisade**.
icy islands: **compagination**.
ideas: **assemblage; body; bundle; camp; chain; cluster; combination; concatenation; hotchpotch; huddle; parcel; profusion; train**.
ideas, good: **heap**.
idioms: **knot; phraseology**.
idle objurgations: **babel**.
idlers: **army**.
idols: **idolatry**.
ignorance: **field**.
ignorant persons: **tail**.
ill humour: **burst; gush**.
ill humours: **conflux**.
ill repute: **house**.
illustrious persons: **sylloge**.
imagery: **host**.
images: **host**.
imagination: **exuberance; syntax**.
imaginations: **phantasmagoria**.
imbecility: **bunch**.
immigrants: **wave(s)**.
immoralities: **drove**.
Imperial Guard, troop of the: **school**.
impertinence: **rhapsody**.

impertinent thoughts, fruitless: **track**.
impossibilities, foolish: **fardel**.
impossibilities, utter: **faggot**.
impotent persons, poor, lame, and: **rank**.
inarticulate speech: **wealth**.
incense: **cloud**.
incidents: **combination**.
incongruities, confusions and: **aggregate**.
inconsistencies and errors: **welter**.
indian corn, ripe: **lingot**.
[Indian mounted troops], sewarry: **cavalcade**.
indigent people: **huddle**.
indignation, grief and: **tumult**.
individuals: **body**.
individuals born at about the same time: **generation**.
infamous falsehoods: **tirade**.
infantry: **cohort; column; phalanx; picket**.
infants: **creche**.
infants at a birth, seven: **septet**.
inference: **pyramid**.
inferior clergy: **body**.
infidels: **plague**.
influence, legislators, those who try to: **lobby**.
information: **cloud; jungle; wealth**.
information, valuable: **abundance**.
ingenuity: **sample**.
inhabitants collectively of a town: **township**.
inhabitants of a town: **town**.
inhabitants of the earth: **world**.
iniquity: **pandemonium; ring; system**.
injured people: **shoal**.
inmates of a harem: **seraglio**.
inmates of a priory: **priorate**.
innkeepers: **closing**.

J

circuit; judicature; miscarriage; panel; sentence; session.
judges and barristers: **mess.**
judicial court: **sitting.**
judicial meeting: **gemote.**
jugglers: **never-thriving.**
junior executives: **strut.**
jurors: **damning.**
jurors, qualified: **rota.**
jurymen: **panel.**
justice: **pile; soupçon.**
justice, organisation for the administration of: **court.**
justices: **miscarriage; quorum; seat.**
jute: **strick.**

K

kangaroos: **mob; troop.**
kempsters: **scolding.**
kernels: **nursery.**
keys: **bunch; bundle.**
keys, organ: **bank; bench.**
kid, white: **mantle.**
kids: **caper.**
kindness: **drop.**
kindred: **grove.**
kine: **drove.**
kinfolk: **kindred.**
kingdom, great: **dignity.**
kingdoms: **colligation; mess.**
kingfishers: **corroboree.**
kings: **bunch; leash.**
kings (playing cards): **pair-royal.**
kisses: **dicker; last; peck; rain; rosary; thrave.**
kitchen: **garniture.**
kitchen, servants engaged in the: **kitchenry.**
kitchen utensils: **battery; kitchenry.**

kittens: **brood; kindle; litter; nest.**
knavery: **consort.**
knaves: **pack; raffle; riff-raff; score; wheen.**
knights: **armoury; banner; chapter; fleet; garrison; knighthood; legion; rout.**
knights, goodly: **sort.**
knights, young: **bachelory.**
Knights Templar: **templary.**
knives: **dicker; tableware.**
knots: **cluster.**
knowledge: **accumulation; book; conglomerate; hill; kilderkin; library; magazine; round; scrap(s); smack; spread; store; wealth.**
knowledge, accidental: **chaos.**
knowledge, divine: **treasury.**
knowledge, general: **budget.**
knowledge, geological: **scantling.**
ky: **bow.**

L

labourers: **corps; gang; squad.**
labourers and harvest waggons: **cortége.**
labours: **conjugation.**
lace: **cascade; coil; drift; purl; torrent; tower.**
lackeys: **cast.**
ladies: **assemblage; bevy; ladyhood; range.**
ladies, fair: **constellation; ring.**
ladies, fine: **power.**
ladies and damoyles: **resort.**
Lady, Chaplet of Our: **sodality.**
lady's hair: **ambush.**
ladyships: **round.**
laity: **order.**
lakes: **chain.**

lakes, crystal: **expanse.**
lambs: **cast; crop; fall; head; myriad; tale; trip.**
lambs skins: **kip.**
lame, and impotent persons, poor: **rank.**
lampoons: **cargo.**
Lancaster: **house.**
lancet windows: **triad.**
land: **butt; muid; parcel; rag.**
landlords: **landlordry.**
landscapes: **series.**
lanes: **clutter.**
lanes, shady: **confluence.**
language: **roll; treasury.**
language, bad: **chorus.**
languages: **detritus; family; hubbub; leash; rag.**
lanthorns: **fleet.**
lapwing: **deceit; desert.**
large load: **crate.**
large stones: **huddle.**
larks: **bevy; exaltation; flight.**
Larrikins: **push.**
Latin metre: **gamut.**
latticework: **treillage.**
laughter: **burst; chorus; flood; gale; peal; riot; symphony; wind.**
laurel: **bosk; chaplet.**
lava: **coil; flood; surge; torrent.**
law: **codex; conservatory; magazine; profession.**
law, civil: **cluster; corpus.**
law, God's: **library.**
law and equity: **fusion.**
lawbooks: **pyramid.**
laws: **body; bulwark; cake; canon; code; digest; repertorium.**
[laws], instruments: **doctrine.**
laws and regulations: **chaos.**
lawyers: **bar; consultation; eloquence; escheat; lurry;**

phalanx; profession; sight; sublety.**
laymen: **laity; power.**
lazaroni ['lepers']: **attroopment.**
lazy servants: **cattle.**
leaders, seven: **septemvirate.**
leaders, three: **triumvirate.**
lead ore: **bing; charge.**
leafy foliage: **frondage.**
learned: **guild.**
learned lives: **zodiac.**
learned men: **academy; clerisy; heap; race; resort.**
learning: **commonwealth; dram; magazine; pittance; scattering; scrap(s); wealth; web.**
leather: **fadge; last.**
leaves: **bob; conglomerate; leafage; levesel; mop; network; sheaf; shower; stook; tussock; verticil.**
leaves, cinnamon: **quill.**
leaves, ivy: **trail.**
leaves, myrtle: **thrave.**
leaves, olive: **chaplet.**
leaves, rose: **garland.**
leaves in a book: **quire.**
leaves of trees: **drift.**
leaves [pages of a book]: **fascicle.**
leavings: **levet.**
lecherous people, filthy: **colluvies.**
lechery: **belt.**
lees: **doylt.**
(legal), authorities: **line.**
legal advisors: **counsel.**
legal profession: **gown; robes.**
legal tribunal: **judicature.**
legates, papal: **legation.**
legends: **family; legendry.**
legislative body: **assembly; parliament.**
legislative body of the United States: **congress.**
legislators, those who try to influence: **lobby.**

lemur: **den.**
lens, prisms or: **battery.**
leopards: **kennel; leap.**
lepers: **colony.**
['lepers'], lazaroni: **attroopment.**
letters: **batch; combination;
    conjugation; file; mass;
    packald; packet; pile; post;
    sheaf; shoal; shower; stack;
    suite.**
letters, men of: **sect.**
leverets: **kindle.**
Leyden jars: **battery.**
liars, Roman: **hive.**
liberties: **bulwark.**
librarians: **catalogue; sheaf;
    shush.**
libraries, university: **consortia.**
library: **bookery; nucleus.**
lice: **flock.**
licentious deities: **rabble.**
lies: **brood; cartload; case; crop;
    embroidery; farrago; pack;
    packet; parcel; peck; string;
    tissue; web.**
lies, slanderous: **file.**
life: **expanse; fount; string; web;
    zodiac.**
life, former: **dash.**
life, public: **theatre.**
life, storms of: **rainbow.**
life, waters of: **river.**
light: **body; dash; drop; robes;
    shower; trail.**
light, golden: **flood.**
light harrows: **gang.**
lightning: **lock; ribbon; shaft;
    trail.**
light persons, mean and: **rabble.**
light rays: **beam; brush; brush.**
lights: **battery.**
lights, cheerful: **gush.**
lights, electric: **bank; battery.**
lights, wax: **constellation.**
like sympathies, persons of: **club.**

lime: **seam.**
limestone: **clamp.**
line, things in a: **queue.**
lineaments, exquisite:
    convention.
linen: **butt; fardel; wad.**
linen articles: **lingerie.**
linen yarn: **bunch; bundle.**
lines: **network; pencil; sheaf.**
lines, railway: **trackage.**
lines, straight: **concatenation.**
lines of verse, three: **tristich.**
linked together, things: **chain.**
linnets: **parcel.**
lions: **den; kennel; litter; pride;
    sawt; sowse; troop.**
lips, open: **pair.**
liquid: **fountain; slash.**
liquid), columns (of: **sheaf.**
liquids: **compound.**
liquor: **parcel.**
listeners: **audience; auditory;
    train.**
list of names: **scroll.**
literary gleanings: **analects.**
literary gossip: **ana.**
literary material: **collection.**
literary matter, worthless:
    garbage.
literary passages: **chrestomathy.**
literary pieces: **posy; potpourri.**
literary pieces or poems: **sylva.**
literary selections: **casket.**
literary works: **cento.**
literary works, three collected
    dramatic or: **triology.**
literature, Athenian: **grove.**
litter: **kindle.**
live peers in Parliament:
    menagerie.
live plants: **quick.**
liveried servants: **squad.**
lives: **myriad.**
lives, learned: **zodiac.**
livestock: **show.**

living: **mass.**
living in the same area, people: **vianage.**
living oracles: **bead-roll.**
living together in a common community, group: **commune.**
load, large: **crate.**
lobbyists: **lobby.**
local authorities: **consortia.**
locks [canals]: **flight.**
locust: **cloud.**
locusts: **army; plague; swarm.**
logic: **system.**
logs: **crop; drive; raft.**
Lollards: **sect.**
long grass: **tussock.**
looks: **battery.**
looks, lovely: **army.**
loose sand: **circus.**
loose stones: **clatter; detritus.**
Lords: **house; seigniory.**
lords: **rout.**
lorries: **fleet.**
lost causes: **train.**
love: **book; shaft.**
love and loyalty: **volley.**
love-lore: **academy.**
lovely looks: **army.**
lovers: **trance; troop.**
low bushes: **nest.**
low hills: **surge.**
low mean people: **rascality.**
loyalty, love and: **volley.**
luck: **mort; peck; scoop.**
lumber: **string; traffic.**
lumbermen: **camp.**
lunar beams: **concentration.**
lupins: **bottle; wad.**
lusts, flattering: **seraglio.**
lyrebirds: **corroboree.**
lyric stage, German: **repertory.**

M

machinery: **bunch.**
machinery and equipment, computer: **hardware.**
mackerel: **mess; pad.**
madder: **poke.**
madness, sense and: **medley.**
magazines: **collocation.**
magistracy: **gown.**
magistrates: **bench; miscarriage.**
magpies: **tiding; tittering.**
maidenhead fern: **tress(es).**
maidens: **carol; rage.**
maidens, fair: **company.**
maidens, holy: **congregation.**
maids: **tail.**
maids, old: **sect.**
maids of honor: **bevy.**
maids of honour: **seraglio.**
mail: **post.**
mail, chain: **stand.**
main part of a group, centre or: **core.**
majestic palms: **grove.**
majesty: **column.**
majority: **generality.**
malefactors: **denomination.**
malevolence: **screed.**
malice: **magazine; shaft.**
mallard: **flight; flush; lute; pudding; sord.**
mallards: **suit.**
Malmsey wine: **butt.**
['malmsey wine'], marlvoisie: **firkin.**
malt: **boll; last; peck; skep; strick; sum.**
mammals: **migration.**
mammals, sea: **school.**
mammon: **helotry.**
managers: **court.**

manchet: **castle.**
mangolds: **clamp; pie.**
mankind: **herd; hive; lump; mass; mob.**
manners, good: **code.**
manufacturing populace: **condensation.**
manure: **pie; seam.**
manure heap: **midden.**
many of the worst acts: **consociation.**
marauders: **cateran.**
march-pane ['marzipan']: **castle.**
mare foals: **meiny.**
mares: **stud.**
mares, breeding: **haras.**
mares, stud of: **race.**
mariners: **ging.**
marines: **army; mess.**
marine shells: **concretion.**
marjorum: **posy.**
market, new growth on the: **sprinkle.**
marl: **darg.**
marlvoisie ['malmsey wine']: **firkin.**
married women: **suit.**
marrows: **tally.**
marsh birds, sea or: **sedge.**
marten skins: **timber.**
martins: **richesse.**
martyrs: **army; calendar; catalogue; consistory; shoal.**
['marzipan'], march-pane: **castle.**
masons: **covin; lodge.**
mass: **compilation.**
mass, coagulated: **congelation.**
masses: **hoi polloi.**
masseurs: **pummel.**
masters: **example.**
masts: **raft.**
masts on the rivers: **wilderness.**
matadors: **pavanne.**
material, literary: **collection.**
materialism: **wave(s).**

materials: **provisions.**
materials or matter, miscellaneous: **miscellanea.**
mathematical tables: **canon.**
mathematicians: **covey; parcel.**
matricides: **triad.**
matrimonial excesses: **nexus.**
matter: **body; coagmentation; parcel.**
matter, dead and stupid: **congeries.**
matter, foul: **colluvies.**
matter, miscellaneous materials or: **miscellanea.**
matter, particles of: **concourse.**
matter, unmethodized: **congestion.**
matter, worthless literary: **garbage.**
matters, ceremonial: **concretion.**
matters, trifling: **small beer.**
maxims: **gnomology.**
mayfly: **hatch.**
mead: **firkin.**
meal: **firlot; grist; score.**
meal, people taking a: **sitting.**
mean and light persons: **rabble.**
mean people, low: **rascality.**
means: **reservoir.**
measles: **dregs.**
meat: **cache; muid; potpourri.**
meat and drink: **convoy.**
meats: **hotchpotch.**
mechanics: **torque.**
mechanisation: **posse.**
medical: **profession.**
medical barks: **seron.**
medical practitioners: **consultation.**
medical specialists: **concilium.**
medicines: **tribe.**
medley, musical: **quodlibet.**
meekness: **mantle.**
meeting, judicial: **gemote.**

meeting, people present at a: **sederunt.**
meeting, race: **scramble.**
meeting of people: **folkmoot.**
melody: **rain.**
melody, delicious: **thread(s).**
melted snow: **escalade.**
members, parts and: **compagination.**
members of a club: **ménage.**
members of a family: **house.**
members of the U.S. Democratic Party: **democracy.**
memoirs, foreign: **compilation.**
memorial brasses: **brass.**
memories: **cluster; round.**
memory: **pool.**
men: **band; battalion; burgonet; coil; confluence; conglomeration; douth; draft; drift; force; handful; host; hotchpotch; knot; manhood; myriad; pare; parliament; push; pyramid; retinue; rush; strength; sum; wedge.**
men, armed: **halt; hosting; legion; stably; stale.**
men, association of: **guild.**
men, body of: **detail.**
men, dead: **hill; quarry.**
men, discarded: **yoke.**
men, distinguished: **crowd.**
men, dozen: **jury.**
men, good: **suit.**
men, holy: **communion; fellowship; hagiocracy.**
men, learned: **academy; clerisy; heap; race; resort.**
men, old: **gerontocracy.**
men, one hundred: **century.**
men, proper: **coil.**
men, rude: **convoy.**
men, secular: **audience.**
men, seven: **septemvirate.**
men, souls of: **migration.**

men, ten: **decemvir.**
men, trained: **cadre.**
men, wicked: **covin.**
men, wise: **junta.**
men and armour: **wappenshaw.**
men in an attacking mood: **threat.**
men in society: **conjugation.**
men-milliners ['dandies']: **confraternity.**
men of letters: **sect.**
men of talents: **resort.**
men of the starboard watch: **starboline.**
men of the Victorian Eleven: **tail-end.**
men of war: **power.**
mental phenomena: **consection.**
mercers: **fraternity.**
merchants: **caravan; convent; faith; merchantry; resort.**
merchant ships: **caravan.**
mercury: **column.**
mercy: **abundance; dram; gob; multitude; well.**
merlins: **cast.**
mermen: **quest.**
merriment: **burst; explosion; flashes; gale; volley.**
merrymakers: **revelrout.**
merrymaking: **mort.**
messengers: **diligence.**
metallic ore: **bing.**
metal ore: **clamp.**
metals: **collocation.**
metaphor and music: **maze.**
metaphors: **mob.**
metaphysics: **tangle.**
meteorites: **swarm.**
meteorologists: **shower.**
meteors: **fall.**
methodical arguments: **congest.**
methodists: **denomination.**
metre, Latin: **gamut.**
metrical romances: **cycle.**

mice: **colony; harvest; nest; regiment; store.**
migration: **trek.**
migrations, Celtic: **van.**
miles: **score.**
militarism: **wave(s).**
military company, fourth part of a: **section.**
military force: **knighthood; militia; were.**
military or naval force: **command.**
military or political body, civil: **establishment.**
milk: **gang; magazine; mess.**
milking cows: **dairy.**
milliners: **fraunch.**
mind: **frame.**
minds: **concent.**
minerals: **suite.**
mines: **bal.**
ministers: **junta; levee; presbytery; synod.**
ministers of Christ: **swarm.**
ministers of state: **cabinet; ministry.**
mink skins: **timber.**
minnows: **shoal.**
minor associations: **truss.**
minstrel poetry: **minstrelsy.**
minstrels: **minstrelsy; troop.**
miracle plays: **cycle.**
miracles: **conjugation; field; nest; packet; shoal.**
mirrors: **belt.**
mirth and war: **racket.**
mirth with sadness: **medley.**
miscellaneous exhibits: **welter.**
miscellaneous materials or matter: **miscellanea.**
mischief: **well.**
miscreants: **canaille.**
miseries: **volley; web.**
misers: **horde.**

misery: **conflux; multitude; sum; theatre.**
misfortunes: **army; tissue.**
misfortunes, crimes, follies, and: **tissue.**
mishaps: **surge.**
misrepresentations: **tissue.**
mist: **bank; river; swathe.**
mistakes: **mass.**
mists, green and grey: **chaos.**
mites: **bite.**
mixture: **mellay.**
mixture, confused: **babel.**
mob: **canaille; cattle; clamjamphine; conflux; frape; hurry; mobile; ochlocracy; plebs.**
mob, fashionable: **squeeze.**
mob-rule: **mobocracy.**
models: **slouch.**
modern plays: **ream.**
modesty: **drop.**
mole burrows: **citadel.**
molecules: **cascade.**
moles: **company; labour.**
monarchy: **frame.**
monasteries: **congregation.**
monastic rules: **canon.**
monastic society: **order.**
money: **balk; bank; brass; bushel; charge; collation; collect; doit; fond; gob; hoard; levy; lock; lump; mass; mint; mort; multitude; oodles; parcel; pile; pittance; pot; power; rag; sight; spill; stack; swag; tribute; wad.**
money, brass: **plague.**
money, prize: **batch; whack.**
money, sum of: **contribution.**
monkeys: **cartload; schemozzle; troop; wilderness.**
monks: **abominable sight; brotherhood; colony; community; confraternity;**

N

nabobs: **nabobery**.
nails: **budget**.
nails, parings of: **gry**.
names: **catalogue; crowd;
    onomasticon**.
names, Christian:
    conglomeration.
names, hard: **heap; shower**.
names, list of: **scroll**.
nastiness: **cataract**.
nastiness, noise and: **shot**.
nation, state, or university,
    governing body of a: **senate**.
national agreements: **entente**.
nations: **colluvies; concourse;
    confederacy; fusion;
    hotchpotch; medley;
    scattering**.
nations, ages and: **assemblage**.
nations, group of: **allies**.
nations, uncircumsized: **cento**.
native officials: **omlah**.
natural history: **body**.
nature: **book; dregs**.
nature, human: **skirt**.
nature, persons of an offensive:
    vermin.
natures: **mob**.
naval commissioned officers:
    ward-room.
naval force, military or:
    command.
necessaries: **provisions**.
needles: **stand**.
negotiation, diplomatic: **web**.
neighbours: **nerve**.
nest, wasps': **vespiary**.
nests, rooks': **rookery**.
nets: **shot**.
nets, fishing: **drift; sagene**.

nettles, sharp: **chaplet**.
network: **sagene**.
new denominations: **vocabulary**.
new doctrines: **covey**.
new growth on the market:
    sprinkle.
new heresies: **fount**.
news: **budget; dicker; scrap(s)**.
news, evil: **cataract**.
newspapers: **file; press**.
newspapers proprietors:
    syndicate.
new thoughts: **crowd**.
nieces: **tribe**.
night: **realm; robes; skirt**.
night, ancient: **dregs**.
nightcaps: **nest**.
nightingales: **rout; watch**.
nightwatchmen: **pallor**.
nine muses: **tripletrine**.
nobility: **port**.
nobility, principal: **bundle**.
noble class: **nobility**.
noble doctrines: **dregs**.
Noble Order of the Garter:
    chapter.
nobles: **aristocracy; rank**.
nobles (coins), English: **pose**.
noble virgins: **chapter**.
noise: **charivari**.
noise and nastiness: **shot**.
noisy assembly: **dovercourt;
    drum**.
noisy dance: **flare-up**.
nomads: **camp**.
nonsense: **pack; realm; ream;
    rhapsody; rigmarole**.
nonsense, bombastic: **tirade**.
noted persons: **galaxy**.
notes: **batch; bundle; screed;
    torrent**.
notes, musical: **gamut**.
nourishment: **magazine;
    reservoir**.
novels: **cargo**.

novelties: **shoal.**
novices: **tirocinium.**
numbers: **column.**
numismatics, Oriental: **corpus.**
nuns: **convent; flap; nunnery;
  superfluity.**
nuns, Holy: **sisterhood.**
nurseries: **nurserydom.**
nurses: **staff.**
nutmegs: **ball.**
nuts: **cluster; gallimaufry;
  hoard.**
nuts and acorns: **provisions.**
nymphs: **retinue.**

oak: **cock; screen; shrubbery.**
oaks: **ring; spring.**
oars: **bank; gang; pair; range;
  suit.**
oathes: **volley.**
oaths: **string; torrent.**
oatmeal: **nieveful; peck.**
oats: **bodge; boll; firlot; garb;
  peck; pook; seam; thrave.**
objectivity: **accrescence.**
objects: **muddle; omnibus.**
objects, five dozen: **tally.**
objects, twelve: **dozen.**
objurgations, idle: **babel.**
obnoxious animal: **vermin.**
obscurity, deep: **mantle.**
observance, conscious: **catena.**
observances: **sorites.**
observations: **parcel.**
observed facts: **colligation.**
occupation: **skill.**
ocean: **dash; symphony.**
oceans), deeps (the: **plump.**
Oddfellows: **temple.**
odds and ends: **cagmag; host.**
offence: **quantity.**

offences: **bead-roll.**
offensive nature, persons of an:
  vermin.
officers: **execution; mess;
  retinue; slate; staff.**
officers, army: **brass.**
officers, naval commissioned:
  ward-room.
officials: **bench; execution;
  hierarchy.**
officials, chief: **aristocracy.**
officials, government:
  bureaucracy.
officials, native: **omlah.**
oil: **congiary; dregs; river.**
Old Guard: **slumber.**
old hags: **hagging.**
old hay: **tump.**
old maids: **sect.**
old men: **gerontocracy.**
old papers and parchments: **heap.**
old saws: **gnomology.**
olive grove: **yield.**
olive leaves: **chaplet.**
olives: **budget; butt; grove.**
omnibuses, cabs, carriages, and
  carts: **traffic.**
one hundred men: **century.**
one hundred things: **century.**
one hundred years: **century.**
ones, young: **passel.**
1,000 troops: **chiliarchy.**
onions: **rope; row; string.**
onlookers: **circle.**
open lips: **pair.**
opera: **ménage.**
opinion: **body; catena; wave(s);
  weight.**
opinion, adherents to an: **consent.**
opinion, persons of the same
  political: **party.**
opinion, popular: **surge.**
opinions: **library; litter;
  mizmaze; rabble; symposium;
  welter.**

opinions, partisan: **olio.**
opinions, superstitious: **lurry.**
opportunity: **gale.**
opposition: **rank.**
opulence: **richesse.**
oracles, living: **bead-roll.**
oranges: **hand.**
orchards and gardens, pleasant:
  variety.
orchard trees: **plump.**
orchids: **coterie.**
order: **genus; party.**
order, religious: **observance.**
order and form: **orb.**
Order of the Garter, Noble:
  chapter.
orders, Holy: **gown.**
ordinances: **capitulary.**
ordnance: **peal.**
ore: **post.**
ore, lead: **bing; charge.**
ore, metal: **clamp.**
ore, metallic: **bing.**
ore, quicksilver: **morsel.**
ore, tin: **bunch.**
organisation for the
  administration of justice: **court.**
organizations, business: **cartel.**
organ keys: **bank; bench.**
organ pipes: **rank; tier.**
organs: **pair.**
orgiasts: **concatenation.**
oriental council of state: **divan.**
Oriental numismatics: **corpus.**
orthopaedists: **brace.**
osiers: **bolt; rank.**
osteopaths: **joint.**
ostlers: **laughter.**
ostrich feathers: **bush.**
otter: **bevy.**
otters: **lodge.**
''Our Fathers'': **belt.**
Our Lady, Chaplet of: **sodality.**
outbuildings: **range.**
outlaws: **band; nest.**

outlaws, Irish: **woodkern.**
ovens: **range.**
owls: **parliament; stare.**
oxbirds: **fling.**
oxen: **drift; drove; herd; meiny;**
  span; team.
oxon: **yoke.**
oyster and scallop shells:
  congregation.
oyster colony: **scalp.**
oyster culture: **park.**
oysterling, young: **park.**
oysters: **bank; bed; brood; cast;**

P

packages: **packery; pile.**
packhorses: **string.**
packs: **packery.**
paddocks, pasturing: **suit.**
pages: **suit.**
[pages of a book], leaves: **fascicle.**
pagodas: **lac.**
paid applauders: **claque.**
pain: **lump.**
pain or pleasure: **nucleus.**
pains: **set.**
paint: **cake; muddle.**
painters: **crew; curse; illusion;**
  madder; misbelief; school.
painting brushes: **sheaf.**
paintings: **canvas; sky.**
paintings, ceiling: **tablature.**
pair: **brace; span.**
palms, majestic: **grove.**
palm trees: **knot.**
pamphleteers: **pair-royal.**
pamphlets: **flock; litter; school;**
  strew.
panegyrics: **cataract.**
papal bulls: **bullary.**
papal legates: **legation.**
paper: **book; budget; bundle;**

patriarchs: **bunch.**
patriotic feelings: **seethe.**
patterers (thieves): **school.**
paupers: **poverty.**
paying 'scot and lot', people:
  scotship.
peace: **multitude.**
peace, perpetual: **harvest.**
peaches: **gush.**
peacocks: **muster; ostentation;
  pride.**
pearls: **network; rain; rope;
  ruck; scatter; scattering;
  string.**
pearly clouds: **scroll.**
pearly sands, coral and: **shaw.**
peas: **hail; mess; mow; reap;
  rick; strike; thrave; wad.**
peasants: **mob; peasantry.**
peat: **gang.**
pebbles: **beach; shingle.**
pedestrians: **square.**
pediments: **labyrinth.**
pedlars: **impertinence;
  malpertness.**
peers: **peerage; quorum; round;
  synod; trinary.**
peers in Parliament, live:
  menagerie.
pekingese: **pomp.**
pellets: **shot.**
pelts: **peltry.**
penance: **scoop.**
pence: **poke.**
penguins: **colony; parcel;
  rookery; town.**
pensioners: **port.**
people: **ancienty; army;
  attroopment; brigade; bulk;
  concourse; confluence;
  congregation; crowd; earth;
  flote; folk; forest; gate;
  generality; globe; heap; jam;
  knot; lump; lurry; maniple;
  mass; meiny; mob; multitude;**

**myriad; nation; nest; nursery;
  parcel; pash; platoon; press;
  public; push; queue; rabble;
  raft; rascal; riff-raff; rota;
  score; shoal; show; slew;
  sprinkling; squad; store;
  stream; strength; tail; thrap;
  threat.**
people, common: **commonalty;
  democracy; herd; hoi polloi;
  plebs; populace; vulgarity.**
people, famous: **constellation.**
people, fashionable: **fashion.**
people, filthy lecherous: **colluvies.**
people, group or association of:
  phalanstery.
people, indigent: **huddle.**
people, injured: **shoal.**
people, low mean: **rascality.**
people, meeting of: **folkmoot.**
people, poor: **power.**
people, savage: **savagedom;
  savagery.**
people, silent: **posse.**
people, standing: **wedge.**
people, worthless: **clamjamphine;
  trash.**
people appointed as trustees:
  trust.
people assembled: **agora.**
people guarding or defending:
  ward.
people in the fashionable world:
  society.
people living in the same area:
  vianage.
people moving: **procession.**
people of fashion: **ton.**
people of good social position:
  quality.
people of the Highlands: **cateran.**
people of the world: **cosmocracy.**
people paying 'scot and lot':
  scotship.

people present at a meeting:
  sederunt.
people taking a meal: **sitting.**
people travelling together: **party.**
people who receive a salary:
  salariat.
people who regularly eat together:
  mess.
pepper: **cark; peck; sprinkling.**
perch: **pack; shoal.**
perfection: **code; girdle.**
performances: **festival.**
performers: **circus.**
performers, composition for three:
  trio.
performers on various
  instruments: **orchestra.**
perfume: **gale.**
perfumes, flower: **potpourri.**
peripatetics: **denomination.**
peristyles: **labyrinth.**
perpetual peace: **harvest.**
person: **multitude.**
personal belongings: **swag.**
personal effects: **traps.**
personalities: **fusillade.**
persons: **alliance; ambush; band;
  confederacy; confusion; galére;
  lede; migration; myriad;
  omnibus; party; quotity.**
persons, association of two or
  more: **partnership.**
persons, better instructed:
  sprinkle.
persons, company of: **assembly.**
persons, five: **pentarchy.**
persons, four or more: **quadrille.**
persons, ignorant: **tail.**
persons, illustrious: **sylloge.**
persons, mean and light: **rabble.**
persons, noted: **galaxy.**
persons, poor, lame, and
  impotent: **rank.**
persons, religious: **convent.**
persons, royal: **royalty.**

persons, sick: **conflux.**
persons, strangely acting: **zoo.**
persons, three: **trinity.**
persons, unit of: **cell.**
persons, vile and wretched:
  mishmash.
persons acquainted with each
  other through some former
  event: **reunion.**
persons authorised to transact
  business: **sitting.**
persons following a profession:
  calling.
persons gathered together with a
  common purpose: **rally.**
persons of ability: **talent.**
persons of an offensive nature:
  vermin.
persons of high rank: **dignity.**
persons of like sympathies: **club.**
persons of the same political
  opinion: **party.**
persons of the same profession:
  order.
persons on horseback: **cavalcade.**
persons sent to a foreign country:
  mission.
persons united by a common rule:
  order.
pestilence: **army.**
petals: **flurry.**
petitions: **magazine.**
petitions, papers and: **maniple.**
petty despots: **brood.**
petty discussions: **crop.**
pews: **pewage.**
phantasies: **foison.**
phantasy: **syntax.**
phantoms: **phantasmagoria;
  phantomry.**
pheasants: **aerie; bouquet; brace;
  eye; game; head; menagerie;
  nide; nye; school; stew;
  warren.**
phenomena, mental: **consection.**

philosophers: **body; clerisy; sect; wrangle.**
philosophy: **patch; system.**
philosophy and rhetoric: **medley.**
photographs: **packet.**
phrase: **collocation.**
phrases: **mint; phraseology; sylva.**
phrases, scriptural: **cento.**
phrases, words and: **ging.**
phrases and pithy precepts, stately: **port.**
physicians: **faculty; sect.**
physicists: **nucleus.**
physick: **fond; profession.**
pianists: **pounding.**
pickets, strike: **cordon.**
pickle: **mickle.**
pickpockets: **school.**
pictures: **olio; rabble; serial; sky; suit.**
pieces, literary: **posy; potpourri.**
pieces, musical: **olio; potpourri; suite.**
pieces or poems, literary: **sylva.**
pies: **pastry.**
piety: **house.**
pigeons: **flight; kit; loft; school.**
pigs: **fare; litter; sounder; team.**
pike: **brace.**
pikemen: **rot; serry.**
pikes: **row; square; stand; tower.**
pilchards: **bulk; school; shoal.**
piled blocks: **confusion.**
piled vanities: **quarry.**
piles: **drift; range.**
pilgrims: **band; caravan; meiny.**
pifings: **spiling.**
pillars: **avenue; balustrade; colonnade; order; pillaring; range; row.**
pineapples: **row.**
pines: **cluster; tuft.**
pine trees: **pinery; pinetum.**
pins: **pastiche.**

pipers: **poverty; skirl.**
pipes: **pipage.**
pipes, organ: **rank; tier.**
pipes and vessels: **compages.**
pirates: **crew; horde; nest.**
pistols: **brace; case.**
pitch: **last.**
pithy precepts, stately phrases and: **port.**
pity: **well.**
place, assembly: **agora.**
places: **colligation.**
plain repetition: **hash.**
plaints: **storm.**
plait: **tress(es).**
planets: **choir; chorus; complex; conjunction; septenary; sisterhood.**
planking, timber: **swale.**
planks: **boarding.**
planted cotton: **stand.**
plants: **clump; diversity; meiny; nursery; packet; race; spring; tuft.**
plants, dried: **herbarium; herbary.**
plants, live: **quick.**
plasterers: **squat.**
plate: **service.**
plate, gilt: **service.**
plate, glass: **bundle.**
plate, silver: **wedge.**
plates: **tableware.**
platitudes, tory: **catena.**
plaudits: **consort.**
players: **company; cry; troop.**
players, bag-pipe: **skirl.**
players, card: **school.**
players, chess: **brood.**
players, poker: **stud.**
players, rugby: **scrum.**
players at a gambling table: **table.**
playing cards: **pack; pair; pair-royal; suit.**
(playing cards), kings: **pair-royal.**

porpoises: **chorus; gam; herd; pod; school; turmoil.**

porridge: **mess.**

porridge], cauld porridge [cold: **claut.**

porridge [cold porridge], cauld: **claut.**

port, mulled: **jorum.**

porter: **pot.**

porters: **gang; safeguard.**

position, people of good social: **quality.**

position in society, rank or: **class.**

possessions: **boodle.**

possibilities: **chapter; circle.**

posts: **forest.**

posts, trading: **line.**

pot: **bow; bowpot; boughpot.**

potage: **mess.**

potatoes: **bag; camp; clamp; hill; patch; pie.**

potters: **confraternity.**

powdered coxcombs: **bevy.**

powdered hair: **mop.**

powder (gunpowder): **magazine.**

power: **accumulation; community; magazine; pyramid; skirt.**

powers: **pomp.**

practices, conceits and: **mishmash.**

practices, superstitious: **branchage.**

practitioners, medical: **consultation.**

prairie dog, burrows of the: **town.**

prairie dogs: **burrow.**

praise: **consort; gale; gush; peal; wind.**

praises: **volley.**

prayer: **convention.**

prayers: **bead-roll; century; chaplet; rosary; storm.**

preachers: **converting.**

precedence: **tail.**

precedent: **myriad.**

precedents, disconnected: **jungle.**

precepts: **body; book.**

precepts, Christian: **codex.**

precepts, scholastic: **rabble.**

precepts, stately phrases and pithy: **port.**

precious stones: **chaplet.**

prejudice: **mass; wave(s).**

prejudice, popular: **tide.**

prejudices: **rank.**

prelacy: **cone.**

prelates: **conclave; pontificality; prelacy; synod.**

presbyterians: **brood.**

present at a meeting, people: **sederunt.**

presumptions, conjectures and great: **plump.**

pretty tales: **sort.**

prey, birds of: **aerie.**

priesthood: **rank.**

priests: **camarilla; chantry; cohort; discretion; hierarchy; mass; priesthood; rabble; raffle; scourge.**

priests, chanting: **trail.**

primroses: **bob.**

princes: **congregation; state.**

principal nobility: **bundle.**

principles: **body; conjuncture; doctrine.**

printers: **chapel; plagiary.**

printer's proofs: **strew.**

(printing), type: **line.**

printing houses: **span.**

printing type: **pillar; stamp.**

priory, inmates of a: **priorate.**

prisms, slender: **tuft.**

prisms or lens: **battery.**

prisoners: **calendar; mort; party; pity.**

private assembly: **conversazione.**

privet: **screen.**

privileged class: **aristocracy.**

Q

R

rabbins [rabbis]: **conclave.**
rabbis: **rabbinate.**
[rabbis], rabbins: **conclave.**
rabbit: **warren.**
rabbits: **burrow; bury; dower;**
  flick; game; head; kindle;
  litter; nest; peltry; rabbitry.
rabble: **canaille; merdaille;**
  posse; revelrout; salvo; scaff-
  raff; tag; traffic.
race: **meeting.**
race, human: **rag; world.**
racehorses: **string; stud.**
race meeting: **scramble.**
racing, seven horses in: **septet.**
racoons: **nursery.**
rafts: **string.**
rage: **outburst.**
rags: **bundle.**
railery: **field.**
rails: **flight.**
railway: **sagene.**
railway lines: **trackage.**
railways: **network; system.**
rain: **brash; cloud; dash; drift;**
  fall; flurry; grist; oncome;
  pash; pencil; plash; rash;
  sheaf; shot; shower; skelp;
  spill; sprinkling; succession;
  swathe; thread(s); torrent.
rain and water: **plague.**
rain clouds: **swirl.**
[rain or water], parny: **dowry.**
rain water: **colluvies.**
raisins: **bunch; frail; lump; sort.**
rank: **degree.**
rank, persons of high: **dignity.**
rank or position in society: **class.**
ranks of soldiers: **serry.**
ranters: **posse.**

rapiers: **case.**
rare conceits: **wilderness.**
rare flowers: **sight.**
rascality, scribbling: **riff-raff.**
rascals: **meiny; rascaldom.**
ratches: **leash.**
rats: **warren.**
ravens: **aerie; unkindness.**
rays: **bundle; cone; quintuplet;**
  scattering; sheaf.
rays, light: **beam; brush; brush.**
readers: **audience; rabble;**
  readership; variety.
readers, young: **horde.**
reapers: **reap.**
reason: **library; show.**
reason and truth: **pittance.**
reasoning: **chain; circuit; train.**
reasons: **mint; rabble; series.**
rebels: **pack.**
receipts, astrology and homely:
  medley.
receive a salary, people who:
  salariat.
reception: **seat.**
reception in a Parisian house,
  gathering or: **salon.**
records, ancient: **archive.**
recrements ['dross; waste
  substance']: **colluvies.**
recruits: **tirocinium.**
red deer: **game.**
red soil: **pocket.**
red tape: **jungle.**
redwing: **crowd.**
reeds: **bunch; clump; faggot;**
  knitch; sheaf; wad.
reflections: **sequence.**
refuse: **doylt; dregs; fullage;**
  garbage; midden; peltry;
  recrement; tip.
refuse/decaying: **cagmag.**
regenerators, social: **cohort.**
regicides: **horde.**
regulations, laws and: **chaos.**

rods, iron: **bundle.**
rods, iron or steel: **faggot.**
rods, steel: **garb.**
roe deer: **great bevy.**
roes: **bevy.**
romances, metrical: **cycle.**
Roman liars: **hive.**
Romans: **riot.**
Rome: **legion; synagogue.**
Romish superstition: **dregs.**
rooks: **building; clamour; rookery.**
rooks' nests: **rookery.**
rooms: **suite.**
roots: **fascicle; knot.**
roots, small: **company.**
rope: **hank.**
ropes: **network; quill; rigging.**
rose leaves: **garland.**
rosemary: **ball; brush.**
roses: **chaplet; posy; rosary; spray; spring; trail.**
roses, golden: **garland.**
round shot: **hail.**
Round Table: **order.**
route: **mobile.**
rowing crew: **eight; four.**
royal, blood: **line.**
royal persons: **royalty.**
rubbish: **burrow; clamjamphine; dump; peltry; sweepings; tip; traffic; trash; tump.**
rude men: **convoy.**
rue: **chaplet.**
ruffians: **gang; rout.**
ruffles: **flurry.**
ruffs: **hill.**
rugby players: **scrum.**
rugby team: **fifteen.**
ruined buildings: **welter.**
ruins: **detritus.**
rule, persons united by a common: **order.**
rules: **canon; code.**
rules, monastic: **canon.**

ruling body: **aristocracy.**
ruling body of ten: **decadarchy.**
ruling body of twelve: **dodecarchy.**
rumour: **packet.**
rumours: **nest.**
runners: **field.**
rupees: **lac.**
rural countryside: **bush.**
rural folk: **rout.**
rushes: **burden; faggot; gavel; tress(es); tuft; whisp.**
rye: **firlot; muid; sheaf; thrave.**

S

sable skins: **timber.**
sacred books: **canon.**
saddest evils: **scheme(s).**
Sadducees, truckling: **pontificality.**
sadness, mirth with: **medley.**
saffron: **dram.**
sage hens: **covey.**
sail: **crowd; press; spread.**
sailing ships: **sailrife.**
sailing vessels: **sail.**
sailors: **army; crew; draft; navy.**
sails: **canvas; cloud; outfit; sail; suit.**
sails, windmill: **sail.**
saints: **calendar; canon.**
Saints: **communion.**
saints: **congregation; consistory; sequence; suit.**
salad: **collation.**
salary, people who receive a: **salariat.**
salesmen: **sample.**
salmon: **bind; brood; firkin; haul; migration; nest; run.**
salt: **boll; chice; clump;**

seats in a church: **sedila.**
seaweed: **sea.**
sea weed: **jungle.**
seaweeds: **kelp.**
secessionists: **secession.**
second causes: **conflux.**
secretaries: **secretariat.**
secret motives: **regiment.**
secrets: **hoard.**
secret thoughts: **cabinet.**
secret tribunal: **areopagy.**
secret will: **cabinet.**
sectaries: **babel; conciliable.**
section, forward: **van.**
secular men: **audience.**
seed: **cast.**
seeds: **mass.**
seigniors: **seigniory.**
selected, things: **selection.**
selections: **faggot.**
selections, literary: **casket.**
selections, musical: **casket.**
selections, poetic: **macaroni.**
self-loving beings: **agglomeration.**
senate, ecclesiastical: **consistory.**
senators: **consistory.**
senior Fellows: **seniority.**
seniors: **seniority.**
senior wranglers: **tetrad.**
sensations: **bundle.**
sense: **soupçon.**
sense and madness: **medley.**
senses: **conservatory.**
sentiments, happy: **train.**
sent to a foreign country, persons:
  mission.
separatists: **knot.**
seraphim: **nest; sodality.**
serfs: **serfage.**
sergeants: **sergeancy; sublety.**
series of comments: **rally.**
serious thought: **well.**
serpents: **brood; multitude; race;**
  serpentry.
serpent tresses: **tangle.**

servants: **family; heap;**
  obeisance; port; power;
  retinue; rout; sequel;
  servantry; servitude; staff.
servants, lazy: **cattle.**
servants, liveried: **squad.**
servants engaged in the kitchen:
  kitchenry.
service, tea: **canteen.**
set of seven: **septet.**
set of three: **pair-royal; tern;**
  ternion; triplet.
set of three: **triangle; trinary;**
  trio.
set of twelve: **zodiac.**
set of twenty: **score.**
sets of dishes: **service.**
settings for a table: **service.**
settlement, collective: **kibbutz.**
settlements, isolated: **aggregation.**
seven, group of: **septenary.**
seven, set of: **septet.**
seven horses in racing: **septet.**
seven infants at a birth: **septet.**
seven leaders: **septemvirate.**
seven men: **septemvirate.**
seventy, group of: **septuagint.**
seven years: **septenary.**
several populations: **conflux.**
several springs: **conflux.**
sewarry [Indian mounted troops]:
  cavalcade.
sewers: **credence; sewerage.**
shade: **cone.**
shades ['colours']: **assortment.**
shadowy hair: **skein.**
shady lanes: **confluence.**
shallow coves (thieves): **school.**
shapes: **rumpus.**
shares: **block; portfolio.**
sharp nettles: **chaplet.**
shawmers: **pluck.**
sheep: **cull; down; drift; drove;**
  flock; fold; head; heap; hurtle;

skins, mink: **timber.**
skins, sable: **timber.**
sky: **phantasmagoria; ribbon.**
slander: **quiver.**
slanderous lies: **file.**
slate: **bunch.**
slaves: **bevy; cattle; coffle; gang; helotry; servitude; string.**
sleet: **shower.**
slender prisms: **tuft.**
slime: **concretion.**
slums: **slumdom.**
small animals: **bed.**
small birds: **roost.**
smallboats: **brood.**
small bubbles: **aggregate.**
small charms: **volley.**
small particles: **grail.**
small roots: **company.**
small ships: **squad.**
small stars: **knot.**
small troubles: **shoal.**
small veins and arteries: **labyrinth.**
small wood, bundle of: **cracker.**
smells, fresh: **gush.**
smoke: **cloud; column; drift; gust; pillar; plume; puff; scroll; torrent; wreath.**
smoke, fire and: **explosion.**
smoke, wood: **swirl.**
smokers: **hack; tabagie.**
smolt: **school.**
smugglers: **set.**
smuggling: **citadel.**
snails: **escargatoire; rout; walk.**
snails and worms: **tribe.**
snakes: **bed; den; sheaf; tier.**
snakes, young: **knot.**
snipe: **leash; walk; whisp.**
snipes: **game.**
snobs: **mob; snobbery.**
snow: **accretion; accumulation; bank; clunch; drift; fall; flurry; girdle; hill; mantle;**

oncome; pash; patch; rain; reek; rick; shower; sprinkle; store; storm; wall; wap; wave(s); wreath.**
snow, melted: **escalade.**
snow and ice: **conservatory.**
snowbirds: **flurry.**
snowflakes: **flurry.**
snuff: **charge; pinch.**
soap: **cake; seron.**
sobs: **storm.**
social gathering: **crush; ruelle; shivoo.**
socialism: **river.**
social position, people of good: **quality.**
social regenerators: **cohort.**
societies: **omnibus.**
society: **column; frame; institution; racket; stratum; tier.**
society, human: **world.**
society, men in: **conjugation.**
society, monastic: **order.**
society, rank or position in: **class.**
society, religious: **connexion.**
soil: **burrow.**
soil, red: **pocket.**
soirée: **conversazione.**
soldiers: **array; battalion; bayonet; boast; company; congregation; crew; decade; draft; file; garrison; gendarmery; globe; maniple; nursery; orb; parade; parcel; patrol; phalanx; picket; platoon; range; rank; ray(s); regiment; rot; rout; soldiery; squad; squadron; store; strength; sum; tierce; troop; vexillation; wall.**
(soldiers), foot: **brigade.**
soldiers, foot: **shot.**
soldiers, horse: **cavalry.**
soldiers, ranks of: **serry.**

stalks of wheat, stumps of the: **stubble.**
standing people: **wedge.**
standing stones: **carol.**
stanzas: **ternary.**
starboard watch, men of the: **starboline.**
starlings: **chattering; cloud; murmuration.**
stars: **break; circle; cleft; cluster; configuration; congeries; constellation; constellation; field; galaxy; multitude; pack; pleiad; shower; sight; spanges; spangle; troop.**
[stars], Copernicus: **circus.**
stars, small: **knot.**
state: **column; commonwealth; tower.**
state, ministers of: **cabinet; ministry.**
state, oriental council of: **divan.**
state, or university, governing body of a nation: **senate.**
state, population of a democratic: **democracy.**
stately aqueducts: **procession.**
stately phrases and pithy precepts: **port.**
state politics: **skein.**
states: **alliance; confederacy.**
statesmen: **disagreement.**
statues: **statuary.**
statutes: **stack.**
statutes and usages: **repertory.**
steel: **blow; burden; sheaf.**
steel rods: **garb.**
steel rods, iron or: **faggot.**
steeples: **wilderness.**
steps: **flight; grece.**
stewards: **provisions; pursuing.**
sticklebacks: **shoal.**
sticks: **bundle; fadge; faggot; frame.**
stiff hairs: **palisade.**

stirring springs: **rally.**
stitches: **clump.**
stoats: **pack; trip.**
stock in trade: **boodle.**
stock-jobbers: **kennel.**
stock jobbers: **assembly.**
stocks: **portfolio.**
Stoics: **denomination.**
stone: **brash; cord.**
stone, blocks of: **confusion.**
stone heap: **bourock.**
stones: **bing; cairn; cascade; cast; clatter; mass; nursery; pile; raise; ruck; shower; volley.**
stones, large: **huddle.**
stones, loose: **clatter; detritus.**
stones, precious: **chaplet.**
stones, standing: **carol.**
stools: **round.**
store: **garrison.**
stories: **catch; doylt; string.**
stories, celestial: **florilegium.**
storks: **flight; muster; phalanx.**
storms: **chain; clamour; magazine.**
storms of life: **rainbow.**
storytellers: **sounding.**
stragglers from an army: **stray.**
straight lines: **concatenation.**
strangely acting persons: **zoo.**
strangers: **band; escort; rabble; rout.**
strangers to the city: **conflux.**
straw: **bolt; bottle; bunch; bundle; handful; knitch; lock; pad; rick; seam; stook; trash; tress(es); truss; wad; wap; whisk; whisp.**
strawberries: **mess.**
streams: **rank.**
streets, quiet: **nest.**
street sweepings: **fullage.**
strike pickets: **cordon.**
strikers: **picket.**

string: **stringing.**
strings: **quintet.**
stripes, decorative bars or:
  barring.
strokes in tennis: **rally.**
strong feeling: **wave(s).**
strumpets: **flourish.**
Stuart: **house.**
students: **class; gown; riot;**
  unemployment.
students, body of teachers and:
  university.
studies: **community.**
studies, school of advanced:
  conservatory.
stud of mares: **race.**
stumps of the stalks of wheat:
  stubble.
styles (architectural): **salad.**
suburbs, scattered: **labyrinth.**
successes, good: **series.**
successes, prosperous: **confluence.**
succession: **chain.**
sugar: **bag; chice; parcel; pot.**
sugar, brown: **cargo.**
sugar, Muscovado: **sum.**
sugar cane: **stand.**
suit, cards of the same: **flush.**
suitors: **mess.**
suits: **clothing.**
Sultan's following: **ragabash.**
sultrying passions: **century.**
summoners: **untruth.**
sum of money: **contribution.**
sun: **tress(es).**
sundry cases: **myriad.**
sunlight: **beam; burst; patch;**
  plash; pool; shaft.
superannuated customs:
  mishmash.
superfluous breath: **abundance.**
supermarkets: **chain.**
superstition: **citadel.**
superstition, gentile: **accrescence.**
superstition, Romish: **dregs.**

superstitions: **bundle; pack.**
superstitious opinions: **lurry.**
superstitious practices:
  branchage.
supper: **scrap(s).**
supporters: **clientage.**
suppositions or assertions: **train.**
surgeons: **faculty; quorum.**
surgeons, tree: **graft.**
surveyors: **camp.**
suspects: **press.**
sustained rhetoric: **gush.**
swallows: **flight; gulp.**
swans: **bank; bevy; drift; eyrar;**
  game; herd; sownder; team;
  wedge.
swearers: **lump.**
swearing: **fusillade.**
sweepings: **doylt.**
sweepings, street: **fullage.**
sweeps, chimney: **confraternity;**
  sweepdom.
sweet affections: **sphere.**
sweet breath: **purl.**
sweetmeats: **confection.**
sweets: **synod.**
sweets, parcel of: **cracker.**
swells: **swelldom.**
swept up, things that are: **sweep.**
swifts: **flock; stream.**
swimming birds: **raft.**
swine: **doylt; drift; drove; dryft;**
  herd; sounder; store; swinery.
swine, tame: **trip.**
swings: **upsy.**
swordsmen: **resort; sodality.**
sycamore trees: **screen.**
sycophants: **compliment; herd.**
syllables: **syllabary.**
symbols: **symbolism.**
syndics: **syndicate.**
synonyms: **synonymy.**
systems, theological: **compilation.**

T

table, players at a gambling:
  table.
Table, Round: **order.**
table, settings for a: **service.**
tables: **nest.**
tables, mathematical: **canon.**
tablets: **book.**
tableware: **plate; service.**
tailors: **disguising;
  proudshowing.**
taking a meal, people: **sitting.**
talents, men of: **resort.**
tales, evening: **rhapsody.**
tales, pretty: **sort.**
talk: **knot; mort; river; spring.**
talks: **round.**
tamarisk: **raft.**
tame swine: **trip.**
tangled eglantine: **trail.**
tanks: **tankage.**
tape, red: **jungle.**
tapsters: **promise.**
tar: **dregs; last; lock.**
Tartars: **horde.**
tarts: **jam; pastry.**
tastes: **hotchpotch.**
taverners: **cajolery; closing.**
[tax collectors], "farmers" of
  public revenue: **farm.**
taxi-cabs: **rank.**
taxis: **charge.**
tea: **blend; break; gulp; pinch;
  pot; tass.**
teachers: **conclave; school.**
teachers and students, body of:
  university.
teal: **bunch; coil; knob; leash;
  spring; string.**
team: **side.**
team, baseball: **nine.**

team, basketball: **five.**
team, cricket: **eleven; team.**
team, football: **eleven.**
team, polo: **four.**
team, rugby: **fifteen.**
tears: **flood; gush; gust; rain;
  river; rush; shower; storm;
  stream; surge; tribute; well.**
teasels: **staff.**
tea service: **canteen.**
teasles: **glean.**
teazles: **bunch.**
teddy bears: **cuddle; hug.**
Te Deums, murder and: **salad.**
teeth: **array; case; choir; gang;
  palisade; rage; rank; row.**
teeth, fair white: **suite.**
teetotalers: **waggon.**
telegraph forms: **sheaf.**
telegraph poles: **forest.**
telegraph wires: **system.**
tempest: **flurry.**
tempest, fell (foul): **plague.**
tempests: **brewage; clutch.**
tempestuous fire: **whirlwind.**
Templar, Knights: **templary.**
Templars: **order.**
temporary blessings: **variety.**
temptation: **gust.**
temptations: **tempest.**
ten, body of: **decury.**
ten, ruling body of: **decadarchy.**
tenants: **tenantry.**
ten days: **decadary.**
tenements: **troop.**
tenets: **doctrine.**
ten men: **decemvir.**
tennis, strokes in: **rally.**
tenses: **consection.**
10,000, group of: **myriad.**
tents: **camp; canvas; choir.**
tents, white: **sea.**
ten years: **decade.**
terns: **ternery.**
terraces: **escalade; flight.**

terraces, rising: **theatre.**
territory: **morsel.**
terror: **fusillade; pomp; rush.**
testimonies: **van.**
text, scriptural: **digest.**
texts: **coacervation; shoal.**
thankfulness and dread: **mingle.**
thanks: **sight.**
thatch: **stook.**
theatre: **sphere.**
theatre, company of a: **ménage.**
theatre boxes: **tier.**
theatre-goers: **queue.**
theatres, provincial: **repertory.**
theatre seats: **row.**
theological systems: **compilation.**
theology: **bulwark.**
theorists: **sect.**
theorists, irreconcilable:
  miscellany.
theory, wild: **rhapsody.**
thickets: **skirt.**
thieves: **den; family; gang; mob;
  pack; quest; school; school;
  skulk.**
(thieves), patterers: **school.**
(thieves), shallow coves: **school.**
thieves and murderers: **sect.**
things: **body; conspiracy;
  multitude; myriad.**
things, disagreeable: **jumble.**
things, five: **quinary.**
things, four: **quaternary.**
things, good: **abundance;
  conjunction; power; train.**
things, one hundred: **century.**
things, six: **senary.**
things, two: **pair.**
things, worldly: **succession.**
things graded according to
  quality, items or: **class.**
things in a line: **queue.**
things linked together: **chain.**
things on show: **display.**
things selected: **selection.**

things that are swept up: **sweep.**
things to eat: **scran.**
things united, three: **triune.**
thinkers: **breed.**
thirty boats, twenty to:
  companionship.
thorns: **burden; bush; faggot;
  tussock.**
those who are alive: **quick.**
thought: **avenue; chain;
  condensation; detritus; web.**
thought, mythological: **stratum.**
thought, serious: **well.**
thoughts: **ana; host; mob; quest;
  scattering; spring; storm;
  throng(s); track; train.**
thoughts, borrowed: **cento.**
thoughts, fine: **nucleus.**
thoughts, fruitless impertinent:
  track.
thoughts, new: **crowd.**
thoughts, secret: **cabinet.**
thread: **clew; knot; lease; skein;
  skein.**
threads, parallel fibres or: **flake.**
threads of silk worms:
  conglomeration.
three: **trine.**
three, group of: **ternary; triad.**
three, set of: **pair-royal; tern;
  ternion; triangle; trinary;
  trio; triplet.**
three children at a birth: **triplet.**
three collected dramatic or literary
  works: **triology.**
three leaders: **triumvirate.**
three lines of verse: **tristich.**
three performers, composition for:
  trio.
three persons: **trinity.**
three things united: **triune.**
three years: **triennium.**
thrushes: **mutation; thrave.**
thunder: **burst; peal; roll.**

thunderous epic: **scrap(s)**.

thyme: **glean**.

tide: **rush**.

tide, floating: **swelling**.

tiger: **swarm**.

tigers: **ambush; den; wilderness**.

timber: **boom; frame; raft; sheaf; stand; standard; tower**.

timber planking: **swale**.

time: **aeon; brood; dregs; drop; hatch; oodles; scantling; scrap(s); sea; spoils**.

time, five children born at the same: **quintuplet**.

time, individuals born at about the same: **generation**.

times: **scheme(s)**.

times, barren: **series**.

tinkers: **wandering**.

tinminers: **pair**.

tinners: **parliament**.

tin ore: **bunch**.

titles: **catalogue**.

toads: **knot; nest**.

toad's eggs: **chaplet**.

toasts: **round**.

tobacco: **bulk; cake; carrot; gage; gush; hand; parcel; sum; tierce; trash; wad**.

together, company who eat: **rancho**.

tomes: **profusion**.

tongues: **clatter; hash; host; mess**.

tongues, sciences and: **sorites**.

tools: **budget; chest; kit**.

tools, tradesmen's: **procession**.

topics: **magazine; quaternary**.

Tories: **scramble**.

torn boughs: **imbroglio**.

tortoises, brass: **trine**.

tory platitudes: **catena**.

tough humours: **coacervation**.

tow: **wad**.

towels: **towelry**.

towers: **cluster; congeries**.

towers of chimney: **babel**.

town, inhabitants collectively of a: **township**.

town, inhabitants of a: **town**.

town or city, corporate body of a: **commonalty**.

town pleasure: **whirlwind**.

trade, stock in: **boodle**.

tradesmen's tools: **procession**.

trading posts: **line**.

tradition, Christian: **corpus**.

traditions: **fardel**.

traditions, ancient: **recrement**.

traditions, dirty: **maze**.

traditions, uncommanded: **rabble**.

traffic: **congestion; jam; rumble**.

tragedies: **scroll**.

train: **tendance**.

trained men: **cadre**.

trains: **race**.

traitors: **confraternity; nest; sort**.

traitors, false: **clan**.

transact business, persons authorised to: **sitting**.

trappers: **brigade**.

trash: **peltry; traffic**.

travellers: **cafila; caravan; fare**.

travelling together, people: **party**.

treasure: **cache; garrison; pose; sum**.

treasures: **mass**.

tree, branches of a: **ramification**.

trees: **avenue; belt; bosk; brush; canopy; clump; colonnade; copse; diversity; festoonery; forest; forest; group; grove; jam; miscellany; palisade; pile; plump; raft; range; rank; screen; shaw; skirt; stand; store; suit; sylva; thicket; toft; toll; tuft; tump; wilderness**.

trees, ash: **ash-holt**.

trees, chestnut: **colonnade**.

24 or 25 sheets of paper: **quire.**
twenty to thirty boats:
  companionship.
twigs: **brash; cow; faggot; fasces;**
  trash; tussock; whisk.
twine: **ball.**
two, body of: **duarchy.**
two or more persons, association
  of: **partnership.**
two things: **pair.**
type: **fount; genus.**
type, printing: **pillar; stamp.**
type, unsorted: **pie.**
type (printing): **line.**
typists: **giggle; pool.**
tyranny: **nest.**

U

ulcers: **community; crop.**
unbelief: **flood.**
uncircumsized nations: **cento.**
uncommanded traditions: **rabble.**
unconnected criticism: **repertory.**
underbrush: **thicket.**
underclothes of women: **lingerie.**
undergraduates: **college.**
understanding: **library;**
  vocabulary.
undertakers: **extreme unction;**
  unction.
unfortunate birds: **nation.**
ungodliness: **nursery.**
unholy passion: **gust.**
unit, cavalry: **sabre.**
united, three things: **triune.**
united by a common rule,
  persons: **order.**
united by common agreement,
  party: **consent.**
United States, legislative body of
  the: **congress.**

unit of persons: **cell.**
university, governing body of a
  nation, state, or: **senate.**
university libraries: **consortia.**
unmethodized matter:
  congestion.
unpleasant food, broken or:
  scran.
unsorted type: **pie.**
upper class: **gentry.**
upright freedom: **tide.**
usages, statutes and: **repertory.**
U.S. Democratic Party, members
  of the: **democracy.**
ushers: **set.**
utensils, culinary: **canteen.**
utensils, kitchen: **battery;**
  kitchenry.
utter impossibilities: **faggot.**

V

vagabonds: **fraternity;**
  vagabondage.
vain hopes: **swelling.**
valets: **valetaille; valetry.**
valour: **theatre.**
valuable information: **abundance.**
vampires: **colony.**
vanities, piled: **quarry.**
vapour: **congregation; pillar;**
  puff; wreath.
vapour, sooty: **grummet.**
vapours: **bunch; robes.**
vapours, floating: **collection.**
various instruments, performers
  on: **orchestra.**
varlets: **gang; varletry.**
vases: **garniture; range.**
vassels: **vassalage.**
vaults: **vaultage.**
vegetables: **herbary; show; skep.**
vegetation, green: **sea.**

vegetation, wild: **savagery.**
vehicles, motor: **fleet; motorcade.**
vehicles, movement of: **traffic.**
veins: **network.**
veins and arteries: **convent.**
veins and arteries, small:
  labyrinth.
vendors: **haggle.**
venom: **bushel.**
verbal arguments: **forest.**
verbosity: **thread(s).**
verdure: **clustering; raft.**
verse: **burden; mess; olio.**
verse, three lines of: **tristich.**
verse, weeping: **strew.**
verse and prose: **analects.**
verses: **cento; derry.**
vertu, articles of: **bijouterie.**
vessels: **conglomeration; craft;**
  echelon; garnish; swarm.
vessels, blood: **colligation.**
vessels, pipes and: **compages.**
vessels, sailing: **sail.**
vessels, war: **escadrille.**
vessels [boats]: **fellowship.**
vestals: **nunnery.**
vicars: **prudence.**
vice: **den.**
vices: **nursery; torrent; variety.**
vices, virtues and: **commixture.**
victims: **covey.**
Victorian Eleven, men of the: **tail-**
  end.
victories: **succession.**
victuals: **mess.**
viewers: **audience.**
vigour, muscular: **outburst.**
vile and wretched persons:
  mishmash.
villages: **villagery.**
villains: **meiny; team.**
villas: **villadom.**
vinegar: **mess.**
vines: **festoon; treillage; vinery.**
violent earthquakes: **theatre.**

violets: **bunch; garniture; gush;**
  mass.
violinists: **string.**
violins: **band.**
viols: **chest; consort.**
vipers: **nest.**
virgins: **carol; consort.**
virgins, noble: **chapter.**
virtue: **canopy.**
virtues: **catalogue; conspiracy;**
  fascicle.
virtues and vices: **commixture.**
virtuosi: **virtuosity.**
visitants: **confluence.**
visitors: **batch; confluence; flood.**
visits: **round; string.**
vociferation: **concert.**
voices: **charm; clamour; clatter;**
  concent; concert; explosion;
  medley.
voices, buzz of: **surge.**
volcanic ash: **cascade.**
volcanic fragments: **agglomerate.**
volcanoes: **rookery.**
voles: **colony.**
volunteer force: **yeomanry.**
vowels: **collocation.**
vulgar politicians: **tribe.**
vultures: **cast; peal.**

W

wages: **pittance.**
waggons: **frame; park; train.**
waggons, carts and: **rumble.**
waggons, labourers and harvest:
  cortége.
waiters: **army; indifference.**
walruses: **huddle; trio.**
war: **peal; rank; spoils; theatre;**
  van.
war, men of: **power.**
war, mirth and: **racket.**

warehouses: **nest.**
wares, cooper's: **coopery.**
warrior, equipment of a: **panoply.**
warriors: **cohort; convent; serry.**
warriors, retinue of: **comitatus.**
warriors who fought from
  chariots: **chariotry.**
war vessels: **escadrille.**
wasps: **bike; nest; society;
  swarm; vespiary.**
wasps' nest: **vespiary.**
waste: **recrement.**
waste substance'], recrements
  ['dross;: **colluvies.**
watch, men of the starboard:
  starboline.
watchmen: **ward; watch.**
water: **accretion; canteen;
  cataract; congregation; dash;
  debacle; exuberance; flood;
  gang; gush; gust; house; mass;
  pat; pillar; plash; pocket; pool;
  purl; push; quaternary; rack;
  reservoir; river; rope; rush;
  shot; shower; spray; spring;
  spurt; surge; swathe; theatre;
  wall.**
water, cold: **gulp.**
water, filthy: **colluvies.**
water, holy: **sprinkle.**
water, jets of: **sheaf.**
water, rain: **colluvies.**
water, rain and: **plague.**
watercolours: **septet.**
water drops: **condensation.**
waterfowl: **bunch; plash;
  triangle.**
watermills: **regiment.**
waters: **accumulation; collection;
  confluence; conflux; load;
  multitude; network; pomp;
  ravel; regiment; string.**
waters, bitter: **brash.**
waters of grace: **spring.**
waters of life: **river.**

watery particles: **congeries.**
wave: **tress(es).**
waves: **tower; wilderness.**
waves, breaking: **roll.**
wavy corn: **expanse.**
wax: **cake.**
wax candles: **galaxy.**
wax lights: **constellation.**
wealth: **accumulation; avenue;
  pile; richesse.**
weapons: **pile.**
weary wretchedness: **wave(s).**
weasels: **pack.**
weather: **gust; parcel.**
weather, dry: **track.**
wedding guests: **convoy.**
weed: **dollop.**
weed, sea: **jungle.**
weeds: **burden; weedery.**
weeks: **warp.**
weeping: **outburst; storm.**
weeping verse: **strew.**
well-doing: **dram.**
whales: **gam; herd; mob; party;
  plump; pod; run; school;
  shoal; tribe.**
whales, bottle-nosed: **grind.**
whales, sperm: **pod.**
whaling ships: **gam.**
wharfs: **nest.**
wharves: **wharfage.**
wheat: **aisle; boll; crop; firlot;
  garb; glean; lock; mow; pook;
  rick; ruck; shock; stand;
  thrave; wad.**
wheat, ears of: **grove.**
wheat, stumps of the stalks of:
  stubble.
whelps: **legion; litter.**
whist: **hand.**
whistlings: **storm.**
white blossom: **pyramid.**
white kid: **mantle.**
white teeth, fair: **suite.**
white tents: **sea.**

whiting: **pod.**
whole world: **theatre.**
whooping, dancing and:
  pandemonium.
whortles: **tump.**
wicked: **rout.**
wicked colts: **haras.**
wicked men: **covin.**
wickedness: **fardel; university.**
widgeon: **bunch; company;**
  flight; knob; trip.
widows: **ambush; viduage.**
wild animals: **venery.**
wild bees: **bike.**
wild birds: **scry.**
wildcats: **destruction; dout.**
wild ducks: **fleet; team; trip.**
wildernesses: **bosk.**
wild fish: **park.**
wild flowers: **embroidery.**
wild fowl: **plump; skein; trip;**
  wedge.
wild geese: **skein; train; wedge.**
wild horses: **haras; tempest.**
wild or foreign animals:
  menagerie.
wild theory: **rhapsody.**
wild vegetation: **savagery.**
will, secret: **cabinet.**
wind: **capful; flurry; gale; gush;**
  gust; orchestra; puff; rush;
  sailful; spurt; stream; tempest;
  torrent.
wind instruments: **wind.**
windmill sails: **sail.**
windows, lancet: **triad.**
winds: **congregation; swathe.**
windsors [chairs]: **knot.**
wine: **case; congiary; dozen;**
  dregs; gulp; muid; pot; sea;
  smack; tass; tierce.
wine, Malmsey: **butt.**
wine, Spanish: **brewage.**
wine bottles: **cellar.**
wine flasks: **canteen.**

Wing Commanders: **flush.**
wings, horse and: **turm.**
winning graces: **pomp.**
wire: **rouleau.**
wire, gold: **hank.**
wires, telegraph: **system.**
wiry grass: **tump.**
wisdom: **well.**
wisdom, cunning: **well.**
wise, speeches: **army.**
wise men: **junta.**
wise professors, canny: **wheen.**
wishes: **farrago.**
wishes, guilty: **brood.**
wit: **dicker; fond; handful;**
  kilderkin; mort; scantling;
  scrap(s); shaft; smack; wealth;
  zodiac.
Witan, assembly or council of the:
  witenagemot.
wit and politeness: **nosegay.**
witches: **cloud; convent; coven;**
  covin; hagging; knot; pack;
  squad.
with sadness, mirth: **medley.**
witnesses: **cloud; detachment;**
  orb; suit.
wits: **breed; junta.**
wits, house of: **calling.**
wives: **brace; community;**
  harem; impatience; non-
  patience; sort.
woe: **gush; suite.**
woes: **catalogue; cluster; field;**
  group; load; parcel; web.
wolves: **head; herd; horde;**
  kennel; pack; rout; troop.
women: **coil; gaggle; gang;**
  gynarchy; gynocracy; litter;
  parliament; regiment;
  sisterhood; womanhood.
women, chattering: **gaggle.**
women, fair: **bevy.**
women, group of: **sorority.**
women, house of: **seraglio.**

women, married: **suit.**
women, silly: **posse.**
women, underclothes of: **lingerie.**
womenhood: **rabble.**
women's club: **sorosis.**
wonders: **dozen.**
wood: **bush; cast; cord; drift; fascine; fathom; knitch; pile; plump; seam; shaw; skirt; spring; stack; tower.**
wood, bundle of small: **cracker.**
wood, field and: **nation.**
woodcock: **flight.**
woodcocks: **fall; game.**
wooded country: **frith.**
wooden items: **treen.**
wood fibres: **top.**
woodland: **bush.**
woodpeckers: **descent.**
woods: **frith.**
wood smoke: **swirl.**
wooing: **brash.**
wool: **ball; cark; fadge; flock; hank; lock; pad; pelage; pocket; poke; skein; trenle.**
wool, combed: **top.**
word, God's: **treasury.**
words: **army; century; circuit; coagmentation; collocation; conglomeration; drop; group; handful; hank; hash; hotchpotch; jumble; multitude; peal; plethora; provisions; rabble; rhapsody; riot; row; scaffolding; series; shot; storm; stream; string; swad; sylva; tangle; tirade; torrent; train; verbiage; volley; wealth.**
words, fiery: **flood.**
words, foreign: **sprinkling.**
words, good: **army; magazine.**
words and actions: **rout.**
words and phrases: **ging.**
work: **feck; plethora; throng(s).**
workers: **cell; factory.**

workmen: **gang.**
works, author's complete: **variorum.**
works, good: **richesse; rosary; tale.**
works, literary: **cento.**
works, three collected dramatic or literary: **triology.**
works of art: **collection.**
world: **concourse; dregs; frame; riff-raff; scramble.**
World, Christian: **onomasticon.**
world, people in the fashionable: **society.**
world, people of the: **cosmocracy.**
World, Sciences of the: **witenagemot.**
world, whole: **theatre.**
worldly things: **succession.**
world of music: **sphere.**
worms: **bed; bob; clew; wreath.**
worms, political: **convocation.**
worms, snails and: **tribe.**
worms, threads of silk: **conglomeration.**
worries: **basinful.**
worship, assembly for: **meeting.**
worshippers: **congregation.**
worshippers, fellow: **connexion.**
worshipping: **mishmash.**
worst acts, many of the: **consociation.**
worsted: **bolt; skein.**
worsted yarn: **hank.**
worthies: **ternary.**
worthless and fabulous scoundrels: **abundance.**
worthless literary matter: **garbage.**
worthless people: **clamjamphine; trash.**
woven brown hair: **garlandry.**
wranglers, senior: **tetrad.**
wrath: **accumulation; explosion; sea; storm.**